COLONIAL WEST INDIAN STUDENTS IN BRITAIN

LLOYD BRAITHWAITE

Foreword by The Hon. Gladstone Mills

UNIVERSITY OF THE WEST INDIES PRESS

Barbados • Jamaica • Trinidad and Tobago

To the University of the West Indies,
colleagues and friends

University of the West Indies Press
1A Aqueduct Flats   Mona
Kingston 7 Jamaica

05 04 03 02 01   5 4 3 2 1

CATALOGUING IN PUBLICATION DATA

Braithwaite, Lloyd
  Colonial West Indian students in Britain / Lloyd Braithwaite.

  p. cm.

  ISBN: 976-640-52-0
  1. West Indian students – Great Britain. I Title.
  LB 2376.6.G7 B72 2001   373.82

Cover and book design by Robert Harris
E-mail: roberth@cwjamaica.com
Set in Plantin Light 10/14 x 24
Printed in Jamaica by Stephenson's Litho Press

Contents

Foreword

In 1945, a few months following the end of World War II (both in Europe and Asia), Britain experienced an inflow of students from her colonies, especially from Africa and the West Indies. Among those from the British Caribbean, a few were scholarship holders and others who preferred to postpone taking up places in tertiary educational institutions in Britain until after the war. A few others too, such as Eugenia Charles, Michael Manley and Milton ('Bob') Cato – all future prime ministers – and Michael (M.G.) Smith and Douglas Hall, future distinguished professors, arrived following a few years spent in Canada at university or in the armed forces.

But the majority of the scholarship students were beneficiaries of the 'mushrooming' of awards flowing from the four-year-old Colonial Development and Welfare Organization (CDW) with headquarters located in Barbados. Established following the Moyne Commission's visit and hearings throughout the region in the wake of the civil disturbances of the mid to late 1930s, the organization's wide-ranging activities included the award of scholarships to the United Kingdom in a variety of fields where the need for trained personnel had been emphasized in the Moyne Report (for example, medicine and nursing, social services, economics).

This scholarship programme was dominated initially by medicals when, in 1943, 14 awards apparently intended for distribution throughout the region were all inadvertently allocated to Jamaica. Benefiting from this bonanza, the Jamaican government decided to assign one to each parish. Hence, the selection of future doctors such as Henry Shaw, Ronald Lampart and Leslie Williams. The error was corrected the following year. Coincidentally, I travelled to Britain in 1944 on the *Queen Elizabeth* with that year's medical scholars which included, among others, Warren (Buddy) Wilson, Robert

Milner and Donald Watler of Jamaica, Noble Sarkar of Trinidad, Andrew Mason of British Honduras, Henry Forde and Colin Vaughn of Barbados, Frank Williams and Balwant Singh of British Guiana (now Guyana).

A year or two after the war, there was another stream which involved the flow of ex-servicemen and women who benefited from the British Further Education and Vocational Training Scheme (FEVT), also in a variety of fields. This was the source of the professional training in medicine of Arthur Wint and Vernon Lindo; in law of Errol Barrow, Ena (Collymore) Woodstock, Uriah Parnell, W. ('Derry') Marsh; Ulric Cross of Trinidad, Dusty Miller of British Guiana; in engineering of Douglas Wint and John Lawrence; in history, of Roy Augier and John Hearne; in economics, of U.V. Campbell; Julian Marryshow of Grenada and Douglas Collins.

Nor were the arts and cultural areas neglected. The British Council and other cultural institutions actively sponsored students in drama, music, dancing, painting and sculpture, while other students managed on their own family resources. Hence, during the period 1945–50 there was an impressive collection which included Louise Bennett-Coverly, Ivy Baxter, Cecil Baugh, Noel Vaz, Hazel Lawson-Street, Julian Barber, Lloyd Hall, Olive Lewin, Fay (Hale) Lindo, Daphne Segre – all of Jamaica; M.P. Aladdin, Edric Connor, Rita (Innis) Coore and Winifred Atwell of Trinidad and Denis Williams of British Guiana.

In addition to this group were the holders of the prestigious Rhodes and national or island scholarships and not an insignificant number of privately funded students. Among the CDW students who arrived in London at summer's end of 1945 were Lloyd Braithwaite from Trinidad, bound for the London School of Economics (LSE). As fas as I recall, he was to join others for the two-year certificate course in Social Science Administration, including Reg Phillips and Winnie Birkbeck Hewitt (Jamaica), Ivor Robinson (British Guiana), Ken Sealy (Trinidad), and others: Sybil Hill-Francis, Rudolph Cousins and Odel Fleming (Jamaica) who had come to London with LSE on the school's return after years of evacuation to Cambridge. Following this programme also, were students from Africa, Ceylon (Sri Lanka), Gibraltar and the United Kingdom.

However, Lloyd eventually transferred to the sociology degree programme. I too arrived in London in 1945 after one year in Cambridge with the school, but reading for the BSc Econ. with specialization in government. This, then, was my first acquaintance with Lloyd Braithwaite; an acquaintance which developed into friendship during two years spent as fellow residents of the large colonial students residence, Nutford House, located between Marble Arch and Edgware Road. Later we would be colleagues for more than three decades, first at Mona, where he became an early recruit to the Institute of Social and Economic Research (ISER) and later (in 1965) professor of sociology. In 1969 he returned to Trinidad as principal of the St Augustine Campus and a pro vice chancellor of the University of the West Indies (UWI) – continuing to teach even after formal retirement in 1984.

In those early postwar years, Britain became the incubator for potential colonial leaders: a propitious environment and seedbed for the germination and emergence of leaders especially of Africa and the West Indies – in politics, other professions and the academy. Nutford House residents included presidents to be, Nigerian Abubaka Tafala Balewa, from Bechuanaland (Botswana) Seretse Khama; Ringadoo (Mauritius); Forbes Burnham (Guyana); Prime Minister Cato (St Vincent); Attorney-General Charles Njonjo (Kenya); Chief Justices Earl Seaton (Bermuda); Telford Georges (Dominica) and Vincent Floissac (St Lucia). Concurrently too, the conditions were propitious for early stirring of West Indian consciousness among students, especially Jamaicans, whose horizon and perspective had hitherto been restricted to their national boundaries.

The population of Nutford House consisted of a mix of young students coming immediately after graduating from secondary school, and older ones with several years work experience. Lloyd Braithwaite fell within the second category. He entered LSE as a mature 26-year-old who, we discovered later, was a qualified solicitor. From the outset he stood out as a mature but open-minded student, possessing an analytical mind, always interested in participating in a discussion while tolerant of the views expressed by others. He was also a very informal person with no regard for the trappings, airs and affectations of high office.

But what I remember most about him at that time were his quiet sense of humour and wit and his facility in cleverly teasing and upsetting some of us, especially the Jamaicans, with expressions of Trinidadian 'picong'. I recall, too, Lloyd's positive presence in discussions in the ISER coffee room when I joined the new Faculty of Social Sciences in 1969. Sadly, this custom of an informal coffee-break discussion ended several years ago.

One of these indelible, but on this occasion less pleasant, memories stemmed from an event which occurred during the Walter Rodney and C.Y. Thomas crises of 1968 and 1969, following the exclusion of these Mona staff members from Jamaica. Lloyd, then pro vice chancellor and I as dean of social sciences were invited to a seminar ostensibly on "The Role of the Social Scientist in the Contemporary Caribbean", with myself as chairman and presentations to be made by two colleagues. During my introduction to an audience bulging at the seams, it became quite clear that the real subject was the future of C.Y. Thomas and that we had been brought there "under false pretences" to provide an imprimatur for the proceedings. The angry audience vented their frustration and rage with intensive attacks on Lloyd and me – while neither of the two presenters attempted to speak. Lloyd and I decided to sit out the 'slings and arrows' though we had every right to leave, considering the circumstances.

In the early years at Mona, Braithwaite was a member of an outstanding group of scholars in the ISER including M.G. Smith and Raymond Smith, Roy Augier and George Roberts. Later he was in a sense, the informal self-effacing 'guru' of a small group of younger intellectuals such as Lloyd Best, Alister McIntyre and Archie Singham. It was in the earlier period that he produced the significant work "Social Stratification in Trinidad and Tobago". It is no accident that during the first few years of the Faculty of Social Sciences, the Department of Sociology was its strongest member.

The background and context depicted suggest, nay indicate that Lloyd Braithwaite was eminently suited for the research involved and the writing of this book. Living in the appropriate and conveniently located laboratories of LSE and the Nutford House colonial students residence, a participant in the meeting which culminated in the formation of the West Indian Students Union (WISU) in December 1945; and given his training in sociology, his enquiring mind was stimulated and challenged.

In fact he conceived the idea as a research student at LSE and I learnt of this interest early in my tenure as liaison officer for West Indian students in the British Isles (1948–51). This post had been created (along with similar positions in respect of other colonial territories), was funded by West Indian governments and located in the Welfare Department of the Colonial Office in London. Lloyd sought information from me from time to time about our students and the assistance and facilities provided officially for them across the United Kingdom and Eire. In fact this book was in the making for the past 50 years.

In this sociological approach, Braithwaite focuses on significant features of the foundations of the future West Indian elite, from among whom would emerge the social, political, professional and cultural leaders of these territories during the 1960s and early 1970s, following the first flush of their assumption of the status of independent states. Concurrently, of course, other future West Indian leaders were also being shaped elsewhere, for instance in Canada and the United States, while the regional University College of the West Indies was still in its fledgling state.

However, the experience of studying and living in Britain was, in some senses, unique. For some students who anticipated a warm welcome from 'Mother', the experience of duplicity and hypocrisy reflected in the attitudes and reactions of the host/hostess induced extreme disappointment and resentment. By contrast, the US approach to blacks was much more direct and honest – though also a source of frustration. Braithwaite illustrates the British approach especially in respect of housing.

For purposes of the study, he concentrates on students' reaction to prejudice and discrimination and in doing so appears to conclude that in general, this reaction was exaggerated. To some extent their allegations tend to be distorted – a function of the general picture of the problems of the group in "adjusting to an alien society". For me, one of Braithwaite's most interesting observations is the development of what he terms a "group culture of protest".

The host attitude of overt contempt for blacks during the late 1940s and early 1950s – the early period of Braithwaite's research and my years as liaison officer – was clearly evident in certain forms of commercial advertisements, such as a poster in the subway on a brand of toothpaste, which depicted black consumers in a derogatory way. The incident which remains indelibly etched in my memory concerns the British Airways large display window on London's Regent Street depicting in lifesize proportions an English traveller being transported on the shoulders of four African natives clothed in 'G-strings'. Action by a Sierra Leone liaison officer and myself, with considerable assistance from a sympathetic British member of Parliament succeeded in having the display removed overnight. But all this occurred over 50 years ago. What is the present situation? Incidentally, I note in his chapter on the Colonial Office Braithwaite's reference to the attitudes adopted by some West Indian students towards their liaison officer. I do not recall being aware of this, though I was certainly conscious of their suspicions and distrust of the Colonial Office staff.

The incipient stirring of West Indian consciousness had been stimulated by the presence of a significant number of students following the end of the war and by the Conference on Closer Association which had taken place in Montego Bay in 1947. These sentiments were reinforced and intensified by the living together of many of them in colonial students' hostels. Capping these events and processes was the formation of the WISU. Braithwaite observes that in the West Indies the only collective representation which had caught the popular imagination was the West Indian cricket team. Further, "the consciousness of belonging to a group called West Indian is something of a relatively late development". Hence, a few students had begun to discuss the desirability of developing a connecting link for the promotion of "cooperation and unity among the people of the region".

It was natural that the new organization would play an active role in relation to the proposals made in the Report of the Commission of Higher Education in the West Indies for the establishment of the University College. But, Braithwaite points out, "the first step towards the formation of an organized opinion on the university came from outside the union (WISU)". However, perhaps the most significant action initiated by the WISU was sending a deputation to the secretary of state for the colonies to discuss the proposals. (The deputation included Forbes Burnham.) Among the issues raised, were the importance of having a university "which fulfilled our social, economic and political needs"; the need to increase the proposed ratio of female students; the appointment of qualified West Indians, if available. Interestingly, West Indies cricket and the UWI have become our strongest regional institutions. Lloyd Braithwaite has indicated that in conducting his research, he had the advantage of being able to observe the behaviour of many of those interviewed on their return home.

Although the major portion of the research which lies at its basis was undertaken long ago, this volume represents more than a historical record. The Colonial Office and its Welfare Department have long disappeared and functions of the latter have presumably been assumed by the high commissions of the former colonial territories, now independent. Some significant conclusions expressed in the penultimate chapter remain valid and relevant currently. Thus, Braithwaite points to the positive effects of an education abroad in the development of self-confidence and of West Indian nationalism. But negative effects also emerge in the possible widening of the gap of consciousness between the middle class student and his or her environment – particularly the 'have nots' of the society. Further, as the author emphasized, the development of the UWI will not mean the end of the significant flow of West Indians to British universities for higher education.

This book should be read for the perceptiveness shown, the quality of analysis provided by the author and its wide ranging coverage of a subject which should be of interest to both the academic and a wider general readership.

Gladstone E. Mills
Emeritus Professor
University of the West Indies, Mona

Preface

The study of colonial students in Britain has excited a great deal of attention. The problem came most to the public eye when in 1951, students at the Hans Crescent hostel went 'on squat', refusing to vacate their rooms as requested; but there were other incidents which attracted attention from time to time. This came as a shock to many concerned people in public education who thought that adequate administrative provision had at last been made to cope with the problem of colonial students.

This study was begun before the interest in colonial students became common and is part of a continuing piece of research on the education of the new elite arising in the West Indies as in so many other colonial areas. Other published studies have concentrated on the problem as primarily one of policy formulation from the point of view of colonial and university administration. The present study is one concerned with the social, political and cultural leaders of a colonial area. Special attention has therefore been paid to the general ideological effects of the education of colonial students in Britain, the emergence of group action, the appeal of communism to colonials and the emergence of West Indian nationalism.

In its original conception, it was hoped to test many of the hypotheses put forward statistically. This has not proved possible. Nonetheless, the study may be of interest, first, because it represents an intensive study of one particular colonial group. It therefore delineates a little more clearly, it is hoped, the interplay between the cultural background of the students and the reaction to British society.

In spite of this, the problems of more general interest to colonial students, for example, the problem of colonial hostels, are also dealt with and, it is hoped, illuminated by this treatment. Second, the study is based not only on interview material but on participant observation over a period of years. Further, because of the high emotional interest aroused by the subject, the thinking surrounding the problem has, so far, primarily been policy oriented rather than sociological-theory oriented. It is hoped that the analysis of the problem in purely sociological terms is a special contribution.

Finally, in the light of the problems of bias (albeit not insurmountable) which arise in the course of sociological field work and of the differential reaction of subjects to different types of interviewers, it may be of some methodological interest to compare (that is, to consider) the results of the study of 'the colonial student problem' by a member of that group.

In the approach to the 'colonial student problem', there is another basic dichotomy. The problem, whether viewed in psychological, political or socio-logical terms, can be regarded either as an analysis of the reaction of the immigrant group itself or from the point of view of the host society. These two approaches are by no means contradictory. Rather, they are mutually complementary. Nonetheless, the issues tend to be confused because of the usual description of the problem as the colonial students' problem as if there were one single problem and one correct approach to it.

In this study, attention has been concentrated not upon the reactions of the host or British society but on those of the temporary student migrants. Naturally, in assessing this reaction it is necessary to take into account the reactions of the host society but the exact details of these are not entered into. On the question of discrimination and prejudice for instance, no effort is made to give the full range of British reactions to coloured colonials or other immigrant groups. The reported evidence of such prejudice and the nature of that prejudice are sufficiently well established to be taken as a given factor. Naturally, an accurate assessment of the 'racialism' of members of the host society is necessary if one is to be able to assess how real or how imaginary are the allegations of prejudice and discrimination made by the colonial student.

The examination of the West Indian student reaction seeks to be larger in scope than a mere study in the reaction to discrimination. Indeed, it seeks to show how the general overall picture of the problems of the group tend to be distorted by the accent on discrimination. One difficulty in assessing the material and its importance arises from the fact that much of the student reaction to the situation is purely temporary. This renders interview material doubly difficult. Sufficient evidence is available to show how students consciously and unconsciously distort the images of their own country and their own social role under the exigencies of adjusting to the situation. Even where participant observation is indulged in as a check on interview material, the difficulty can only be partially overcome since overt behaviour is often itself merely an expression of temporary adjustment to the situation.

In this respect, the writer has been fortunate to be able to observe the behaviour of many of the interviewees and members of West Indian student organizations on their return to the home country. This has led to a degree of caution in appraising the material and to an increased understanding which would hardly have been achieved otherwise.

Introduction

The West Indian Student in Britain

The Problem in its More General Setting

A generation ago, the problem of the overeducation of the colonial was considered to be an acute one. People interested in the development of the colonies stressed the fact that the 'educated African' for instance, did not fit easily into either the indigenous social structure or the framework of administration then established. Sometimes the problem was conceived as one of so changing the administrative structure that he could be more easily absorbed, or of so changing the structure of native institutions that he would become, albeit indirectly, more closely associated with the administration and hence play a more useful role. Sometimes, the problem was conceived as one of giving less education to the African so that there would be less personal maladjustment, less personal unhappiness among the Africans. The higher education of Africans – so the argument ran – was both rendering the education of Africans unhappy and making more difficult for the administration, the constructive tasks of administering justice and raising the levels of training. Perhaps due to good fortune, to divine providence, or to some innate quality, the task of the administration of the so-called backward peoples of the globe had fallen into the hands of European powers. This task would occupy them for several years, "perhaps even generations to come".[1] It was within the context of feeling and sentiment that the higher educational facilities for people in the colonies were conceived. But the problem was in reality larger than the colonial issue. Large areas of the world not directly under the control of the imperial powers came indirectly under their influence through the trusteeship of the League of Nations. Classed as backward, they were placed under the tutelage of the imperial powers because of their inability to sustain themselves under the strenuous conditions of the modern world.

The perspectives of the people in the colonies and in the trustee nations were, however, somewhat different. Within all the colonies and trusteeship territories, there developed nationalist demands either for independence or for a marked increase in participation in the administration of the territories.

The educated African, for instance, was considered maladjusted precisely because he challenged the European conception of his role in the colonial area. He felt competent to play a larger part in the governing of his area; he articulated his demands more clearly; he challenged the European not merely by a revival of primitive nativism – although nationalism had its nativistic aspects – but by an assertion (whether well or ill grounded) of the equal capacity of the African to take part in the running of his own affairs on the national level.

There can be little doubt that there were many oddities and absurdities in the case made out by the colonies for independence and increased self-government. Indeed, part of this study will be concerned with showing how in one particular area certain nationalist conceptions arise. These enabled hostile critics to pillory the educated representative of the so-called backward peoples in what appeared to the latter to be the most cruel fashion. The difficulties of the 'marginal man', the man of two worlds participating in both worlds and master of none were stressed. The doctor who believed in witchcraft, the lawyer who in secret session might consult the oracles appeared more ludicrous than the simple native untouched by European hand. If this were to be the result of higher education, perhaps it was a little premature to think in terms of higher education. So much remained to do to raise the standards of the mass of the people that it was possible sometimes to pose the question of higher education versus mass education as if there were a necessary antithesis between the two.

Nonetheless, higher education in the British colonies at any rate continued to be available to the colonial. Within the British universities, the tradition of hospitality to foreigners – long established and still unquestioned – meant that private citizens were able to obtain a higher education, no matter how inadequate might be the public provision in the colonial territory. Moreover, the problems of colonial administration within a liberal imperial framework were such that the creation of an educated African class, able and willing to profit from higher education, was almost a necessity.

The importance of the liberal tradition cannot be over stressed. In spite of the simple denunciations of imperialism which are fashionable (and not merely in colonial circles) it is clear that the process of imperial control worked within a normative framework which precluded or rendered difficult certain of the more dubious features of imperialism and facilitated the long-term development of self-government. This process has long been stressed by popular apologists for imperialism. The path of development of nationhood in the case of India for instance has been stressed as one of the glories of British imperial rule. Such claims cause hostility among most colonials and are considered an affront. Yet they contain much substance.

The logic of the development (granted, the maintenance of the democratic framework) in the United Kingdom appears impeccable. There is, indeed, from a sociological point of view nothing surprising in this development, but it presents as an 'inevitable' a development which could conceivably have taken a different form. After-the-event logic is not appreciated particularly by colonial participants. It resembles (in reverse) the inevitability of the Marxists. In the case of the latter, the belief in inevitability acts as a source of encouragement and a spur to action on the part of the revolutionary. In the imperial case, the logic of inevitable development appears to the radical colonial to be an invitation to cease his radical activity.[2] It appears to accept on its face value the argument of the administration that they are in fact training the people for self-government. But he is concerned less with praise for their achievement than in pointing out their sins of omission.

Further, the colonial or other representative of the 'backward' community is assured of the fact that his struggle has not been without results. His immediate perspective tends to dominate everything. He seeks to win a battle in a given situation; *everything* appears to depend upon the struggle in which he is engaged. He does in fact appreciate the moral framework established by the imperial powers. Indeed, much of his strategy and tactics are dictated by a realistic appreciation of the situation. But ideologically, he cannot concede anything to the enemy. He turns a blind eye to the facts when it is convenient. The establishment of Indian independence appears to him to be really the product of the self-sacrifice and devotion to the Indian nationalist cause.

Moreover, the contribution of the imperial power has often been mis-stated. Nationalism has been imported into the colonies both directly and indirectly. Ideas of nationalism, democracy and self-government have often had their origin and support in people from the metropolitan community. The sources of these ideas are many and various; and their relative strength still remains to be properly assessed. One of the sources (and in the light of subsequent developments we can say one of the most important sources) was precisely the education of colonials abroad.

Again, by the mere setting up of certain administrative areas, the imperial government served to bring about 'national' sentiment. It is true that the development of nationalism in the colonies did not always follow these purely administrative boundaries but the existence of a central administration as a frame did produce some form of unity of common sentiment.

Nationalism as one of the main cultural patterns of the West came to be taken over by the colonial country. This development of colonial nationalism has often been deplored, but it is an almost inevitable result of culture contact in the imperial-colonial relationship. The educated colonial who becomes the leader of colonial nationalism comes to be much criticized; it should be remembered that he is a logical product of a situation not of his making. This does not lessen his moral responsibility or reduce his blame worthiness; it does however reflect on the self-righteousness of his critics and place him socio-logically in his proper context. The criticism against the colonial who has received higher education is similar to that directed against the educated African in general. The latter has often been criticized for possessing a false scale of values, instead of serving his people, he thinks in terms of self-advancement; instead of going in for technical education, he wishes to become a clerk.[3] This false scale of values appears even more dubious when it appears to masquerade under a group affiliation with a systematic ideological justification.

This sort of criticism which developed against the educated colonial is illustrated by one who has had experience in the problems of administration of backward territories. W.R. Crocker in his book *On Governing Colonies* (1947), strikes heavily at the 'evolué' or 'evolués' who are the product of the colonial system. He observes that there are differences in the colonial policies of metropolitan countries. He comments with favour on the British policy of social distance, and criticizes the French for their assimilationist and socially egalitarian position. Characteristic pictures of 'evolués' dressed stiffly and uncomfortably in European dress are reproduced and stories belittling them are retailed with little disguised relish.

The general criticisms are followed by a more explicit evaluation of educational policy. Of the British system he writes:

> The special evils of British educational practices have been fourfold.
>
> First, the multiplication of the quasi literate clerk class and the neglect of vocational education and with it the neglect of the village schools and of the countryman in general. Second, the imposition of more or less unmodified curricula taken in bloc from English schools and designed for English certificates (the setting and marking of these examination papers which is or was done in England by people who had never seen Africa!); the cult of the certificate as Lord Harlech called it when he was Under-Secretary of State. Third (it is part of the same mentality), the sending, often on scholarships at Government expense, of Africans to England. Some Africans, especially of the Sierra Leone Tribe, who are now quite Europeanized do well there; but to send Africans in the numbers sent from the Gold Coast and Nigeria is good neither for the individuals concerned nor for their country. Fourth, the uncontrolled or insufficiently controlled Mission school. (Crocker 1947: 56)

This does not mean that Mr Crocker is opposed to all higher education but he wishes the education to be related to the government and personally, to the special place of the African. He is not unsympathetic to the provision of technical education but he regards the Africanization of the administrative service as something that is developing, perhaps too quickly.

> Official policy has declared for maximum Africanization to the limit of the possible. Officials on the spot are less confident about the wisdom of the policy and criticism notably on the grounds of compatibility is rife.
>
> There is a strong case for those who argue that the time has not yet come for Africanizing the Administrative service. It is conceivable that an African medical or engineering officer will carry out his technical duties not less efficiently than the European. But the Administrative Officer is more than a technical officer – he is the British Raj. (Crocker 1947: 129)

In keeping with this somewhat negative evaluation of the role of the educated 'evolué', he dismisses them as being of little importance. "The new elite in Bakar, or Elizabethville is more noisy than numerous" (Crocker 1947: 145).

The case of Mr Crocker is interesting because the book appeared in the postwar world less than ten years ago. The position appears ludicrous now in the light of the general developments in the colonial and underdeveloped areas generally and in West Africa in particular. Indeed, Crocker himself within a few years of the publication of the book radically revised his position and published another book *Self-Government for the Colonies* (1949), in which the case for self-government was persuasively put. The reasons given by Crocker for his change of position are interesting. They are contact with American Negroes and the political developments within the United Nations.

The fact brings into prominence one of the main points of difference between the contemporary colonial elite and the imperial conservatives. This is the difference in time perspective. The conservative is convinced of the good that he is doing, of the altruism in which he or his country is acting and he sincerely believes that ultimately the people under his country's guidance will be led into truly civilized progress. Surveying the backwardness of the colonies, the formidable nature of the task and conceiving of the problem as precisely one in which his own country will play a role in solving, his perspectives are long-term; the task appears immense and he speaks in terms of 'ultimate' self-government. The colonial radical leader on the other hand is concerned primarily with his own role, or at least the role of the group with which he identifies. He claims that this group has a special role to play and he compares this special role with the total task of developing his country. Without formulating it as pithily, he is aware that in the long run we are all dead. He is interested in the here and now.

Developments in the international field have led to an increased consciousness of the role of the colonial elite. The problem of the educated African, for instance, is now perceived as a major problem, not because of their maladjustment but because they are perceived as a powerful 'elite'. A few years ago, they were dismissed with passing references. Now, special studies are in progress on the African as well as other elites of the underdeveloped areas. In point of fact, these elites were indeed "more noisy than numerous", but because of changes in the social structure their noise was able to win a sympathetic enough response from the mass of the people.

In one sense, the problems of the colonial elite must be considered within the context of the development of relations between more technically developed and underdeveloped areas. For instance, the problem of differential salaries and allowances inevitably arises whether the country is independent or in varying degrees of political dependence. The question of expatriation allowances, for instance, is one of the highly charged emotional subjects for the colonial elite. It is interesting therefore to see that the same problem arose and was one of the points of dispute in the Tito–Stalin controversy. Even in areas like the West Indies where no formal differential has existed, the subject is charged with high emotional interest and enters in a scarcely veiled fashion into all questions affecting the terms of administrative service.

Again, the problem can be conceived in a much wider setting as one of the vast processes of intercultural education in which certain major countries like the United States and Britain play a major role. The education of foreign students in the United States parallels in many important respects the problems of colonial students in the metropolitan countries, and although there are also important differences, a comparison of the situation in the United States and Britain should be rewarding.

The position with regard to the American studies (they will be examined below) has recently been described in the bulletin of the Carnegie Foundation:

> What of the foreign student in America? One of the striking developments since the end of World War II has been a threefold increase in the number of young men and women who come from abroad to pursue their studies at American colleges and universities. Last year, a census taken by the Institute of International Education showed 34,000 students from 129 nations enrolled in 1,452 institutions of higher learning – some in every state in the Union.
>
> Half of these are on their own resources. Others are on government aid and from sources in the USA. Some are given college and university scholarships, USA government grants, civic and community organization awards and foundation funds.
>
> One thread that runs through all the student exchange programmes, both public and private, is the belief that much more is involved than just formal schooling and the acquisition of knowledge.
>
> The goals of exchange, naturally, are numerous and various. Ranking high however, is the hope that exchange of students can help to build greater international understanding and goodwill. Undoubtedly, most Americans welcome the presence of students from abroad, and probably go on to assume that the 34,000

young men and women studying on our (i.e. America's) campuses will return to their home countries with increased understanding of and respect for the United States, its people and its institutions.

REACTIONS TO AMERICA

Most foreign students do respond favourably to their American experience. As would be expected, there are a few exceptions. What are the factors which may lead these few to acquire distorted, or at least incomplete views of the United States? How can these factors be controlled?

These are just a few of the many questions which the Social Science Research Council asked a group of educators and social scientists to consider some three years ago.

Under the guidance of a committee chaired by Ralph L. Beals, explanatory studies were begun with financial support from the Ford and Rockefeller Foundations and Carnegie Corporation. The studies which are being conducted by M. Brewster Smith are primarily directed toward delineating the process of learning and adjustment entailed in foreign study and identifying the major factors that affect its outcome.

Some results of the investigations into one aspect of the overall problem – how foreign students see the United States – have already been reported in various journals, and the Council has plans for the publication of several formal reports within the coming month.

The evidence is as yet by no means conclusive, but it seems to show that at least in some cases students find their stay in this country a vexing, baffling and frustrating experience and they may go home with resentful, even hostile attitudes toward the United States.

As an illustration of the type of problem that may arise, one may take the case of a Japanese student who is an intellectual, a member of the upper socioeconomic class and who has a strong admiration for certain aspects of American culture.

His decision to attend an American college is the most crucial one of his life thus far. His family and friends wish him well, and he leaves for the United States with high expectations. Arriving at the College Campus, he experiences all the normal bewilderment of any new student, American or foreign, facing the necessity of finding living quarters, adjusting to his studies, and making a place for himself in the student community.

This student, for example, comes from a country that sets great store by ceremonial politeness. Personal relationships are subtle and intricate and social obligations are held in most delicate balance. The easy friendliness of Americans almost certainly surprises –maybe even frightens –him a bit. He hesitates to accept a proffered invitation for fear that he may not be able to repay it properly. His hesitation may be interpreted as standoffishness and the reaction may be a show of pique. Now thoroughly confused, our Japanese student may tend to withdraw into himself and his defensive gesture may confound the misunderstanding.

When he completes his education and returns to Japan, a whole new set of problems may now confront him. Business ventures in Japan, to a far greater extent than in this country, are organized along family or 'clique' lines. If he has lost touch, if he has not been integrated into the pattern of family and personal relationships, his opportunities for advancement in business or professional life may be hindered. Again, his American studies may be better suited to the culture and technology of the United States, than to conditions as he finds them in Japan. He may find that his American education has left him something of a 'foreigner' in his own land. His ultimate reaction to his American experience, if not actually hostile, at least may be – understandably – 'mixed'.

Problems of various types are mentioned by students from different areas. Students from India were students in this country and returned Indian students were observed in their own country under a project independently conceived and supported by the Hazen Foundation.[4]

Typical reactions are described by M. Brewster Smith:

Equally affronted by American ignorance of their homeland and by what passes for informal discussions of it in the public media, these students are likely to develop a view of America that is more a reflex of their defensive needs, than a reflection of personal experience. These are the students who cite American race relations as a counter to criticisms of caste, American materialism to balance home-country poverty – and so on through a long list of standard reactions to the probing of standard 'sensitive areas'.

In contrast, Mr Smith reports, "Scandinavian students exemplify the other extreme. Coming to America with few doubts about their national worth they characteristically take a much more realistic matter-of-fact view of their American experience."

So far, we have been stressing the importance of the colonial elite and assuming that the elite is identical with those who have received higher education. It is clear that this is not entirely the case. The term elite is one which sociologists have come to use in a special way. In common speech, the term tends to refer to the people with 'social' influence and to the 'upper class' in terms of social status. As used in general sociology however, the term has come to mean those who play a special role in the social system, in particular generalized roles of leadership and roles involving the use of power and authority. In this sense, it can be seen that although many of the elite in colonial areas possess higher education, and give ideological leadership and high level inspiration to the nationalist movement, these roles are by no means exclusively confined to those with academic experience.

It is clear also that in most colonies, we are seeing or have seen a change in conception of the social roles of those who have received higher education. In most areas (in spite of the cultural differences and the consequent rejection of some of the Western trained) the association with the metropolitan power brought high status. Those with professional or academic education in the institutions of the West appear to form at an early date a social elite in the narrow sense of the term. In the course of time, members of this group come to play in ever increasing numbers, a special elite role in the sociological sense of the term.

This particular process has never received the scholarly attention it deserves. Anthropologists with their particular frame of reference were more concerned in practice with tribal and community studies. The question was so intimately bound up with the political life of the community that it called for a certain amount of political comment. But the fact that it became a 'political' question made it the subject for assertion and counter assertion rather than scholarly reflection. Among the sociologists, there was some concern with the problem as evidenced in *The Marginal Man* (1937) by Stonequist, a work which was inspired by Robert E. Park (1923). In any case, the unfortunate division then existing between those academics concentrating on the study of primitive society and the sociologists making a study of Western industrialized society hindered the development of sociological interest in the subject.

Further, the involvement of so many educated colonials in the political development of the community meant that there was little reflective or revealing work on the psychological processes involved. Thus A.R. Desai, in his *Social Background of Indian Nationalism* (1948), pays no special attention to an analysis of the special role of the Western educated in fostering and developing the cause of Indian nationalism. Only one study that the writer is aware of paid the question serious attention. For the rest, there is perhaps as much sociological insight and contribution to the subject in the book by the journalist Payne, *Richer in Asia,* as is to be found anywhere else.

Fortunately, in one or two cases, we have revealing autobiographies which give some insight into the problems faced by students from underdeveloped areas, in particular, the autobiographies of Gandhi (1940), Nehru (1936), and Edward Attiyah (1946).

In the case of the West Indies, there is much indirect evidence of the role of the educated colonial in introducing ideas of political reform into the community. However, in only one case has there been any explicit discussion of the problem in a psychologically revealing fashion.

One of the most interesting, sensitive, and psychologically penetrating accounts of the reaction of the 'colonial' student to his experience in England is that of Edward Attiyah in *An Arab Tells His Story* (1946). Although the background of the writer is so very different in some respects from that of the West Indian, there are many similarities. In the case of Attiyah, he grew up in Syria without any sense of national consciousness. As a Christian Syrian, his awareness of collective relationships was not national at all. "Christians versus Moslems – this was my first notion of collective human relationships" (Attiyah 1946: 10). In much the same way, many West Indians became conscious of racial factors, of the antagonism between white and coloured before they became aware of any national identity. The author experienced the same identification with Britain which was as commonplace a generation ago in the West Indies. His choice was England but others chose to identify themselves with France. In much the same manner, 'radicalism' in the West Indies glorified 'American' success, military and economic, or (more rarely) French assimilationist policy and counter-posed this to the decadent British admired by their rivals, the loyalists and conservatives (Attiyah 1946: 27).

In this 'counter-national' atmosphere as Attiyah calls it, there was

> a regular stream of well-educated Syrians, in many cases professional men, leaving Syria in quest of wider and freer fields of work. For every Syrian who was out to stay and work at home when he had finished his education, there was one who looked forward to going abroad. Indeed you first tried to find work outside of Syria and only stayed at home if you could not get away. (Attiyah 1946: 26)

The attachment to England and English ideals was reinforced by education in an English school at Alexandria. Victoria College was followed by a sojourn at Oxford where the favourable impression of Britain was reinforced by an enjoyable study of the modern greats. Attiyah met with minimum prejudice but having fallen in love with an English girl, he came up against the problem of the prejudices against mixed marriages. He feared opposition both at home and from the English family into which he proposed to enter. The situation he described can be paralleled by many a colonial student. Yet in practice, the stiffer opposition came from his own family.

The agreeable impression created by his stay in England naturally did not predispose him to radicalism. It was only later that his radicalism developed. It was not that he was not aware of prejudices among the British. Even before leaving Syria, he had heard of British prejudices. His father admired the British profoundly but held the view that they considered themselves superior to him socially and racially. He therefore avoided intimate contact with them. He writes:

> It was very painful for me to hear that the British looked down on us. I tried to persuade myself that it was not true, that anyhow it was not true of the majority of Englishmen . . . My first reactions to reported instances of the contempt of Englishmen for Syrians were those of resentment, of hatred for the particular offender. I felt that somehow the insult touched me personally, since an English- man who despised one Syrian would despise another, would despise me. It was not a question of standing up for my own dignity as an individual.
>
> But as various little incidents and the feelings they aroused sank into my mind, I myself began to be conscious of a feeling of contempt for Easterners, and to be half ashamed of being one. My desire to identify myself with the English people, to become more and more English in my habits and ways, to adopt England and be adopted by her was greatly intensified by these feelings. Had I been a nationalist, had I had any strong feeling of solidarity with other Syrians, of love for my country and my race, my reaction, I suppose, would have been the very opposite of this. I should then have reacted by hating Englishmen and asserting my nationality with a fanatical aggressiveness and a pretended belief in its superiority. But I was not and never had been a nationalist. (Attiyah 1946: 42)

In England, these feelings of shame were smoothed out by contacts on the basis of equality with fellow students and friends. But even in the favourable picture of life at Oxford given by Attiyah, there is some suggestion of feelings of difference and colonial solidarity. However, it was only on his return to the East that radical feelings developed. Having obtained a job at Gordon College, Khartoum, he found that there was a sharp division between the British and non-British staff. The British tutors each had separate offices while the Syrians shared a common room. Attiyah believed that the British tutors, recent graduates from Oxford and Cambridge would befriend him, but as he noted:

> My expectations were disappointed. The British Tutors did not show any desire
> to know me. They nodded with a polite smile when we met in the corridors, and
> once during a football match which we were all watching, one of them spoke to
> me a few words, asking me what college I had been at, but for four or five months
> that was all the human intercourse I had with them. Towards the end of the school
> year, they did invite me to dinner once at their mess, but by that time it was clear
> to me that the kind of friendship I wanted and had hoped to find among them was
> out of the question. (Attiyah 1946: 137)

The crisis came when the governor general of the Sudan visited the school
and reviewed a physical display by the students. The non-British staff had to
be content to watch the proceedings from the common room while the British
staff attended and were presented to the governor general. Attiyah immediately joined a Syrian club and became a nationalist.

> The new affiliation was not recognized by the tribe I had for so long tried to belong
> to . . . here things were different. I was regarded by the British community as a
> foreigner. Its doors were closed to me . . .
>
> Mortification was not slow in turning into resentment. The domain from which
> I was excluded began to arouse my hostility. The dwellers in that land began to
> assume in my eyes the aspect of forbidding and arrogant strangers, their sump-
> tuous houses and spacious gardens, the character of feudal castles housing an alien
> and haughty aristocracy. The manifestations of British privilege and British
> prestige began to gall me, and for the first time I began to experience towards the
> British Empire the hostile feelings of a subject who resents its rule and its might,
> because he has no share in them. What I had taken a personal pride in till then
> was becoming now the enemy of my pride, and I began to rebel against the glory
> I could not be associated with. (Attiyah 1946: 137)

To add to the complications, we find that this radicalism of Attiyah in
response to discrimination on his return 'home' was only temporary. He
eventually obtained employment in the Sudanese government in a congenial
job which allowed him to make use of his personal experience in order to
interpret the Sudanese to the British and vice versa.

Lest we care to think of Attiyah's case as typical, we should perhaps cite
the case of one of his most outstanding pupils, Mowaiya who also went away
to study English literature at the American university at Beirut, only to find
the life of a literary giant in Cairo difficult and a lack of hospitality to his ideas
when he returned home. Maturity and responsible office were not for him. He
ended up in a lunatic asylum.

The experiences of Attiyah are paralleled in some respects by those of Gandhi. Here too we find an initial attempt at assimilation followed by disillusionment on return home.[5] Gandhi, having achieved a certain degree of adjustment to Western conditions, returned to India to find that the status system there was completely different to that in England. While in that country, he had become acquainted with an Englishman who had a brother working as a magistrate in the district in which Gandhi intended to practice. Gandhi received a letter of introduction to the latter. However, on presenting it on his return to the homeland, he received a hostile and unfriendly reception because in presenting it he had violated the prescribed norms and status system. Consequently, he was ordered out of the magistrate's office and had to seek employment in another city. Hence his visit to South Africa.

These instances, interesting in themselves, should warn us against too narrow an approach to the problem of the education of colonials in Britain. The role of this education abroad in promoting nationalism is a complex one, and cannot be explained purely in terms of the reaction to prejudice and to problems of adjustment.

In the case of the West Indies, there have been few people who have articulated their experiences in Britain. Undoubtedly for the majority, the contact with the larger world must have been something of a shock. It is clear, however, that the drive towards assimilation was the dominant theme; that a nationalism sufficient to sustain and make articulate the radical theme had not yet come into existence. A few examples of the move towards radicalism would appear to have been directed towards a much broader colonial reaction. This was reflected in the attachment of students to the League of Coloured Peoples. In one instance, we have an account of the process by which this awareness and identification with the larger colonial world takes place. In his book *The Evolution of the Negro* (1929), Mr N.E. Cameron of British Guiana gives an incidental account of these processes:

> While I was in England I had many conversations with African students and thereby discovered that the bulk of African people were illiterate; the desire then entered into me to go as a sort of educational missionary to some part of this continent. The finest part and the part most in need of such assistance seemed to be Liberia.
>
> The state of my ignorance and preconceived notions is best brought out by my surprise to find that the people lived in huts in settled countries and cultivated the soil instead of wandering about in forests and eating the raw flesh of wild beasts.

I found that West Indians in particular were loth to believe many things I told them, considering that these things did not fall in with their preconceived notions. For instance they would hardly believe that the Africans as early as 1450 and before were making cloth, and though the poorest wore only the absolute minimum, those better off were clad in their own way.

At times I was even humorous. When some writer described the inhabitants of fishing villages as naked, I asked myself "How is it that these Christians instead of regarding the people as savages did not consider them as approximating to the perfection of Adam and Eve?" I was humorous here, because by now I had known that the art of cloth-making was widespread over these countries.

I mention that with regard to our past, we usually adopt ostrich tactics but we are sometimes forcibly reminded of it by certain European workers, thus, one editor wrote that this country was being partly governed by 'descendants of slaves' and more than one referred to the people as such.

I remember a most interesting conversation I had with one of my supervisors which he concluded with "What I should like to see in the African is the spirit of *self-help*. Let him show what he can do and I shall respect him for it". Beautiful words and quite fair though respect must also be given to what the African has done as brought out in their work.

Still more interesting was an address which I heard delivered by an anthropologist. In the course of his remarks he said, 'What an Englishman likes is pride in self, pride in race, *pride in your own traditions*. To see people talking with pride of their own achievements is his heart's delight, but he definitely cannot bear the fact of coloured Americans trying to be 'White men' and merely imitating Europeans." Fine! I was pleasantly surprised to hear this as I used to think that Englishmen, and for that matter Europeans in general, saw nothing good and beautiful in things that were quite different from their own and that they interpreted differences as inferiority. (Cameron 1959: vii–xii)

Again, in a recent speech outlining the nature of his relationships with the Caribbean Commission,[6] Dr Eric Williams, one of the outstanding intellectuals of the British Caribbean, states that while a student he had belonged to no political party but had, at Oxford, attended meetings of the All-India Students Organization. There is some indication in the rest of the speech that this outstanding West Indian nationalist also developed something of a 'colonial' identification. He quotes from his notes on an interview which he had with a British official in Washington and notes that the latter never expected a colonial to speak to him in that manner.

The process of the development of West Indian nationalism through contact with the larger world abroad is a much wider one than that of the higher education of students. The growth of West Indian nationalism among emigrant groups in the West Indies is a subject worthy of investigation. Those with higher education and most easily able to establish status on their return home have frequently done so and this is the reason for the importance of this group.

It is clear however, that in the case of Cipriani and Butler in Trinidad, Manley, Nethersole, Bustamante and Richard Hart in Jamaica, that experience of the larger world has been instrumental in the function of national feeling as well as in the self-confidence necessary for effective leadership. In the case of Cipriani for instance, it was his role as advocate of West Indians at court martials during World War I which led to his reputation as a fearless advocate of the people opposed to racial discrimination. It was this reputation which led to his initiation into politics as a radical labour candidate opposed to the conservative Major Rust.

The vice principal of the University College of the West Indies has also given an account of his own reaction to the nationalism of the British people. In an article discussing the rise and significance of West Indian nationalism, he describes how during the last war he observed the reaction of the British people.

> They knew that their country was in need of them and I felt that because they knew this they marched all the more proudly . . . As I watched I saw that they did not march alone . . .
>
> . . . This, I said to myself, is the meaning of history. Here is a nation which can face the present because it knows how to draw upon the reservoirs of courage and of spiritual power from its past.
>
> After the parade I marched straight back to my lodgings, a gloomy room in the basement of a gloomy building near Hyde Park. My mind turned to the island of my birth, to the lands of the Caribbean, to the people of the West Indies, and I looked back at my own life and thought of the way in which I had slowly discovered that I was a West Indian, that this was my home and these people my people.

In the absence of other articulate expressions of the reaction of the West Indian elite, the only possible way of evaluating their reaction to experiences in Britain is by going out, meeting them, interviewing and observing. The report which follows is the result of such an effort.

Chapter 1

The Nature
of the Problem

The Problem as a Political Problem

The problem of the education of colonial students in Britain is very often seen as a political problem; as one of cementing or preventing the disruption of ties between the mother country and the colonial territories. If we take the West Indies for instance, it is clear that education in the metropolitan country is valued as a means of furthering the development of the colony along sound lines. Hence the provision of study courses in the United Kingdom (UK) through study leave; the condition that open scholarships could be held only in the UK or some other Commonwealth country; the provision of special training courses for civil servants; the special scholarships and visits of observation by leaders in the trade union and so on.

On the other hand, this process of educating the colonial in Britain immediately brings up the problem of how far education in Britain results not in a cementing of the relationships between the colonies and the mother country on the one hand but in causing national disaffection in the colony. Many people believe that the bitterness resulting from racial discrimination in the UK may be a factor disrupting the political tie.

In any case, the broad political responsibility of the Colonial Office for the colonial student population was accepted in principle, as can be seen by the establishment of a separate Welfare Department of the Colonial Office, primarily concerned with dealing with the problems of the colonial student population.

The idea that ignorant landladies could in fact affect the political unity of the Empire, at first confined to a few radical thinkers, has become widespread. Correspondingly, the notion has gained credence that favourable experience of life in the UK should be provided out of sheer political expediency. Legal, administrative and institutional controls immediately suggest themselves in this context.

The Liberal Approach to the Problem

Sometimes, but not always, this essentially political approach is associated with a 'liberal' approach to race relations. Indeed, frequently the liberal approach in race relations is essentially a nonpolitical one. That is, the problem is conceived as one of liberal principle; of the individual assuming a tolerant attitude in race relations. The essential liberal approach, however, frequently appears to be one lacking in warmth, insight and understanding. In the first place, the liberal, taking his stand in principle, tends to feel self-righteous in his role and hence self-conscious. Moreover, because of his stand in principle, he tends to be concerned primarily with his own role and sense of moral obligation. Sometimes therefore, his stand on principle is embarrassing to those whom it is intended to benefit. In any case, it blinds him to that sympathetic insight which would render the contradictory and sometimes puzzling behaviour of the coloured person comprehensible. In general for instance, the liberal defines the problem of race relations as one of good interpersonal relations regardless of race and colour. He therefore tends to look with especial favour upon this type of relationship entered into by the West Indian as successful adjustment. Insofar as good interpersonal relationships becomes a matter of policy, it tends to become one of opposition on principle to segregated hostels, of seeing manifestations of prejudice as due to stupidity and ignorance. The oversensitivity of the colonial and his aggressiveness tends to be judged on the basis of equality and stupidity and ignorance likewise condemned.

It will be part of the argument to show that the definition of the problem as one of liberalism in interpersonal relations is essentially a false one. In the first place, the 'successful adjustment' of the colonial may be bought at too high a price – both in individual and social terms – and in the second place, this approach, while appearing superficially correct, violates in effect the principle of equality on which it is superficially based. It tends to place the stress and responsibility for adjustment on the minority group. Equality of treatment of both groups makes sense in fact, only if both groups are similarly placed. In terms of depth and intensity of feeling and in terms of the power relations between the groups with which the individuals are identified, it is a mistake to regard the immigrants from the colonial society and the members of the host society as being essentially on the same footing. This view of the problem as a political one apparently inspired the researchers of Political and Economic Planning (PEP).[7] It is assumed – without an intimate knowledge of the social structure of the various territories – that the students in the UK will play an important part in the life of their countries when they return. Although this is the case in many instances, this is not universally so and one suspects that there could be less preoccupation with the problem if there were some scientific means of assessing the true weight of the 'educated colonial' in the political relationship.

This evaluation of the problem is encouraged by the fact that many students away from their homes have fantastic conceptions of their own roles in the home country; conceptions in many cases only possible because of their absence from the government which they profess to know and to be able to influence so well.

Although sufficiently precise information was not forthcoming from the present investigation, an attempt will be made in this paper to put the political aspect in its proper perspective.

Student Definition of Their Problems

The definition by the students of their own problems can only be taken as a partial guide to the source of their discontent. Elsewhere, we have indicated how acceptable the political definition of the problem was with its exaggerated stress on the special role of the colonial student. The definition of the problem is also subject to other forms of distortion, both on the conscious and unconscious levels.

To all newly arrived students, the problem of material provision looms large. There is a stress on climatic factors, the question of adequate clothes and the provision of food. However, it should be observed that the stress on these matters frequently increases. Minor irritations are evaluated within the total context of the individual's expectations and aspirations. They can either be taken in their stride or exaggerated into something of great importance. Naturally, the adjustment in point of detail affects all students but some, as soon as they have affected a personal adjustment to the situation, forget about the matter while others continued to grouse.

Food was a particular case in point. The plentiful use of sugar in the West Indies was not common in Britain and during the war and early postwar years there was a shortage of sugar which made "the cup of lousy unsweetened tea" of the calypsonian unacceptable to the West Indian. The cup of unsweetened tea either became a symbol to newcomers of the status of the well adjusted or on the other hand, became a common cause of complaint and solidarity between the newly arrived and older discontented sojourners.

Frequently indeed, the newcomers although preoccupied with the problems of adjustment to the new situation, evaluated their problems in realist terms until they learnt from older students that there were legitimate grouses and these were symbolic affirmations of colonial solidarity. The fact that these problems loom large in the reports of the students should not be taken seriously. How relative these complaints are can be gathered by the fact that at the University College of the West Indies similar distortions and complaints can be observed among students arriving in Jamaica from the other islands. These students complain on the basis of a slight difference in temperature, of the cold and their inability to study effectively on that account. There is also the fact that the problems of loneliness and discrimination sometimes raise such a range of problems among the newly arrived, that they pin this general discontent upon one feature of the environment.

The Psychological Approach to the Problem

From an academic point of view, it would be possible to analyse the problems of adjustment from the psychological point of view. Such an approach would take into account the varying personality types which compose the student population, the level of experience of the host society, the differential reaction of the various personality types to the same situation and the range of similar reactions of different personality types. If quantitative studies using control groups are not possible, it would still be possible on an impressionistic basis and through case studies to delineate a little more clearly the nature of the problems of adjustment of students.

The prime focus of this study, however, has been sociological rather than psychological. Nonetheless, some attention has been given to these problems, because of their intrinsic interest, their importance from the point of view of policy formulation, and their relevance for understanding some of the sociological problems involved.

The Sociological Approach to the Problem

The problem of the integration of foreign and of coloured students into the UK community can be regarded as a purely sociological problem. It is a process similar to others going on all over the world and the reactions of minority groups to the host country and vice versa in itself demands attention.

But the narrowly conceived political approach to the problem can be placed in a more broadly conceived sociological context. Quite apart from the problem of the political relationship, we need to know what it means to a dependent community to have most of its highly placed professional people educated in a metropolitan community. The role of the radical leader in politics must come in for consideration but as part of a wider relationship. This alone can place the question of radicalism in its true perspective. The study is here conceived therefore as essentially a preliminary to the study of the emergence of a new elite in the British West Indies.

In addition, however, the study is sociological in its perspectives because it seeks not merely to give an account of the individual's reaction to his problems of adjustment, but to describe as well the process of group formation and group action, and the development of a group 'culture of protest' as a result of the situation in which the West Indian students find themselves.

Chapter 2

The Background
of the
Students

After the failure of several attempts to settle white European labour in the West Indies, the social structure of the islands developed into one in which there was a distinct cleavage within the society. At the bottom of the social scale stood the slaves with interesting social differentiations among themselves. Occupying something of an intermediate position were the free coloureds. At the upper end of the scale there were the white groups. The majority of owners of the properties in the island were absentee proprietors who left the management of their plantations to attorneys while they resided in England. The orientation of the most influential section of the society therefore was not towards the islands from which they drew their wealth but towards the 'mother country'. This orientation led to a great neglect of educational facilities in the area.[8]

Ideally, the children of the whites were educated in the UK. Not all of the whites in the colonies were able to afford this, consequently some provision was made in the region for the education of the whites. On the whole, educational facilities for the slaves were nonexistent until a few years before the abolition of slavery.

With the abolition of slavery, there was a great concern for the adequate provision of education for the masses of the people. Both missionary endeavour and governmental concern had a greater task before them than they could manage. Nonetheless, there developed in nearly all the colonies a framework for elementary education and in the late nineteenth and early twentieth century there was much concern for the implementation of adult education. Inevitably, the administrative practices and the context of education drew heavily on English experience. From early, criticism of the lack of adaptation to the local environment varied.

The overall effect and function of the educational system in the second half of the nineteenth century and the first half of the twentieth was to create three quite separate streams:

(1) In the first place there was the elementary school system which provided for a certain number of the lower class.

(2) Second, there was the secondary school system.

(3) Third, there was the provision for higher education abroad, chiefly for the learned professions.

The Function of Elementary Education

The elementary school system in its early stages was more concerned with supplying a minimum standard of literacy. The impact of the primary school was much greater in the towns where differentiation meant that functional literacy was of some economic importance and, in an area so largely dependent on external markets, literacy assumed some importance for the countryside as well. But, by and large, in spite of the attempts to introduce agricultural education into the schools, the contribution was rather in the direction of providing basic skills rather than content.

In so far as there was limited occupational mobility, the elementary school served a special function within 'working class' or 'lower class' occupations. There was also a certain mobility from the lower classes into the middle class. Nearly all the elementary school teachers were recruited from people who had passed through the elementary school.

Moreover, there was some limited mobility within the system. This was more marked in some islands than in others, but everywhere there was talk of the educational ladder, the provision of free places in the secondary school for brilliant pupils from the elementary school and of scholarships for study at universities abroad. The facilities thus provided were limited in scope but were sufficiently large to make a difference psychologically. People felt in many territories that there was in fact a career open to the talented once the successes of a few outstanding cases became generally known.

The Objectives of Secondary Education

As regards secondary education, there was some official concern as well. This was reflected not only in the establishment of government secondary schools (Queen's Royal College in Trinidad; Queen's College, British Guiana; Cornwall College, Jamaica), but also in the liberal grants which were given to recognized secondary schools.

The precise objectives of secondary education have never been clear. In all cases, the provision of secondary education would appear to bear some relation to the market for the graduates of such schools. In a modern industrialized society, the necessity of an 'elementary' or 'primary' education is obvious in a purely material sense. Moreover, failure to provide such education would go against the grain of the ideology of achievement and equality of opportunity which to a certain extent must develop in a highly industrialized society. At the same time, there is a special demand for certain levels of education both technical and general which is not satisfied by the provision of elementary education and by a labour supply that is merely literate. Consequently, special institutions are developed or transformed for the purpose of meeting the demand.

This function of secondary education tends to be confused because of three facts:

(a)   The function of supplying general education at the secondary level is needed in the preindustrial society as well. The carry over of many of the institutions from a preindustrial era, and, in many cases, the prestige attached to these institutions leads to an assumption of the continuity of function of the school. In a sense there is continuity but there are also important changes in social function. In the second place, the fact that there is a limited market only for graduates of secondary schools precludes the development of such education on the scale which would make it acceptable in a democratic society.

(b)   There has never been any controversy over the development of technical education beyond the primary level. In the case of secondary education, we can look upon it as a special type of vocational training for which the imbibing of certain of these cultural and literary traditions is required (for example, teaching, administration).

(c) These literary traditions of the secondary school have been inherited from a more sharply class divided society and this unfortunately has beclouded the issue. The provision of education appears, in a democratic society, as the provision of careers open to the talented and the limitations of secondary or grammar school education appears to have a class bias.

The function of the secondary school in the West Indies tends to be shrouded in the same class controversy as in the UK. But here, the relevance of supply to demand is much more keenly felt. From the governmental point of view, there is a strict limit on the provision of funds. There is need for the provision of higher education on a limited scale and the idea that there should be public provision of universal primary education is widespread.

From the point of view of the mass of the people, secondary education was viewed in an entirely vocational perspective. It was regarded as a means of training for entry into the professions or into the local civil service. It was realized by nearly everyone that the number of opportunities in this field were sharply limited. The radical agitation never developed for the spread of secondary education to all areas. Rather, it concentrated on making available to outstanding pupils of the lower classes a share in the limited opportunities provided by the society.

Tertiary Education

Although the orientation was towards higher education abroad, there was provision in the area itself for some forms of higher education. During the seventeenth century, there was a request by Codrington for the establishment of a college for the training of ministers of religion. The relics of this request are now to be seen in Codrington College, Barbados. where a limited number of pupils take degrees in classics and theology. The place functions primarily as a theological training centre for the Church of England. But the institution also supplies a limited number of teachers of classics. There is also an occasional lecture in oratory in order to keep to the terms of the trust, but there were also earlier attempts to make provision for higher education in the area.

The Imperial College of Tropical Agriculture was established in 1921. This college was imperial in perspective. It was intended to serve the whole of the colonial empire by giving postgraduate training to agricultural officers. The fact that it was situated within the West Indies was largely accidental. However, the exact purpose was not very clear in the minds of the general public of the area who felt that the Imperial College owed a special obligation. Partly on account of this local pressure and partly because the college existed to serve the West Indies as well as the rest of the colonial empire, special courses were run for a diploma of the Imperial College. Eventually, the students of the course reached degree standard. Scholarships were granted by the various governments and in many USA and Canadian universities, the diploma was accepted as being equivalent to a degree.

In the 1870s, there was a proposal for a university college in Jamaica but this failed because of sectarian differences. Later, in the last decade of the nineteenth century there were attempts to start a university college which would train people for the external examination of the University of London, but this too ended in failure after having produced only 30 graduates. Those attempts at university education were all abortive. In 1932, the position in Jamaica was described thus:[9]

- 248 Public aid for university and collegiate education in Jamaica is confined to the expenditure from scholarships. One Rhodes Scholarship is also available annually.

- 249 There are no institutions of university standard. The training colleges for teachers are not affiliated. The only other institutions of collegiate rank are those training for the Ministry.

- 250 There was formerly a university college in connection with the Jamaica College for boys from which during its existence from 1890–1902 thirty students passed. Special students studying for external examinations of the University of London may still be taken, but the block grant of £700 given in special recognition of their work to the school has long been absorbed in its general purposes.

- 251 The student who wishes to pursue his education beyond the secondary state must therefore, with the exception of those who study privately for examinations of Arts, Science and Law, look outside Jamaica. The question of a West Indian university was revived at the First West Indian Conference in 1929, which recorded its opinions that the governments concerned should consider further the desirability of such an establishment. Proposals have also been made in Jamaica from time to time for the foundation of institutions.

The same picture could be drawn of any of the other colonies.

It was not until 1948 that a university college of some standing and with some prospects of success was established in the area. Apart from these provisions for local education, the only other means of obtaining qualifications was by study for the external degree of the University of London with or without supervision. Provision existed for the local training of the lesser professions eg solicitors, surveyors, druggists, teachers, but for first class professional education the student had to proceed abroad.

The mere fact that students for the most respected professions had to go abroad would have given the problem of education abroad a very special status. Its importance was increased by the fact that due to the limited educational ladder that had been created, education abroad assumed a very special significance for the social structure. After emancipation, the social structure remained one in which the European element in the West Indian population remained to a large extent socially, politically and economically dominant. However, the coloured middle class came – in spite of temporary setbacks – to play an increasingly important role in the social order.

The Role of Scholarships

In this connection, the rise of the professions is of especial importance. The provision of free places in the secondary school and of public scholarships allowed a certain number of individuals to rise to the highest points in the professions of medicine and law. There are many reasons why these professions were especially attractive to coloured West Indians. Suffice it to say that lawyers and doctors possessed a special prestige in the society, and the independence which successful private practice in one of these professions entailed was looked upon almost as a supreme value. We must remember that in a society in which there was only a limited form of social mobility the few opportunities that existed became a focus of attention. Everyone followed in the small community the career of the poor boy who through examination successes was able to rise to the height of a profession. Moreover, these successes were obviously based solely on merit in a society in which contacts and connections were of paramount importance in rising to influential positions.

Because of the fact that particularistic ties limited entry and development in spheres where independence could not be so easily achieved, all of the humbler people who had opportunity gravitated to law and medicine. But even among those successful in business, the high evaluation of the professional man was something lacking. It was the only form of independent prestige which required no further validation. As a result of this, all open scholarships tended to result in an increase in the number of doctors and lawyers. In some of the larger islands, separate scholarships were given for science and for arts, but all led in the same direction – towards the professions. Where it was desired to direct scholarship winners into a given field, this had to be specifically provided for. The Government of Trinidad, for instance, gave special agricultural scholarships to the Imperial College, special grants to surveyors in training; the Government of Jamaica created a separate agricultural scholarship.

So great was the emotion surrounding the open scholarships, and so great was the identification of the community with the successful candidate, that any attempts to lay down conditions to the winner of the scholarship in the interests of the community were consistently opposed. Fortunately, the considerable expansion in scholarship opportunities that has taken place during the last few years has not been on the basis of this tradition. The open scholarship which allows the winner to wander wherever he wills continues but in addition, special facilities in a variety of fields have been created. Special scholarships for those engaged in social welfare work have been created. There are separate teachers' scholarships. Special civil service scholarships have been created in the areas. In some cases, these involve degree courses but in most cases what is envisaged is a shorthand course of training for those who are likely to rise to positions of prominence within the civil service.

The New Social Consciousness

One of the main reasons for this high demand for university graduates has been the increase in social consciousness in the area. The disturbances of the thirties have caused a rapid demand for the development of welfare services and for increased standards of living. One result of this has been an expansion of the administrative machine which has come at a time when there is a world shortage of such skills due to the excessive development on the demand side. Another result of this rise in social consciousness is a strong desire for upward mobility. Hence there has not only been a rise in the number of professions and courses pursued but also an increased influx into the newly created professions.

The nature of many of these new courses can be criticized and some evaluation will be attempted elsewhere in a discussion of the role which a West Indian university can play in training a new elite (in the sociological sense) for the area. Suffice it to say that in most cases, the courses are of short duration and that in effect they are placed in a different category to the bulk of the students. However, because of the special role in administration played by those subjected to these courses, these experiences of the UK are of great importance.

In the discussions which follow, no specific reference is made to certain groups who technically do not belong to the student group but who should receive some consideration. In many of the islands and territories all members of the civil service who have reached a certain level become entitled to a free passage to the UK for themselves, their wives and children. The origin of the pattern was the leave to which the UK colonial officer was entitled after a term of duty. Because there was no formal distinction based on country of origin, 'home' leave to the UK became attached to certain statuses rather than to the ethnic group. With the West Indianization of the service, this right has been conceded to the new colonials in the senior posts.

The reactions of these temporary visitors are hardly any different from those doing short courses. However, they tend to be more inclined to be impressed by the host society and this to some extent counter-balances the critical attitude developed as a result of the hardships during the initial period of adjustment.

Increase in University Training in the Postwar Period

Some idea of the change of scale of university education can be seen by comparing the position in the year before the war. Before the war, the number of students from the area could not have been more than a couple hundred. In the postwar world, the number had increased so that in the immediate postwar period there were over two thousand students in England preparing for some sort of profession but not all of these were university students. The students from the West Indies come from a society in which they are well aware of racial and class distinctions; where it would be correct to say in one sense, that the social order is based upon race. It is a society, however, in which the racial and colour groupings do not necessarily coincide with marked cultural differences and indeed, one in which the coloured middle class from which the bulk of the students come, considers itself completely Westernized and basically British in its culture.

We have seen that it is a society of limited educational opportunity and the numbers involved in higher education are very small compared to the total population. Further, it must be remembered that higher education in England has in later years been supplemented by an extensive use of the opportunities offered by Canada and the USA. Moreover, there has been the recent development of the University College of the West Indies. Nonetheless, it remains true to say that higher education in Britain enjoys higher respect in the West Indies, British degrees are more highly honoured and the influence

Table 2.1: Students at UWI by territory of orgin, 1954

Territory	Universities and Medical Schools		Colleges, Technical and Training Schools		Inns of Court		Nurses		Total No. of Scholars	Total No. of Private Students	Grand Total
	Scholars	Pvt. Stud.	Scholars	Pvt. Stud.	Scholars	Pvt. Stud.	Scholars	Pvt. Stud.	Scholars	Pvt. Stud.	
	(1)	(2)	(3)	(4)	(5)	(6)	(7)	(8)	(9)	(10)	(11)
WEST INDIES											
Bahamas	4	6	3	1	–	4	–	1	7	12	19
Barbados	9	34	3	8	–	7	1	16	13	65	78
Bermuda	3	4	1	4	–	1	2	1	6	10	16
British Guiana	23	52	16	18	1	34	11	14	51	118	169
British Honduras	2	2	5	–	–	1	2	1	9	4	13
Jamaica	68	84	34	43	1	24	14	180	117	331	448
Leeward Islands	9	4	1	4	–	5	3	4	13	17	30
T'dad & T'bgo	49	100	21	39	–	27	22	16	92	182	274
Windward Islands	26	13	2	4	–	7	11	4	39	28	67
TOTAL	193	299	86	121	2	110	66	237	347	767	1,114

Source: UWI Report, 1954.

and esteem of those who have studied in Britain is greater than that of any other group.

Table 2.1, taken from the report on the official visitors to the University College in 1954, gives the numbers of students and their distribution according to the territory from which they come.

A comparison with the numbers involved in Canada, the USA and the West Indies immediately suggests itself. But the problems of classification and comparison are so great that this task must be reserved for another occasion.

Preparing the Student for Life in Britain

A great deal of importance has rightly been laid on the preparation or lack of preparation of the colonial student for life in Britain. For instance, following the general concern with the problems, the British Council has been giving in the various West Indian islands, orientation courses designed to help students adjust to conditions in the UK. There are two difficulties with such courses. First, they tend to stress the 'information' aspects to the neglect of more subtle psychological preparation. Second, they are only one of a variety of sources through which the student comes to develop certain expectations.

The Sources of Ideas about England

Occasionally, ideas about England were reported as having been obtained through contact with English people in the colonies. It is clear, however, that with a few exceptions such contacts were perfunctory and, for the most part, consisted of advice as to which were the best universities to attend, what sorts of clothing should be worn and the like.

Sometimes the advice given by such persons although accurate and well-meaning produced unfortunate results. One student for instance, coming from an island with the most rigid of racial barriers was advised by several English people of high standing, including an archbishop and another member of the clergy, that he should choose England rather than the USA because of the absence of the problem of racial discrimination there. Having arrived in the UK, this student (who had more English friends than most other West Indian students) conceived of the problem of discrimination as being his major problem. Here, the 'information' and interpretation given may be described as correct, but with the particular background of aspiration, expectation and information it was interpreted as misleading.

Another difficulty arises from the fact that the experiences of the older generations of students were usually of a different character, and the values and attitudes of students of today were not entirely in line with those of older persons. When students were few in number, the problems they faced were somewhat different. It would appear that the drive to integration was much greater and the resistance to integration much less. In many cases friendships and marriages were formed.

In any case, on return to the West Indies there was little discussion of problems of discrimination or adjustment. Back at home, it was not congenial to give stories which placed the individual in an unfortunate light, particularly when the context of events was unlikely to be appreciated. On the contrary, the student on his return had status thrust upon him and to admit less than full participation in all that was best in British life was to deal a blow not only to the self but also to friends and well-wishers. The interpretation of any such event was in terms of personal defect. Everybody else reported back successful adjustment. Something was wrong with the individual who was unhappy or suffered from discrimination.

Among the more privileged of this group there were some who had relatives and friends who had studied in or visited the UK. There can be little doubt that these people were the source of some of the major misconceptions of the students in the UK. First, their experience of the UK was fundamentally different from that of the generation of West Indian students in universities in the period immediately after the Second World War. Even postgraduate students who had completed their courses during the war and returned to the United Kingdom were aware of vast changes that had taken place.

The ideas which such contacts provided were from a period when West Indian students were in a small minority. Although the problem of 'visibility' in racial prejudice does not now command the stage in the same fashion as it did some years ago, there can be little doubt of the significance of numbers and of the perception of numbers in the definition of a racial situation. The West Indian student proceeding to Britain nowadays is not merely faced with the problem of adjusting to the host society but of defining his own attitudes to the substantial group of West Indians he now finds in England. On the other side, certain of the stereotypes held by English people which tended to see the foreign coloured student as the exceptional outstanding member of his community, if not indeed a member of the native aristocracy, have perforce been undergoing change because of the large influx of colonial and foreign students since the end of the Second World War. Further, there were innumerable things to compensate (among the older generation of students) for any misfortunes that had befallen the individual. There was a selective memory and through harping on the pleasant and the prestige giving, the unpleasant was pushed into the background and forgotten.

All in all, then, the ideas spread by those who had been educated abroad did not help the student who was proceeding to the UK after the Second World War. Indeed, the particular preoccupation of the West Indian with 'marrying light' accentuated the distortion of the situation. Because of this preoccupation, there was a tremendous emotional interest in the affairs of people who had married white wives. Innumerable stories circulated about them. The context and significance of these stories will be discussed elsewhere. Suffice it to point out that the myth grew that so far from there being any real racial prejudice, the English girl was waiting, eager and willing to ensnare the West Indian professional.

But apart from these cases where there had been some contact, the main sources of ideas about Britain held by the students were those also held by the majority of West Indians. England was a place where everything was superior. 'Proper' English was spoken; they were superior in sport; they were the source of 'West Indian' culture; materially and morally they were in some sense superior to the island communities.

Some of the students had become influenced by the new developments in the political life of the West Indies and had imbibed a certain amount of nationalist fervour. But as some admitted, this nationalism did not interfere seriously with their judgement of England as being a superior place, to which it was highly desirous to journey and in whose life it was an honour to be allowed to participate. Even where parents had been educated abroad, there was still room for misunderstanding. Thus, one student who claimed "to find life very much as I expected to find it from reading about it and hearing accounts from my parents of what I did find", went on to give misconceptions of university life that he held.

Well, for one thing, I never expected to find this completely impersonal attitude. I had got an idea of a university from my father who had been to Oxford, but I did not know really what to expect. I suppose I had an idea of London colleges being strung out about the place but I never expected to find it such a mechanical affair, people just meeting two or three times a week and then disappearing to their separate houses. I did not know it was such a sausage factory, completely mechanical.

The great difficulty about the 'ideas' which students have about England is that the relative accuracy or inaccuracy of the information is of relatively little account. The reasonable evaluation of the students' experience depends not upon whether 'true' factual material was presented to him but on the emotional significance which this has for him. There are some things which can only be learnt by experience and the placing of isolated facts in perspective is a process which can be facilitated by the impartation. In the presenting of factual information, a great deal of attention should therefore be placed upon the mental set of the student. Indeed, it may be stated that it is perhaps more important to give to the incoming student some insight into his own psychological processes than to give him details of social organization of the host society. The 'ideas' which the student brings to England are a complex of intricate sentiments so bound up with his personal life history, expectations and the values of the culture of the society from which he comes that it would be wrong to regard them as purely intellectual in origin. In some senses, it would be correct to say that if education in the UK should be concerned with producing good West Indians, only good West Indians can in fact profit most suitably from education in the UK.

Experience in the West Indies would indicate that there is no single source of ideas or attitudes and that in spite of the general drive to social mobility and prestige arising from their privileged position as recipients of higher education, there is a certain amount of individual variation of approach to experiences in Britain. Relevant factors are the personality characteristics of the individual, his background or experience in situations involving race and colour, his hopes and aspirations, his degree of group identification and self-assurance before leaving for his homeland.

The Importance of Level of Expectation

The question of level of expectation is of crucial importance for understanding the reaction of the West Indian student. Where there is an expectation of a high level of discomfort or of discrimination, the reaction to the experience of

discrimination and discomfort is less marked. On the whole, however, the level
of expectation of the West Indian student is extremely high. In a colonial or
subordinate territory, it is almost inevitable that the metropolitan country and
everything associated with it will enjoy high prestige. The student going to the
metropolitan country is thinking in terms of getting a profession or of
improving his position in an already chosen profession. He believes that by
going to England he will acquire some of these values of the larger world which
he has come to admire so much. This admiration of the metropolitan centre
is very high in the West Indies because its economy is so highly integrated and
dependent upon the mother country; because its social structure and culture
approximates so closely, in many respects, to that of Britain and, above all
because of the political relationship.

Due to the dependence of the West Indies on imported manufactured goods
to such a high degree, the West Indian was constantly and continuously being
drawn into admiration for the outside world. Quite apart from the fact that
traditionally there was little respect for things produced locally, the crux of the
matter was that the West Indian student was accustomed to use nothing or very
little that was produced at home. All the pressures of advertisement and
propaganda encouraged the tendencies to think of the metropolitan community as superior. The most prized possession of the individual, whether it was
a certificate or educational and professional competence or merely a material
possession, all bore the stamp "Made in England". Campaigns for the
promotion of British trade accentuated the belief in the quality of British
goods. Even some of the local goods produced for export came back as
finished products bearing the brand "Made in England".

Further, the West Indian, during the period of his history had been stripped
of a large portion of his cultural heritage. There was little that was distinctive
in his culture. Consequently, there was little left for him to do but to show
pride in his total acquisition of Western culture. In spite of the rise of
nationalism which seeks to accentuate whatever differences exist, this drive to
show oneself a complete master of Western and particularly British culture
continues unabated.

The political relationship of course was one which stressed the inferiority
— however temporarily conceived — of the colonial area. All the main directives
of policy, as well as the leading administrators of all the West Indian colonies
came from the UK. As a consequence, among all students there was a pride

at having had the privilege of visiting the UK and attending British universities. They therefore entered the UK thinking of themselves as being specially privileged to enter into such intimate relationships with the British people.

On the whole, the mythology of the society tended to lead people to think of the English people at home as being in some sense superior to those in the colony. Real Englishmen were more tolerant than their representatives in the colonies and certainly more so than the local whites.

The Nature and Reaction of the Host Society

The personal background of the student and the level of expectation of the student are of importance in understanding his reaction to the host society. His perceptions of this society are coloured by these background factors and by the immediate problems with which he is faced. Much of this must be called misperception. Yet, this should not blind us to the fact that a really important factor is the reaction of the host society to the stranger in its midst.

It must be remembered that the majority of the student group is to be found in London or other industrialized centres. The impersonality of the urban area has long been emphasized by sociologists. It is not appreciated in an academic sense by the West Indian (or other colonial students). This impersonality of life in the urban areas renders difficult intimate contact with a family group and groups of families such as the individual has been accustomed to at home. The impersonality is interpreted as hostility, and this increases further the anxiety with which the student is beset. The student finds that the private castle of the English home is not so easy to penetrate. Even where intimate friendships are developed, the barrier to acceptance within the home is not always overcome.

The private and personal reaction of the individual was not enough to ensure adjustment. Consequently, there were official and unofficial agencies which sought to ease the strain of adjustment for the student.

The Agencies Offering Hospitality

It is perhaps fortunate that the fate of the colonial student did not depend purely upon the hospitality of the individual British family. There were in existence a multiplicity of agencies which sought to put foreign students at home. Some were primarily concerned with visitors from the colonies, but others threw their nets wider and catered for the colonial student only incidentally. Among the most important of these was the Victoria League. The aim and object of this organization which was Commonwealth-wide in scope was to cement the bonds of friendship between the different areas of the Commonwealth. Although the headquarters of the association was in England, there were branch organizations in other parts of the Common-wealth. Most of these were in the dominion but there was a branch in Jamaica. In spite of this, however, the majority of students had never heard of the Victoria League before they came to England. Even among the Jamaicans, the League was not known among the social class from which the bulk of the students were drawn but was very largely identified with the upper classes.

The East-West Fellowship Council was not so organized. Although enjoy-ing high patronage, it did not have the high prestige of the Colonial Office, nor did its programme of introducing foreigners into British homes meet with much initial success. In this case, the reaction among West Indian students at any rate was to resent 'hospitality' offered in an impersonal sense. As time wore on however, the persistence of its organizers was rewarded by increased interest by West Indians.

Chapter 3

The Problem of Discrimination

Types and Forms of Discrimination

Nearly all students report that they have experienced some form of discrimination. The problem of assessing the exact extent of such discrimination is difficult because many of these reported experiences may not have been acts of discrimination at all. Thus it was commonly observed that newly arrived students complained excessively of being stared at, pointed at or otherwise singled out for observations. Their extreme self-consciousness in the new situation caused them to notice and record every commonplace glance in their direction as an indication of curiosity and even of hostility. Similarly, delays in service at the restaurant were believed to be due to colour hostility. Nonetheless, even when the subjective factor is allowed for, the elements of discrimination and prejudice are clear.

Discrimination in Public Places

Of course, in the public transport system of London nothing like racial discrimination could be found but incidents occurred with the passengers which could be given a racial interpretation. Thus in buses and trains, places next to coloured students were frequently the last to be occupied and seats would be vacated as soon as coloured travellers sat near. Of course, there was much room for misinterpretation here. Less equivocal was the remark of passengers, "I suppose it is the penalty for having an Empire" or incidents such as when a drunk woman for minutes on end shouted to a group of coloured passengers, "Why don't you get out of this train? That is what is wrong with this country, we have too many black men. Why don't you go home to your country?"

Restaurants

On the whole, there were few reported incidents connected with restaurants. One academic has reported his inability to entertain "a prime minister of a colonial territory" and during the period there was an incident reported in the popular press in which a lecturer at the School of Oriental and African Studies was refused admission to a public restaurant. The situation never arose sharply for a number of reasons. First, there was provision for cheap meals in hostels and canteens and secondly, the places in which such discrimination was likely to occur were beyond the reach of most colonial students. Indeed, relationships in the public restaurants were such that much light-hearted banter could take place.[10] Again, there were some restaurants which relied heavily on West Indian patronage. For the most part, West Indians when they thought in terms of going out patronized Indian and Chinese restaurants where a cosmopolitan atmosphere prevailed.

Nonetheless, the fear of discrimination existed among many students and certainly limited their participation. Moreover, because of this fear of discrimination there was a tendency to patronize those restaurants where coloured persons had been known to patronize. This tendency to flock to recognized places awakened the anxieties of the pioneers who sought out good or cheap restaurants only to find that their presence encouraged other coloured patrons to attend. There was no guarantee that the proprietors who accepted one or a few coloured clients would welcome an invasion.

Barber Shops

The same sort of problem arose in connection with barber shops. There were no cases in which students were actually turned away but getting a haircut was an intimate affair which brought racial characteristics very much to the fore. West Indians are extremely sensitive to questions of hair. From childhood, anxieties are expressed as to whether the child has 'good' or European type hair or 'bad', 'nigger' hair. It is a preoccupation which arises sharply again at adolescence. For the younger generation, the question of adequate barbering was therefore more acute but, in general, all West Indians posed a concern about a good haircut which was incomprehensible to the outsider. Some idea of the sensitivity of West Indians on this point can be gathered from the fact that one student who had got what he considered to be a bad haircut systematically awoke early in the mornings, came in to the hostel late at nights, paying in consequence for two sets of meals in order to avoid the ridicule of his friends. On another occasion, a student, having announced that it was his birthday, went out to get a special haircut. His instructions to the barber to take a great deal off was interpreted in absolute and not in relative terms. He returned to his hostel to find himself a public laughing stock.

Of course, the British barbers faced a serious problem when confronted by kinky hair. There was the problem of broken combs and even of total inability to comb the hair of the West Indian at all. The niceties of differentiation made by the West Indian did not make sense. The tradition developed of giving what West Indians came to call a 'machine' or 'African' haircut, much to the annoyance of the recipients. This was good enough for the Africans with their 'bad' hair – to treat them thus was to place them on the same status as the despised Africans.

In spite of this, many barber shops endeavoured to attract a coloured clientele, actually soliciting customers from some of the colonial hostels. But here, the same problem arose as in the case of the restaurants. Once a barber shop was known to be free of discrimination, coloured students flocked to the place. Sometimes, far from finding security they found their anxieties aroused by the efforts raised to stem the tide. Hints would be dropped or remarks such as, "I don't object to cutting black people's hair but I don't want to have so many blacks in my shop."

As a reaction to this, some students actually took to doing their own barbering. A Jamaican barber was actually discovered but as he depended on a primarily white clientele, he showed the same hostility to having too many coloured students and showed it in a perhaps more uncouth manner. Eventually, an enterprising Jamaican polisher took up barbering as a part-time occupation and attended colonial students' hostels expressly for this purpose.

Accommodation

The question of the hostels for colonial students will be dealt with separately. Here, we merely note that the area in which students felt that they experienced the most discrimination was on the question of accommodation. There were very few incidents of actual overt discrimination. The matter was usually handled politely. Where students sought accommodation through regular university channels there was much less likelihood that discrimination would be encountered. Otherwise, there was an almost universal experience. Occasionally, there was the odd landlady who would make offensive remarks or shake her head violently as soon as she saw that her applicants were coloured. On the whole, relations were polite and cordial but this did not make the experience of discrimination less gruelling. Indeed, every case of refusal had to be evaluated as a potential act of discrimination.

One incident which gained a great deal of notoriety was known in student circles as "the case of the Yugoslav general". A group of young female medical students went to an agent who gave them the address of a vacant flat. On telephoning the owner, they were welcomed and invited to come to see the flat which they could have if they wished. On arrival, the proprietress welcomed them, invited them in for tea and told them that she would have been most delighted to rent them the house since her husband had himself been a doctor. However, the fact was that since the telephone conversation, she had to give special consideration to the case of a Yugoslav general who was a personal friend of her husband. The general was wounded during the war and was now bereft of housing and had, because of his invalid condition, to live on a ground floor flat. She would have to give him priority, she was afraid.

The girls accepted her story and her hospitality was taken as genuine. They returned to the agent to state that the flat had already been let. However, the agent insisted that this was not the case. So convinced were they by the story of the Yugoslav general that they preferred to believe the landlord rather than the agent. The next day however, they were besieged by doubts and rang again to discover whether the flat was still vacant. To their astonishment, they were again invited to come and see the flat for it was still unoccupied.

This technique of checking by telephone on refusals was something commonly employed by students even though they sometimes had to disguise their voices. Searching for accommodation on the basis of polite refusals was costly not only in terms of the psychological strain involved but also in terms of time and money. Consequently, many students in defence took to the habit of explaining over the telephone that they were coloured, so that the position might be made clear from the outset. All complications were not avoided in this fashion however. One landlady, on being told on the telephone that the enquirers were coloured replied that she did not rent her rooms to niggers. On other occasions, confusion arose over the use of the term West Indian. Students would say over the telephone that they were coloured West Indians only to find out that the landlord was willing to take Indians and not Negroes.

In a situation in which there was so much anxiety, students tended to take the first accommodation that was available to them. This was one way in which the price of available accommodation was shot up. It was hoped in the course of this study to indicate quantitatively whether colonial students paid more for comparable lodgings than English or other foreign students. This did not prove possible although a relatively easy task. It was the impression of the observer both that the colonial student in 'digs' paid more for his lodgings and that he paid more for comparable lodgings as well. With regard to the first question, the early acceptance of lodgings whether ideally suited or not meant that frequently higher charges were paid than otherwise. But in addition, there were landlords quite willing to exploit the position. Landladies would frequently push up their prices as soon as they saw that the applicant was coloured. Sometimes this was apparently done merely in the hope of putting the students off but there was also the deliberate pursuit of coloured guests because of their presumed capacity or necessity to pay more. Some landlords approached the Colonial Office seeking coloured people and advertisements appeared on notice boards which specified that coloured guests were welcome or that 'coloured tenants only need apply'.

The Evidence of Discrimination

In spite of the politeness, it was fairly patent without the use of the telephone check that prejudice existed with regard to accommodation. Many notice boards and newspaper advertisements carried statements that coloured persons were not wanted or Europeans and British preferred.

Because of the fear of hurt when directly involved, students sometimes got others to ring up landlords on their behalf. If this was an English person or a student with an English sounding voice, the question would sometimes be asked whether the students were coloured or not. Because those telephoning were not directly involved, they could carry on a conversation with greater ease and would hear enquiry and doubt as to the desirability of taking coloured guests.

Usually, the blame for discrimination came from fear of how other guests in the house would react and what neighbours would think. In spite of the fact that some landlords appeared specifically to want to exploit the colonial market, there were others who feared a drop in standards and hence in income once colonial people were accepted. The nature of some of the reported conversations would indicate that there was a real concern and not a mere rationalization or excuse for not offering the flat.

The contradictory positions of these two types of landlord might be both quite legitimately held. To a landlord who systematically exploited the colonial market, there were rich rewards to be had but for the landlord already established as primarily serving a British clientele there was the fear of repercussions among other guests. As in similar situations in other parts of the world, the genuine anxiety displayed was not increasingly a reflection of the objective situation. Indeed, because of the divergence so often found between expressed attitude and actual behaviour[11] we would expect some anxieties to be misplaced, even when they did not reflect the projection of the individual's own prejudice.

The Focus on Discrimination

In spite of the extent of the discrimination, the evaluation of the problem of the students in the UK as a problem of discrimination and of the ways of meeting it is a false one. This is partly because of the differential reaction to discrimination but even more so because discrimination becomes a rationalization for the individual and a means of ideological justification.

The basic problem of the individual is the disruption of his primary-group relationships. This does not always appear to him to be the core of his problem but a comparison with the exactly similar reactions of single Europeans in somewhat similar situations in the West Indies would indicate that the factor of prejudice has been much overplayed.

The disruption of these relationships and the failure to enter into satisfactory new ones create in the individual a high level of anxiety and sense of personal dissatisfaction. This is projected onto the environment and blame for the poverty of adjustment is placed on external sources. This mechanism serves to reduce the level of anxiety so that we are faced with the peculiar situation that the individual becomes more comfortable with the belief that he is in a more difficult situation than that which in fact actually exists.

The loneliness which afflicts the student is frequently commented upon by the newly arrived student before he learns to give accepted group definitions of the situation. The loneliness was particularly marked in the case of the girls, many of whom give accounts of their periods of quiet weeping in response to the loneliness of the situation. In this situation, students are forced to rely on their friends to a fairly high degree. Here again, there is a special problem in the case of girls because there was a tendency to develop strong emotional attachments to any male who befriended them. This led to a more permissive sexual atmosphere than would otherwise have obtained. Again, the students' moral code was greatly assisted by certain 'external aids to morality'. Here again, Lewin's conception of the personality as a combination of 'own forces' and 'induced' forces is of some relevance. The moral code of the individual was reinforced in the West Indies by the pressures to conformity in the small community. In the freer, more anonymous atmosphere of the big city, the 'induced' forces or external pressures on the individual's personality were removed. This affected male and female alike but the latter more deeply. The girls seemed to have been more sensitive to these pressures in the West Indian environment. Many a girl found herself drifting about against her will and, in surprise, into a situation which would not have been contemplated in the West Indies.

The disruption of personal relationships and the need for their re-establishment was one of the reasons colonial students resented so much the stereotype of 'colonial' and 'native' and reference to "your people". It seemed to look upon the individual merely as part of a group whereas the emotional need of the student was to be treated as an individual. Even where the best will in the world was evidenced there was some irritation at this treatment. Thus when students were offered 'hospitality' at an English home in an anonymous fashion without the invitee needing to establish any personal relationship, this hospitality was rejected, although in many cases students were, psychologically, desperately in need of such hospitality. An invitation from someone who had taken the trouble to visit personally, or to indicate a special line of interest had a much greater chance of being accepted.

The desire on the part of the student was never one of friendship at all costs although in the cases of desperate loneliness this sometimes developed. The student wished to be taken and accepted at his own evaluation. This is one of the reasons students were frequently able to enter into closer and more intimate relationships with foreigners with a different background who on the surface would appear to have less in common than the fellow Britisher. The great emotional need of the moment was an appreciation of his position of loneliness and it was easy to develop a bond of friendship with others similarly placed. Sometimes, this alliance led to strange bedfellows.

Thus a dark-skinned girl from the West Indies explained how on arrival in the UK she was beset by loneliness. Even at her college dining hall she ate her meals for several months by herself. One day while having lunch, she was surprised to hear the clatter of cutlery opposite to her, for the places at the dining table in her vicinity were usually deserted. Her surprise increased further when she looked up and discovered that it was a white student and male. Such intimacy of contact although rare had been experienced before when there was a crush in the dining hall, but this student actually initiated the conversation. He asked to be excused but he was from Johannesburg; he felt extremely isolated and lonely; he could not understand the British and their attitudes to foreigners and he felt that she as a colonial would understand his plight and befriend him.

The reaction of being able to accept friendship only at their own evaluation of themselves was something not peculiar to the West Indian student. Thus M.A. Meng, a student from Peking, was extremely lonely and desperately in need of friendship. He became friendly with West Indian students whom he sought out because in his loneliness he feared that he would have a nervous breakdown. He had introductions to many Britishers through his father but he found that the acceptance of hospitality from these friends (and particularly from American friends in Britain) generated more hostility than it did intimacy. Their definition of the Chinese situation, their constant preoccupation with the political relationship of China to the Western world seemed to him to be their sole interest in contacting him. They never showed any sensitivity to his own personal emotional needs. It was not that these problems did not concern him. On the contrary, his West Indian friends thought that he was particularly obsessed with these things and could speak about nothing else. Once personal intimacy was established he could dwell on these things but in the presence of the white foreigner, concern with these things stamped him a Chinese, different, a member of a group and not an individual.

This desire for intimacy was one of the reasons why the term colonial came to be often rejected by the student. West Indians certainly felt themselves superior as a group to most of the other colonials and resented the fact that they were stamped in one form or fashion 'colonial'. Resentment at this collective designation tended to disappear, however, as it came to be recognized that a fellow colonial was one who readily understood all of the individual's immediate problems. Although the use of the term continued to be opposed, it actually became interchangeable with West Indians in many conversations. Indeed, on occasions, it was used to mean all foreign subjects of coloured extraction.

The association of coloured and colonial was one not confined to the students themselves. The case of Tom Jenkins, a Negro student from the USA who visited the UK in order to collect research material, served to illustrate this. One subject in which he was particularly interested was the question of interracial marriages. He approached someone at the Colonial Office (not the welfare department) who grew panicky at the thought of someone researching so dangerous a subject. The official got in touch with a West Indian considered of greater maturity and explained that she felt that she had a special protective responsibility as he was a coloured student and therefore in need of Colonial Office care and protection.

The need for solidarity arising out of this loneliness and inability to meet English people as friends and equals is amusingly illustrated by the case of one Chinese student from Malaya. On arrival in the UK, he was placed temporarily in a colonial students' hostel but after a few weeks he was asked to leave and arrangements made to accommodate him in a private boarding house. However, he was most unhappy there and agitated for admission into another colonial hostel. On arrival there, he told a group of West Indian students that he was glad to be with them because "he wanted to be with his own people". At that time, there were no Chinese or Malayans staying in this hostel at all.

It is clear from this that the factors hindering integration were not entirely the fault of the host society. Colonials took over the popular stereotype of the

English as being cold, reserved, and capable of making conversation only in terms of the weather. This satisfied them that the fault lay entirely with the British but, it was clear that there were emotional blockages on the part of the majority of students themselves. They thought in stereotypes as well. Every individual Englishman or woman they encountered was interpreted as the British. There was a selective perception of events. For instance, one student was extremely unhappy and built up a picture of the British as hostile, prejudiced and separated by an impassable gulf from the colonial. If he met any student who had a different point of view, he shed his contact and sought more congenial company which could reinforce his views.

Undoubtedly, one of the main reasons for this was the preoccupation with the colour question which the student brought with him. There was a strong tendency to negative self-evaluation and this was projected out onto the environment. The extreme sensitivity to colour questions can be gauged by the fact that one student of intermediate racial status, on being asked in the restaurant, "black or white?", with regard to his coffee, interpreted this as a reference to his skin colour.

The establishment of primary-group relations was also rendered more difficult by the fact that most West Indian students had few sustained extra curricular interests which could serve as points of contact. The student was able to hold his own academically but his attitude to examinations caused him to stick to the beaten path. His competitive attitude towards his fellow students also did not facilitate entry into intimate relations.

The Stereotype

Investigations carried out by impeccable sources have served to show the existence of a considerable body of prejudice in England. Dr Kenneth Little's pioneer study of *Negroes in Britain* (1947), which dealt primarily with the colour question in Cardiff, has been followed by A.V. Richmond's *Colour Prejudice in Britain* (1954) which dealt with the position of the West Indian worker in Liverpool. Besides these, studies have been conducted of resident immigrant communities in North Shields (Collins)[12] and Liverpool (Senior and Manley)[13] and London (Banton).[14]

The picture painted by these researchers confirms the general impression of observers of the existence of discrimination particularly in the spheres of employment and accommodation. We have seen that students soon become aware of the existence of discrimination with regard to accommodation, but on the whole they live relatively sheltered lives. Nonetheless, students manage to get a fairly accurate idea of the nature of the beliefs which the British hold about them. Even where people are on their guard, they sometimes betray their real attitudes. This revelation of attitudes range from the humorous to the tragic. On the one hand, there was the student who heard an older child correcting his younger companion, "Don't call him a blackie, two blackies told me that." Or, the Canadian soldier who called the student aside in the pub to explain to him that the English were prejudiced but that he, as a Canadian, was free of prejudice. "In Canada we are different," he said, "In Canada we call niggers coloured gentlemen." In the course of their lives, the students inevitably come upon the sensitivity to race in the society. The shop assistant sniggers when the book *Adam in the Wood Pile* is asked for. The landlady betrays her ignorance and on becoming friendly confides her misconceptions. Thus one student was asked whether it was true that in Africa men had tails. This annoyed him intensely and his reply, although rude and lending itself to other reactions, was satisfactory to the landlady. "Yes," he said, "All African men have tails but they wear them in front."

Even in the case where students have a minimum of contact with English people, they come up against the abysmal ignorance of the colonies and of the stereotypical views of coloured people. Thus maids and porters at hostels and at universities lumped coloured people all together. The visits of members of the Royal Family was confused so greatly that it became apparent to all that the ignorance of the colonial empire was profound. It is true that there might be a bias in such contacts but the effect remained the same nonetheless.

However, where there was contact it was with a more educated public. Thus the writer had the opportunity of sitting once at dinner next to an acting parliamentary under-secretary for dominion affairs. This dinner was a climax to the conference The Democratic Future of the British Empire. In the course of conversation, it became clear that he did not know the difference between Trinidad and Jamaica because he conceived of the former as being the capital of the latter. He expressed surprise at the fact that English was the main language in Jamaica and Trinidad. On the other side of the student was the wife of a member of Parliament who had recently returned from the West Indies. She was somewhat appalled and embarrassed by this display of ignorance, and so, turned in explanation to say apologetically that one had really to go out to the colonies in order to know what they were really like. Whereupon the acting parliamentary under-secretary included her in the conversation enquiring whether while she was in Jamaica she had been able to go out in the sun!

This ignorance displayed in high quarters was later confirmed by a government sponsored survey about knowledge of the British colonies and Commonwealth. This survey revealed a failure to appreciate the difference between dominions and colonies and a gross ignorance of the geography and political status of the various parts of the Commonwealth.

This same student also had the experience of visiting a school. He was introduced by one of the teachers to another as a visitor from the colonies. The teacher was sharply reprimanded by her colleagues. "Colonies," she said in surprise, as if in apology to the student, "We don't say colonies any longer, they are all dominions now."

This question of factual information about the colonies has more implications than at first appears. In studies on race relations, it has been found that the mere exposure to information is of relatively minor importance in reducing prejudice – at least among the very prejudiced. Sometimes prejudiced stereotypes exist through mere misinformation and this is cleared up as soon as adequate information is available. In the case of the colonial areas, these aspects of factual information have a special emotional content.

The generation of West Indian students with which we are concerned grew up in an educational system which stressed the connection with the British Empire. Frequently, there was a greater acquaintance with British geography and history than there was with the history and geography of their own lands. The educational system helped a great deal in linking the child's world of thought to the metropolitan power. In their ignorance, the West Indians believed that this regard for the mother country was reciprocated by a like concern with each of the territories. It is clearly impossible for the child in the British school to possess a detached picture of the life of all the British colonies. A little reflection on the part of the West Indian should have brought out the fact that the special relationship of each colonial territory could not be duplicated. As it was, the ignorance of the British people with regard to the details of the Caribbean was used as a stick to beat the British with. It was clear, some held, that the British educational system was inferior to that of the

West Indies. Instances where West Indians were more acquainted with the geography of the British Isles than residents were frequently quoted. Their ignorance of their own history and geography disturbed such individuals not at all. In the ignorance prevailing in the UK, they were able to parade their knowledge without much reflection as to how limited it really was.

The question of factual information on empire relations was of less importance than the appreciation that the symbolism of empire meant something entirely different. In spite of the radical interpretation of Empire Day, there can be no doubt that the symbolic significance of this day had an entirely different emotional interest to the West Indian than it had for the Britisher.

In some of the West Indian Islands, Empire Day was declared a public holiday; in all the islands, it was a school holiday and a day of special songs and rejoicing. Even among those who disagreed with the celebrations, the fuss that was made on the official side was taken as indicating the degree of importance attached by the British to the colonial relationship. It came as a shock to most West Indians to find that Empire Day was a day of minor consequence to the mother country. The newspapers gave it no publicity – there were few public celebrations of any kind. The West Indian felt that he had been deceived, that he had been deliberately inculcated with a loyalty to the Empire while no one in the 'mother country' cared about its development except when the occasion arose to demonstrate 'their' strength and superiority.

Another set of ideas which were particularly galling was the belief in the natural inferiority of the half-caste. It would sometimes be explained that the British were not prejudiced but merely opposed to interracial marriages. There was a popular story among many of the students that Professor C.E.M. Joad had written in one of the popular newspapers that he was prepared to accept the coloured man as a brother but not as a brother-in-law. This was interpreted by most students to be the general standpoint of the Britisher.

The belief in the natural inferiority of the half-caste appeared to be a rationalization of the refusal to accept the coloured man into the most intimate of social relations. This interpretation had double consequences. In the first place, interracial marriage had a special emotional interest for the West Indian because of the system of social stratification. Second, most of the West Indians in Britain were half-castes anyway because of the interracial mixture – not necessarily by marriage – which had taken place in these islands.

Another of the more popular conceptions which caused minor resentment but usually amusement was the belief found among school children that the blackness of the Negro was due to his failure to wash. Thus students would be described by small children as dirty. Or, the latter would take their spittle and attempt to rub off the dirt. This equation of blackness with dirt can easily be understood among white children. As far as the writer knows, the psychological effects of this equation in an explanation of racial prejudice have not been fully explored.

Among the ideas about 'colonials', there were a few specific ideas about West Indians which were especially irritating. For instance, the idea of some liberal-minded Englishmen was that the prime desire of all West Indians was to achieve integration at whatever cost, with the host society. The picture of the lonely colonial crying in the wilderness and awaiting entry into the promised land was largely correct but nonetheless irritating. The idea that prejudice and discrimination could be overcome by showing that "we are not all that wrong" smacked to the recipient of this generosity too much of patronage. Thus well-meaning attempts to protect people from racial discrimination or to show the "better side of Britain" left the West Indian largely unmoved. It was felt that here as in other cases, the real task that awaited liberal Englishmen was the re-education of their followers. It was not that the West Indians were opposed to entering into amicable relationships with liberal-minded English people – it was that they objected to seeing the colonial-British relationship as of primary importance without a sympathetic insightful understanding of the position of the individual. The liberalism was acceptable but in so far as it was accompanied by the stereotyped image of the colonial, rather than the concrete individual, rejected.

Not all the beliefs were equally harmful. Thus most students heard of and many experienced the belief that there were particular good qualities about being black. Sometimes students would be stopped in order that they might be touched and in this way give good luck. There was the occasional belief that the blacker men possessed esoteric wisdom denied to the whites. This was the basis of some white patronage of coloured doctors for instance. The writer had the experience of being asked to address a special society to explain occult science since it was known that 'you people' possessed secrets not available to the Western mind.

Another fairly common stereotype was that the student (when not considered merely as a native) was an exceptional person in his homeland. Many students were able to capitalize on the credulity of the English in this regard. This belief had its origin perhaps in the days when only the sons of wealthy colonials were able to visit and study in the UK.

The stereotypical view of the colonials was paralleled by the stereotypical ideas about colonials themselves. One can imagine the reaction of the student who in spite of the emotional difficulties involved, was giving his loyalty to the Empire when he heard himself being casually described as a black foreigner. Moreover, the individual became aware directly or indirectly of those special derogatory names for people of his kind: "ink spots", "blackies", "nigger", "wog".

There was a special resentment in the West Indian because he fell into the general stereotype of colonial and not in a special category of West Indian. He wished to be considered separately precisely because he considered himself superior to other colonials and to people in backward territories. The basis of this belief was the fact that they had shed their barbaric customs – African or otherwise – that they commanded a civilized language – English – and felt more or less at home in British culture. It came as a severe shock to many when they were asked whether they spoke English at home. The idea that the West Indies like nearly all the other colonial areas possessed an indigenous language or languages of their own appalled them. Of course, not all the fault lay on the West Indian side. This was so for this ignorance of the language or background of the West Indies was usually coupled with a naive simplicity which made it safer to believe that the West Indian had been able to acquire fluency and proficiency in the reading and writing of English during a short sea journey or after a short period of a few weeks in the UK. Indeed, it gave the West Indian a special pleasure to demonstrate the stupidity of the Englishman by leading him up this particular garden path.

Other Stereotypes

The idea of all colonials as 'natives' was linked with some of the beliefs that all natives lived in a state of primitive savagery. Thus students found they were asked questions such as whether they wore clothes at home or whether it was true that they lived in trees at home. The civilizing mission of Britain in putting down cannibalism, intertribal warfare, headhunting, witchcraft and so on were the facts which appeared to have struck the imagination of the Britisher. It was clear that he did not appreciate that the terms colony and native covered a wide range of territories differing greatly in culture and state of civilization.

The West Indian student soon sensed the complex of ideas with the connotation of inferiority that surrounded the word 'native'. There was no other word and stereotype − not even the use of the term nigger which generated so much emotion. So great was the resentment at the general use of this term that some students enjoyed themselves by constantly using the term 'native' to refer to the members of the British Isles themselves − usually much to the annoyance and occasionally, the protest of their hosts. This stereotypical picture of the inferior native displayed itself on many occasions. Thus one student found that it was assumed not only that he did not know English but that he was ignorant of the most elementary facts of life. The stereotype of the native without appreciation of differences was to be found even among the radical group so that a Negro student was congratulated at a communist meeting for having achieved Indian independence. The communists in their thinking had the stereotype of the 'native' in reverse; the picture being that of the oppressed 'native', the colonial striving everywhere to overthrow the colonial regime.

Moreover, the culture of the whole group was saturated with the stereotype of the black man as inferior even where no viciousness of thought or sentiment was implied. For instance, one maid in a colonial students' hostel consistently called upon the students to 'play the white man' oblivious of the incongruity of the situation. Another student expressed his shock when, visiting a friend's home for the vacation, he heard them casually speaking of working like a nigger. These terms have come into such general usage that it is difficult to determine how much emotional significance is still retained in them. In the first instance, it was doubtful if the girl fully realized the implications of the phrase she was using. Again, the phrase 'work like a nigger' is not unknown in the West Indies. The use of such phrases in the UK where the individual was particularly sensitive to racial issues led to a philosophical wondering of the implications of language as reflecting social phenomenon. Again, on the screen and on the radio, the stereotype of the native often appeared to give offence which would perhaps be overlooked in the West Indies but not in the UK.

The popular advertisements frequently carried stereotypes. In the case of a British Overseas Airways Corporation (BOAC) advertisement, student representation was used to stop a depiction of natives considered offensive. In another case, a visiting coloured American student wrote to one of the companies which advertised a coloured boy with a big white grin in a peculiar position. In reply, the student was informed that he did not understand the British position in the matter. The British, unlike the Americans, were free of prejudice. The picture was considered inoffensive and had exactly the same connotation as "Ten Little Nigger Boys".

A young barrister, after recounting his first experience of discrimination in England, wondered in retrospect whether there had not been genuine misunderstanding of the situation after all. Even after qualification, he noticed the tendency in himself to place the blame on colour. He related the following experience which he had shortly after qualifying.

> I was cross examining a fellow and before the judge had time to finish writing down the answer, I asked him another question. He shouted at me, "Wait!" I immediately thought that this must have been on account of colour so I gave him back. I threw down my papers and when he was finished he said gruffly, "Go on" . . . I took my time about taking up my papers. Later on, I learnt that that was how he treated every young barrister.

Perhaps the question which irritated most (after that of whether English was spoken at home) was the enquiry of when the student was likely to go back home. Such enquiries may have been directed with the best intentions – on the assumption that students were really desirous of returning to their homeland as quickly as possible. The question however was usually interpreted to mean that coloured people were not wanted in Britain and that the person putting the question did not wish to conceive of the colonial as having an equal right to remain within the heart of the Empire.

Here again, the special background of the student must be held in mind. Whatever the difficulties of adjustment faced, there were few West Indian students who did not toy with the idea of remaining in the UK. To go to England was the lifelong ambition of most West Indians – if they dared to aspire to so high a thought. Many thought in their adolescent years of reaching there through the field of sport or through scholarships. Having reached England, they knew that their status both among newcomers as well as back home in the West Indies depended on how long they remained in England.

The teacher doing a course in education knew the additional prestige – and possible pay – she would have if she could say that she had held her own independent of any patronage in an English school. It was the same in the other professions. Consequently, the suspicion that he was merely being tolerated as a penalty for Empire and not as a right touched off a degree of emotions and resentment which the questioner never intended and usually never suspected.

Language

The question of language goes deeper than the mere resentment that the West Indian is not considered English-speaking. In most areas of the West Indies there is a tremendous dialect problem. There are the problems of Hindi patois, notably in Trinidad and British Guiana, French patois in St Lucia and Dominica, and problems of English patois in nearly all the islands and territories. Indeed, there are few people who approximate anything to the standard of public school English. This numerically small proportion of people, for a variety of reasons which we need not detail here, have to sustain a terrific struggle to prevent themselves and their children from being swamped by the pervasive influences of the local dialect. There is therefore, among West Indians, a high sensitivity to speech which betrays 'inferior' origins.

At the same time, members of the middle class are sufficiently secure in their command of the tongue and sufficiently insular to regard themselves as speaking 'correct' English. On the whole, the really standard, British Broadcasting Corporation (BBC) English or the 'Oxford' accent is regarded as not proper English at all, but as essentially a dialect variant of a few upper class people. English as spoken in the individual territory is taken as correct.

The position is one then of curious ambivalence, of a struggle for proper speech by the people who nonetheless have no essential conception of what is 'proper' since no real generally accepted standards exist. Consequently, there is variation in the accents of individuals from the same island and territory. There are also variations among different islands; some territories produce a larger number of people anxious to conform to 'English' standards of 'English'. Some students self-consciously seek to drop their local accents and assimilate to public school English. If they are in contact with other West

Indians, this exposes them to the ridicule, joking, and possibly even contempt of their fellow West Indians. At the same time, many were anxious to obtain badges and symbols of their sojourn in the 'mother country' and the conspicuous one of language was sometimes not neglected. This question of speech was also affected by their orientation to home and those who came from areas where 'improved' speech was welcome cultivated changes in accent and pronunciation, while others coming from more Americanized or anti-British areas preferred to denounce "the imitation of Englishmen".

Thus, one president of the West Indian Students Union (WISU) strongly criticized those who were not making the best use of their opportunities. There were some who were not even making use of the opportunity to improve their speech. On the other hand, a young lady improved her speech until she spoke such standard English that she was jealously admired by many English students at her school. In the social circle of the particular island from which she came, this would have brought her prestige but she was transferred to another island. There, she found her 'English' accent ridiculed and attacked. Interracial marriage is the only other subject which provokes so much interest, both among the students themselves as well as in middle class circles in the West Indies concerned with the problem of education abroad.

Among the students themselves, there tends either to be an aggressive assertion of West Indian English or a complete capitulation before the standards of public school English. As an illustration of the first reaction, we have the case of a student who even at home sought to speak standard English. However, on his arrival in Britain, he became a nationalist and affected the coarse speech of the lower class of his island. As an illustration of the second, we may take the case of a student who after a few weeks in Canada developed a strong Canadian accent. On his return home on vacation, he was strongly criticized and abandoned this accent.

In spite of this, the majority of the students find that their accents are changed through having to make themselves intelligible and acceptable to English contacts. Students who are not conscious of having made any changes in their form of speech are sometimes surprised when on return home, or on greeting new arrivals in the UK, they are told that they have adopted an 'English' accent. Wherever such changes occur the West Indian not exposed to these influences tends to condemn them as an affectation assumed for the purpose of enhancing status.

Sometimes the problem of accent took on peculiar forms. One student for instance, had two sharply distinguishable forms of speech, one of these reserved for when he was speaking to English friends, and one for when he was speaking to West Indians. Of this he was quite unaware and he considered in all honesty that he had one consistent manner of speech.

In other cases, we find students embarrassed by their local variations who nonetheless are afraid to consciously modify their speech pattern through fear of ridicule. Hence they speak in a jokingly affected manner aping the upper class English all the time. After doing this for a number of years, their 'normal' speech approximated to this caricature.

On the question of speech there was the same amount of rationalization as in the case of the interracial marriage. Those who changed their speech usually justified it on the grounds of a natural process consequent upon residence in a foreign land. It is a noteworthy fact, however, that mere length of residence could not be taken as an adequate guide to changes in speech.

Among the factors which appeared to be relevant to these changes were the following:

(a) The evaluation of the British group as a whole and in particular the special group with which the individual came most in contact.

(b) The evaluation of the individual's own social group and its particular form of speech.

(c) The individual's primary group relations. Individuals at residential colleges appeared to be greatly influenced by the speech of fellow students. However, that the individual's primary group relationship was not the sole determining factor can be seen in the fact that prolonged residence and friendships in colonial hostels did not preclude changes in speech. The lawyer for instance, may not have entered into any but purely formal relationships with Englishmen at his Inn, but he had the professional model of the English barrister before him and this influenced his speech.

(d) Individuals seemed to vary in the effect that primary group contacts had upon them. Some students for instance changed their accents from time to time, according to whether the group with which they had the most intimate relations were primarily English or West Indian.

Types of Adjustment

It has often been taken for granted by those who have a 'liberal' approach to the problem that the problem of the colonial student is essentially one of moving away from his fellows and obtaining friendships in the host country. The criterion of healthy adjustment here employed is an *a priori* one, and does not take into account either the peculiar background or the specific problem of adjustment of the student.

In general, those students who make good adjustments with English people are subject to as much psychological strain and distortion of perception and emotion as those who remain attached to their fellow colonials. For instance, one West Indian student became secretary of the conservative party in the district in which he lived and was well adjusted to the local government. He was engaged to a local girl as well. In order to maintain his precarious adjustment, he was forced to sever all his contacts with his countrymen. Moreover, in order to justify this, he had to build up an exaggerated and distorted picture of the West Indians in London. He averred that prejudice did not exist and pointed to his successful adjustment as proof. It was not that this student was not aware of the facts because on deeper interviewing he was able to cite many instances of racial prejudice which he had himself experienced.

Another student, as similarly 'well adjusted', although in much closer contact with West Indians, also averred that the English people were free of prejudice and, in the same breath, related the story he had just heard in the bus which clearly showed evidence of prejudice. At the time, a play called *Deep Are the Roots* dealing with the racial problem in the USA was running and one of the passengers had declared that she had heard of it as a good play but that it was inadvisable to go to see it because a lot of coloured people were attending performances and "one doesn't know who one will sit by". In another case, a leading intellectual denounced all those students and others who openly protested against discrimination. In terms of the sociology of the affair, it was their sensitivity and inability to behave normally that produced discrimination which was very largely a figment of their own imagination.

These minor observations sometimes lead not merely to psychological self-deception but to open subterfuge. Thus one student, having married an English woman, decided to take up permanent residence in Britain. Here again, his 'successful adjustment' caused him to paint a lurid picture of the lives of the students in order to rationalize his desire to sever contact with them. He kept his wife closely guarded from people who were among his most intimate friends at home. If he happened to meet them on the street, he would pretend that his wife was merely a casual acquaintance and treat her as such. Or, he would leave her after finishing his chat with his coloured friend arranging to meet her elsewhere. Never would he voluntarily introduce his wife to a coloured person and all his friends who visited England were received and entertained in his office not his home.

All four of the cases cited here were of men who had married English girls. This was not however in itself a product of this type of adjustment, although it may be taken as an indication of the lack of balance which sometimes resulted from interracial marriages.

This type of successful adjustment depends upon a conception of the self and one's group which can hardly be described as psychologically healthy, or in keeping with the idea of 'freedom of personality' so often advocated by liberal democracy. The success of adjustment is achieved in practice by an accentuation of that negative evaluation of the self and of the group which has already done such psychological damage in the West Indies. Deviations to the right rather than to the left of the path to maturity may be more acceptable to the host society but this does not render them any more healthy.

Both among the successful adjusters and those favouring this type of adjustment, there is essentially a belief in the superiority of the host group. In public speeches, it is sometimes referred to as the 'best in British culture'. More generally, the equation of the best in British culture with the casual everyday intimacy of a British home is made with an ease which makes the observer wonder sometimes if all things British were best. Students who have successfully adjusted in the past may become devoted to the mid-morning break or early morning tea or many of the other superficialities of life. This was not, however, the primary purpose for which they were receiving education. Whether the adjustment of the student can be considered good or bad can be interpreted psychologically as being free from internal conflict, etc. or from the point of view of the purpose for which the individual is being trained. This involves a discussion of the purposes of higher education for colonials, and cannot be settled in the abstract.

Moreover, the adjustment achieved by these individuals is not open to the group of West Indian students as a whole. It would depend on an actual physical dispersion of West Indians and on the severance of contacts with other West Indians. In the circumstances, this was impossible. Many of the 'successful adjusters' also used the belief shared by their British contacts that they were exceptional people. They accepted the negative evaluation of the group given by the host society but pointed out that while the judgement was correct it did not apply to all West Indians. In a liberal society where prejudice was not particularly virulent this was an eminently successful approach. Here again, it would be impossible for large numbers to cultivate this line of approach.

In practice, this type of adjustment was only made by those who so valued integration into white society that they were prepared to subordinate all other loyalties to this end. Not all who were predisposed this way made this adjustment, but nearly all that did adjust had been thus predisposed.

The Changing Pattern of Discrimination

Throughout the West Indies there is the tendency, more marked in some islands than elsewhere, of making extremely sharp differentiation between different shades of colour. These discriminations are important because they explain a great deal of the reactions which take place among West Indian students.

A great many of the fair-skinned persons who have spent the greater part of their lives separating themselves from their more dark-skinned compatriots and seeking the company of fairer persons, regard the continuation of this process as one of the major tasks of their visit to the UK.

Within the UK, it is found that these colour discriminations are not as sharp or are at least different from those of the West Indies. One of the main results of this colour differentiation is to make the West Indian more sensitive to minute shades than the English. A certain resentment is felt towards those near whites who pass or can pass for white.

More usually, all coloured people are classified as one group although the specific classification as a black surprised those who were not so classified in their colony of origin. MP, for instance, was a scholarship winner from one of the islands who was fairer than some of his colleagues at school. In the West

Indies he had little to do with them but in London he was thrown together with them. One day, while walking along with one of his darker-skinned colleagues, some school children pointed to them saying, "Look at those two niggers." For the first time, this individual reported, he knew that he was a black man. As a reaction to his discrimination against his darker brethren, he became violently Negro-nationalist and a strong advocate of socialism.

There was also the case of V, a fair-skinned girl who, during the period of her voyage to the UK and during her early period there, showed what critical West Indians would describe as a typically 'snob attitude'. However, many fair-coloured people find it easier to pass for white in English society than they would do in some of the territories at home.

Where the individual is fair enough to pass this raises characteristic problems. Sometimes the individual classifying himself as coloured feels that this fact is patent and obvious to all. Later, when the Britisher realizes he is coloured he is accused of deception. The experience of JB represents a good case in point. JB was a fair West Indian who obtained lodgings in a house where she was the only guest. She was served meals with the rest of the family and enjoyed the whole week. At the weekend, however, her boyfriend, also fair but more obviously coloured, visited her. Immediately, the family cut off all relations with her, served her a week's notice, accused her of deception and from henceforth she had her meals served in her own rooms. In another case, a fair West Indian who was married to an Englishman sought lodgings through a friend who stated they were not coloured. The wife was pregnant and the student, who would not otherwise have resorted to such a subterfuge, nonetheless retained his relationship with his coloured friends. When they visited him there was the same shocked surprise and the same loss of accommodation – at a critical time.

Even where people are obviously coloured, there is sometimes a distinction made between fair and dark coloured. Thus a Polish landlady who had declared over the telephone that she had no objection to coloured students, declared to some West Indians that she was prepared to rent them the flat. However, she had just rejected an African doctor because "his skin was too dark".

Of course, such a reaction, although general is not inevitable. Some of the fairer group although obviously coloured seek, in the face of this discrimination, to put out that they are different and to educate the English people to a proper scale of values. The position 'at home' is explained to their English friends, some of whom fall in line with those explanations. When this is done a particularly bitter feeling develops against such individuals on the part of other West Indians.

The case of MAO provides an example of this. On arrival in the UK, her first contacts were with West Indians, but having been thrown in a predominantly English institution her whole outlook changed sharply. Within a few months, she had shed all traces of a West Indian accent and dropped most of her West Indian friends – a fact which provoked some bitterness. She became friendly with an Englishman. Although the latter desired to mix with as many West Indians as possible, she made strenuous efforts to seal off contact with them.

Here is another case of a student fair enough to pass for white under certain circumstances. Before going to the UK, he had spent some time in the USA. He reported only one experience of overt discrimination. As he related:

Only on one[15] occasion when I was in . . . At first, the people thought I was a government spy, then worst of all they thought I was a communist spy, when a man appeared on the scene who appeared to be living without any visible means of support. When they heard I was a West Indian, the whole village just went wild; they invited us here and there and everywhere. Everything went well until Mary was speaking to the landlady one day – there were three of them, three old fogies – and said, "It is alright but if you are coloured like Adrian". From that time! It was about two months before the baby was born. Until the baby was born, they spoke not a word to me and immediately they gave us notice. On another occasion, some people rented a flat to my brother and myself and when they discovered we were coloured they just gave us notice to quit. One time my brother and I went to a nightclub with another fellow considerably darker than us and there we came up against this sort of thing: "You and you can come in but not you".

In giving this account, the student flushed and showed strong resentment, "I mean that sort of thing just gets me. My blood boils. I hear similar incidents I just remember in Canada." Asked whether he expected *such* discrimination between shades of colour in England this student replied:

Frankly no. I was accustomed to this American way of thinking. You are either on one side of the fence or the other, so I was quite surprised to find that they had this West Indian habit of discriminating between shades.

Well that sort of thing gets me mad. Very often I am having conversations with people who don't know I am coloured and when I tell them that, you can see them as if struggling to say, "For God's sake, don't tell me that you are coloured, you are destroying everything." My reaction to that is usually to terminate the conversation. (Here, the student stressed the point but appeared embarrassed as if not speaking the truth.) I generally get very angry when that occurs. I suppose it is my sense of guilt about it, seeing that so often people take it for granted that I am not coloured, and I don't worry to disillusion them, especially when I was in the United States. In New York, I was having a good time and having the best of both possible worlds. I mean I was just out for a good time and didn't care about these things but the guilt feelings must be there causing me to feel angry.

The White West Indian Student

Usually, discussions have been carried on as if all West Indian students are coloured. One of the interesting things about 'race relations' is the way in which biological symbols become attached to groups and consequently cause a real confusion between cultural and racial characteristics. Social-psychological research still has to offer a really adequate explanation of why this should be so. In the analysis of the problem of the West Indian student, such a confusion frequently occurs.

The West Indian population is composed of many different racial groups and a comparison of the problems faced by these different ethnic and racial groups should give an indication of some of the real problems involved.

For many of the white students, the problems are almost identical with those of the coloured, even though the colour question does not enter. If the white West Indian does not face the problem of interracial marriage, he faces what is almost an international marriage and an intercultural marriage as well. Usually, he discovers that his background is such that he does not like the pace of life of the big city. So many of his most important emotional experiences were rooted in the West Indies that he came to look upon himself as a coloured. He was faced with the same differences in routine of everyday life, he had to make the same adjustments in matters of food and climate. Often, in matters of speech, he had difficulty in making himself fully understood. He found the same stereotypes about colonial society to anger and irritate him. He too had a problem in making friends and coping with the loneliness of the big city.

Thus one student expressed the same homesickness, showed neurotic symptoms and had to return home; another found herself the roommate of coloured persons with whom she would have had only the most perfunctory of contacts. While some fled all contact with West Indians and sought to shed their colonial origin, others found themselves active in West Indian organizations. Indeed, the identification with and interest in things West Indian was not confined to native white West Indians. Some colonial officials who had spent protracted periods with West Indians to some extent found themselves strangers in their homeland and were glad to maintain West Indian contacts.

One literary person who could not technically be called a student can be taken as illustrating how deeply creolized some of the whites in the West Indies could be. He boasted in manner similar to the coloured colonial that while writing and working in New York, he slept with all the girls working in the office. "The creole boy can hold his own!" was the way he put it.

In one or two cases, we get the same radical redefinition of the situation where whites faced with the problems of adjustment, became communists or extreme left wing. This leads to a redefinition of the situation in terms largely at variance with the definition of the social situation in the West Indies.

Some white West Indians, like fair coloured people, are primarily interested in integration into English society, but a great many find themselves asserting their solidarity with their fellow colonials. It is perhaps this group of West Indian whites which faces the most difficult problems. They are torn between two incompatible worlds and are in a position somewhat similar to that of the 'successfully adjusted' coloured groups. It was the experience of many coloured West Indian students that they came more in touch with local whites in the UK than they did in their home country. Sometimes, this was due to the prior arrival of a coloured person who could help in simple matters.

Among the white students, there is also the conflict about whether they should return to the colonies or remain in the UK. Family ties, the pace of life in the small community, the prestige and status which would be accorded them, all pull in the same direction. The prestige of anonymous participation in the big city and so on, pull in the direction of staying in the 'mother country'.

The West Indian white of several generations has come to consider England as home. If his parents happened to be government officials or very wealthy, it is possible that he has had some prior contact with the UK. Even so, however, his contact has been under the most sheltered conditions. If, as in some of the islands he happened to be of European rather than English descent, the enthusiasm for the 'mother country' was tempered by other considerations. Thus, there are French whites in Trinidad who feel closer kinship to the

French Republic. Even among some of those critical of France, it is on the grounds that the French Revolution was a mistake.

By and large, however, the white person in the West Indies had two 'homes': the home of everyday experience in which most of his significant emotional experiences were rooted and the home of the imagination and of prestigious connection.

The Other Ethnic Groups

Culturally, the West Indian students do not constitute a homogeneous group. The most important cultural difference is that between the Indian and Negro groups. The Indian student has all the problems which the creole West Indian faces and something more.

One of the most important of these problems is the question of food. Dietary differences do not assume much importance in the West Indies. Most people eat at home and hence individual or group peculiarities about food are of little consequence. In London, the student finds that he has to rely heavily on public conveniences for his food. Many Indian students were vegetarians or at least accustomed to somewhat different food. Such food was available in London at the various restaurants scattered around the city, but those restaurants catered for a select clientele and prices were therefore prohibitive from an everyday point of view.

Sometimes, where the student came from humble surroundings, the whole question of table etiquette arose. Where a student ate with his hands at home, he had to adjust to the terrific array. Among the lower class and lower middle class students, this was frequently a problem, but with the Indians, it assumed a special significance. One Indian, on his way to the UK, sugared his soup and acted in such an attention drawing fashion that his fellow West Indian guests had to take him in hand and coach him in the elements of table etiquette. On another occasion, a student was so puzzled by the intricacies of the menu that although forced to come to the table, he invariably retreated after a few minutes. Sometimes, this led students to prepare meals for themselves rather than face the double problem of food that they did not like and a table etiquette they did not understand.

In the case of other foreign students who possessed more of their national culture than the Indians of the West Indies, the problem was more severe.

Thus Ma Meng, a Chinese, preferred to stay at home and prepare his meals which he ate in his national dress. He only ventured out into public restaurants if forced by a crisis or if accompanied by a friend in whom he had confidence.

Indeed, in the case of the Indian students, the question was somewhat the reverse. Where the students were identified or identified themselves as Indians, they were expected to possess their own national dress. This proved irksome to some Indians from the West Indies who took pride in the fact that they had shed this evidence of lowly station. Some proceeded to adopt Indian national costume so that they might show themselves truly Indian. Hence Indian girls finding that the sari was considered a beautiful form of dress and commanded respect from the British, wore them for the first time in England.

The crises in identification were more marked with the Indians than the other creole groups. Their position as a minority in the West Indies was not clearly defined, and the sense of Indian nationalism and self-identification which was emerging was accompanied by the sharing of many of the creole and Western values. In England, they found that the West Indies or larger community with which they tried to identify themselves was relatively unknown as compared to India itself. It became profitable therefore to make the identification with mother India. This in itself had problems. On the whole, Indians tended to look down upon the West Indians because they had lost so much of their cultural heritage and because of the peculiar nature of Indian immigration to the West Indies. In any case, the West Indian found that he had more in common with the Indian from Mauritius or South Africa than he had with the Indian from the homeland.

Second, having appropriated Indian affiliation, he was faced with the necessity of affirming a culture with which he was basically unfamiliar. In some cases, this led to a diversion from study into a reading of Indian literature. In one case, it led to the acceptance of an appointment in India. This girl had been a prominent member of the youth movement in the colonies and had accepted the task of representing her colony at an international youth congress. While at home, the split between the Indian and nonIndian sections of the youth movement affected her not at all. In England, she felt the need to identify herself as Indian and consequently refused to represent the colony's youth at the international gathering. On her arrival in India, the young lady realized what a wide cultural gulf separated the Indians in India from the

Indians in the West Indies. On her return to England, she continued to wear her *sari* and otherwise identify herself as Indian to the British public. On the other hand, she became a fierce West Indian nationalist, holding that the first loyalty of the Indians in the West Indies should be to their adopted country.

This crisis in identification for the Indian caused the majority of the group to adopt this standpoint. In spite of the affirmation of West Indian nationality, early experiences and identifications made any conscious attempt to minimise racial conflict difficult to achieve.

A small conference of the more broadminded of West Indian Indians, designed to consciously encourage the pursuit of cooperation among the ethnic groups, broke down because of the Hindu identification and loyalty of a leading member of the group. This individual launched into a strong attack on the Christian members of the group. They had betrayed their Indian heritage by becoming converted to Christianity. They were the prime cause of racial intolerance in the West Indies. Because of their insecurity, they were bound to affirm racialism. On the other hand, he as a Hindu, well read and learned in the scriptures could afford to be tolerant since he basked in the security of Hindu culture.

The precise result of the crisis of identification with the Indians varied in accordance with the personality structure and the primary group affiliations of the students in London. Although self-identification as Indian was increased, education in England in fact rendered such students much more westernized than they would otherwise have been.

Two students affirmed on arrival in the UK a vegetarianism which those who knew them at home affirmed that they never possessed. This vegetarianism began on board the ship in an attempt to differentiate themselves from the segregated coloured students. Because of their vegetarianism, they were served at a special table separate from the rest. This continued to be exploited on arrival. However, several years of residence soon caused a sharp shift in attitudes. In sexual relations, this led to alliances of a more or less permanent character with girls belonging to different ethnic groups – one was white, the other coloured.

Similarly, another Indian student at first refused to attend dances, much to the annoyance of his creole friends, on the grounds that "Indians don't dance". He was at pains to point out the superiority of the Indian system with its stress on chastity and so on. Within a few months, however, he had learnt to dance and embarked on a career of promiscuity strangely at variance with his earlier convictions.

The Chinese Student

The problems facing the Indian student were much more acute than those facing the Chinese. In the first place, fellow Chinese students, both from the West Indies and China proper, were fewer in number than the Indian. Secondly, most of the Chinese who went to study in the UK were those who had already lost most of their cultural heritage and were therefore almost completely Europeanized. Again, except in Jamaica, the Chinese in the West Indies have not been important politically, thus their position has not generated a great deal of emotion. Nonetheless, the same problems of identification arose. In at least one case, it turned the radicalism of the student in a communist direction through identification with developments in China. This student adopted a position of supporting all Eastern manifestations of culture as appeared to the West. Consequently, he introduced his statement on points of Muslim law, about which he knew nothing, on the general grounds of its superiority.

The West Indian Student as the 'Marginal Man'

Stonequist (1937) introduced the concept of the 'marginal man' to explain a certain phenomenon. The racial and cultural hybrid was perched between two worlds on the margins of both. He was a 'marginal man'.

Using this concept, Stonequist sought to synthesize a great deal of material dealing with the problems of acculturation. The concept, originally popular and conceived as having some theoretical value, has largely fallen into disuse with the rise of new theoretical forms of reference. Nonetheless, it occasionally comes up for reconsideration. Broom has attempted a reformulation of the concept, and in popular textbooks it is still privileged.

The use of the term is of special relevance to our problem here because the application of the concept to the West Indies by Stonequist has been expanded by Simey, in his book *Welfare and Planning in the West Indies,* and other writers. The difficulty about using the concept of 'marginal man' is that it leads to two hopeless confusions of categories.

First, there is the confusion between 'racial' and 'cultural' characteristics. The two, although often coincidental, do not necessarily coincide. Indeed, insofar as the concept 'marginal man' points in a primitive fashion to empirical problems of real importance, it is precisely the destruction of relations between biological and cultural hybridity which is of real significance.

The concept 'marginal man' also tends to confuse sociological categories necessary for the analysis of a social system and psychological categories more appropriate for the analysis of the system of personality structure. For instance, the term 'marginal man' is sometimes used to refer to a certain type of social role. The social role of an accommodating leader between two conflicting groups may cause the term 'marginal man' to be applied to such accommodating leaders. On the other hand, it is clear that such accommodating social roles can be played by a large variety of personality types. Such a role, from the psychological point of view, may be one congenial or conflictual to the personality of the individual undertaking such a role. The concept of the 'marginal man' tends to confuse the performance of certain marginal social roles with the question of personality.

This confusion is further accentuated when the term 'marginal man' is employed to describe the sort of personality problems which arise through the process of acculturation or through the performance of certain of these marginal social roles. Here, insofar as the concept 'marginal man' points to the fact that the whole life organization of the individual is coloured or may be coloured by the problems of acculturation or the performance of marginal roles, it points to a real problem. But, this problem is readily amenable to analysis in terms of a theory of personality structure which can render the analysis more fruitful than by the use of ad hoc conceptions like 'marginal man'.

The term 'marginal man' has been used loosely to describe the whole of the West Indies, in the sense that the West Indies forms a cultural area which is part of the Western world but with significant differences. The term has also been used to describe the position of the educated colonial generally, including the West Indian who is educated abroad. It is clear, however, that such a formulation of the problem ignores important differences between groups of West Indians. From the point of view of the reactions of the students themselves to their problems of adjustment, the question of personality and differences in types of personality are of supreme importance. The concept 'marginal man' tends to be a ragbag category in which all are lumped together.

The concept 'marginal man' has also tended to be used to describe the man of two worlds' in situations where there are sharp cultural or social differences which pose a dilemma of choice for the individual. The characteristic problem of the West Indian is one of deciding to which group he shall give his full allegiance but the dilemma is not posed through sharp cultural differences but through the similarity of culture. This was recognized to a large extent by Stonequist because in tracing the natural life cycle of the 'marginal man', he noted as critical the creation of barriers which prevented him from achieving participation in the superior culture. Something of the sort takes place in the case of the West Indian. Because of the similarity of cultural heritage, he looks forward to and expects a fuller sharing of the life in Britain. His expectations may not be altogether reasonable, but they are almost inevitable in the circumstances. Failing to achieve the integration, there is the falling back on the nationalism of the subordinate group in some cases. But this, as we have seen, is only one of a variety of reactions to the situation.

It should be noted that all racial groups are in a sense 'marginal'. The white West Indian finds that there is something of a cultural and even more of a psychological barrier. In his case, the question of cultural difference is not so important as that of group identification. Of course, there must be some minimum of cultural differences, some symbol to form such an identification but objective barriers such as racial discrimination and so on then, are not. The problem is one of level of expectation; of self-valuation of the 'self-regarding sentiment'; of evaluation of one's reference groups. The psychological problem of the reaction of the white West Indian is susceptible to analysis in these terms.

With regard to the coloured West Indian, there are likely to be a few more cultural differences but of greater significance than this is the question of colour or racial difference. One of the reasons which makes the question of race relations important both psychologically and sociologically is the permanence of the symbolism of race as compared with some other cultural characteristics. It has frequently been commented on that cultural differences come to play the same role as social differences. Because of this, indeed, there is some rational basis for the popular confusion of 'racial' and 'social' groups. But, at least in countries and conditions where there is a drive for assimilation, the existence of physical symbols which cannot be dissimulated differentiates the racial from cultural problems.

It is this distinctness and permanence of physical symbols which lead the question of race relations to have such psychological importance. The physical dimensions of the body and their sound evaluation are of central importance in the development of a self-conception. Because of this centrality, it is important both from the point of view of the drive towards establishment of relations with others as well as the drive toward autonomy, as Angyal had put it. Any barriers, real or imagined, that are based on physical appearance are likely to generate a great deal of emotion. The individual has to live continually with and come to terms with his physical appearance. It is rarely that he can forget it and hence the apparent obsession with the racial question.

Of course, sensitivity to racial discrimination is in itself a cultural matter, but once racial questions become culturally defined in this fashion, their peculiar characteristics come into play. In any case, the West Indies is an area where racial and colour differences assume a special psychological importance. It is clear that here too, the concept of 'marginal man' is not sufficiently refined for a really illuminating analysis. In so far as the 'marginal man' is a psychological conception and points to the permanence of the conflict, it has some bearing on this point. In situations where racial and cultural discrimination exist, the 'racially' different individual *must* forever live with the conflict. With the culturally different individual, there is the possibility of escape. In the case of the 'racial' individual, this is impossible. Hence we have seen that the 'successfully adjusted' West Indian student is placed in a peculiarly difficult position. Even where, however, the culturally different individual does not take advantage of the possibility of escape, the existence of the rejected opportunity makes a great difference. It permits the individual a greater deal of self-respect than in the racial situation. The position here is more comparable with the case of volunteer Negroes or people capable of passing for white in the USA, who prefer to accept the social classification of colour differences. Such a conception permits the personal involvement of the individual to wear an altruistic mask, and high ethical conceptions can be conceived as the driving force behind the individual's life organization.

Such differences are observable in white West Indians *vis à vis* coloured West Indians. Of course, this point must not be exaggerated because coloured West Indian students still have the possibility of rationalizing their emotional preoccupations. This is one source of the association of student radicalism with the labour movement. The West Indian society is a highly stratified society and therefore the turn towards the masses is one which can most easily be paraded as altruistic and self-sacrificing.

In the case of Indian and Chinese students, it is clear that the concept of 'marginal man' has perhaps more significance for the Indian student in the UK. Here, the cultural differences assume the greatest importance of all the groups.

Reactions to Discrimination

The reactions to discrimination varied in accordance with the personality and values of the person being discriminated against as well as with the situation in which the individual found himself.

For instance, on one occasion a group of three students were walking together when some small children started shouting out "blackie" after them. The reactions of the three students were quite different. One wished to strike the offending children. Another was angry but preferred to curse the British generally; the third was amusedly tolerant and taunted the children good-humouredly as "whities".

Sometimes, the open act of discrimination produced a momentary spell of anger. For instance, where one individual was actually stoned by school children, he swore that he would kill one of them if he was able to lay hands on them. On the other hand, the students themselves were conscious of being in a minority and overt resorts to violence were rare. More usually, it was the discriminated person who had to be protected. Occasionally, students were subject to physical attack by people with no other motivation than that of "beating up a nigger". Thus in a pub on one occasion, an Irish man of proletarian stock had to stand up in support of some West Indians who were about to be thrown out of a bar which was being patronized by white American soldiers who objected to their presence. On another occasion, a student was subjected to unprovoked physical attack in 'the tube', but was afraid to retaliate. Occasionally, there was a resort to like violence. Thus one student reported that he had been accosted in a threatening manner by a drunk just out from a pub. The man had used insulting remarks about 'nigger' and a fight had ensued in which the student had got the better of the fray. A crowd collected and a policeman turned up as well. The latter, on hearing of the cause of the dispute told the student that it served the fellow right and allowed him to proceed on his way.

Such incidents were few and far between but every now and then the fear of violence appeared among the student population. Thus groups have followed coloured students in the street calling out threateningly "Mau Mau". On another occasion, a fascist group started holding mass meetings in the vicinity of a colonial students' hostel, and this aroused not entirely ungrounded fears.

The damage which was done was psychological rather than physical. On the whole, in Britain, there were few episodes which were traumatic for the individual. There were students who panicked on arrival in the country and wished to go back home, but there was no association of such a reaction with traumatic racial discrimination.

Among West Indian students, there were reports of traumatic incidents but all of these concerned individuals who had experienced discrimination in Canada or the USA. This was particularly true of people who had passed through the USA. Such students had experienced or knew friends who had experienced the refusal to be served meals or dishes in restaurants and bars; the serving of water and then the breaking of the glass. They had experienced differential access to other public facilities in transport, cinemas and so on. One student who experienced such discrimination found himself in a relatively deserted railway station in the southern states where the crowd of white and coloured passengers assembled as was the custom, without regard to racial distinction. Gradually, people started noticing the signs "white only", "coloured only". In this student' s case, the refusal to be categorized together with the fear of violating the customs of the country, led to his taking to the bush to urinate. Among this same crowd was a coloured student, himself the product of an interracial marriage, who experienced the breaking of his glass in a public restaurant after he had used it. For the next twenty-four hours, he remained in a stupor just walking in an agitated fashion and speaking to no one. Such traumatic experiences were often commented on, but by and large those who had experienced discrimination in the USA were pleasantly surprised by the situation in the UK.

The reactions to overt forms of discrimination ranged from the desire to be integrated with the host society on the one hand, to the complete radical communist position on the other. Yet, there is a sense in which we can speak of a group reaction to the situation.

On the whole, it can be said that the experience of discrimination did not confer status within the West Indian group. Indeed, the experience of discrimination was something personally painful. It was not something that was accepted philosophically – as in the nature of things. Moreover, students knew that there was a differential incidence of prejudice and there was always the suspicion that the person experiencing discrimination might have brought it upon himself. There was no anxiety therefore to report incidents of discrimination unless these were acts of prejudice which all the students had themselves experienced. This does not imply that students did not speak about acts of discrimination which they had suffered. But, the motivation for this seemed more to arise from the desire to share their anxieties with sympathetic listeners.

It was the reaction to discrimination which brought status to the group. If the act of discrimination had been successfully countered, or some sort of protest registered, the individual in relating his story could present himself as a hero. The one way in which the recounting of the experience of discrimination itself could bring status, was if the student could throw some new angle on the subject, as for instance if he had detected some subtle form of prejudice which might otherwise have passed unnoticed. In so far as the reports showed up 'those British' as prejudiced and portrayed the enemy in its true colours, it was a form of protest.

Indeed, far from status arising from persecution there was even a tendency to identify with the 'aggressor'. Jokes were often directed against those who had experienced discrimination as occurred with a group of students who were employed in the making of a film. One student was rejected because he was not dark enough and another was reported to have been told, "Roll them eyes, darkie" – a fact which his friends, to his great annoyance, did not allow him to forget.

The Neat Dichotomy of Black and White

To most of the students who come to the UK expecting a great deal of discrimination, the position as it exists comes as a pleasant surprise. This is not invariably the case, particularly to those who have had long residence in the USA. It would appear that after the initial shock and resentment against discrimination as practised in that country, there is an accommodation to the situation there. While there is continued resentment at being placed as second class citizens, there are few disadvantages once one abides by the rules of the game. Indeed, it was part of the rationalization of students who had experienced discrimination in the USA that there was even an advantage. One student for instance described how he enjoyed a long ride in comfort while other white passengers stood in discomfort.

On arrival in the UK, some students find the task of sizing up the situation –so difficult for all incoming students –doubly difficult. The politeness of the English is deduced as hypocrisy, especially as they hear from their fellow students so many stories about the discrimination which does not appear on the surface. Suspicious because of the stories, they are hesitant about each situation and preoccupied with evaluating the motive and intentions of those with whom they come in contact. Some even pine for the more open discrimination that they had experienced, because then they knew where they stood, while here there was the anxiety of defining each situation anew.

The Smallness of the Group and its Consequences

While overt acts of discrimination were rare, this must not be interpreted to mean that the isolated act was not of considerable significance. The West Indian immigrant group was a very small one and except for those individuals who cut themselves off from all contact, there was a high degree of interaction among members. One consequence of this was that such acts of discrimination were magnified considerably. Nothing went unnoticed, and to the group preoccupied with racial questions, there was continual comment on any incident that occurred. Usually, in the course of being retailed, the stories became embellished and distorted but such embellishments as did occur were all in the direction of depicting the British as a wicked, perfidious people.

The Reaction of the Dark-Skinned

Among the majority, there is a certain joy at the rejection of those who would otherwise practice shade discrimination. Indeed, the dark-skinned are so keenly aware of this discrimination of fellow West Indians that they sometimes rush to the defence of the British as being free from colour prejudice.

For instance, KL was a medical student who had made his way through scholarships. In the UK, although he mixed freely with male students, he felt that the fair-skinned West Indian girls were still prejudiced against him. He imagined slights in some cases and even when friendship was openly proposed this was considered to be merely a temporary concession to circumstance. He declared himself more at home with white Britishers than with other West Indians.

The same process of differentiation and consequent bitterness can be seen in relations between the Indians and the Negro community. Many Indians are like the fair-skinned coloured who feel that they can escape discrimination if they retain their separate ethnic identity.

Thus when a party of mixed Negro and Indian students travelled to the UK via the USA, there was complete mixing of the students until arrival at the port of entry in the USA. Their turbans – never worn in their home countries – suddenly appeared in an effort to avoid discrimination. The Negro students had not had an inkling of this and deeply resented it. The calculation of the Indians was not entirely without foundation because they were offered Pullman accommodation. Again, one Indian student was reported to have secured the eviction of a Negro student in order to find a place for one of his Indian friends by alleging to the landlady that the Indians constituted an aristocracy in the West Indies and that the Negroes were a despised slave class. The greatest bitterness was provoked by those Indian students who, in Canada, had 'exposed' the creole girls by explaining to the ignorant Canadians that they pressed their hair.

Such discrimination – or at least the belief in such discrimination – had on one occasion political repercussions. Thus allegations about discrimination by the Colonial Office and the West Indian governments in favour of Indian students rather than Negroes were made on this basis. In one year, the awards of medical scholarships were given to Indian and fair-skinned West Indians. This may have been merely coincidence but the explanation given by some of the students concerned gained currency. These alleged that the Canadian university authorities faced a different problem. There were many promising West Indian students who had completed their premedical course but had difficulty in getting into medical school. One of the problems was the question of colour. Hence, when the Canadian university authorities were asked to recommend students for medical scholarships to the UK, they proposed those students who would be more acceptable – in terms of Canadian experience.

Discrimination: Trauma and Persistent Anxiety

The open and public acts of discrimination are often thought to be those of the greatest psychological significance. The traumatic episodes of rejection in love, or the landlady slamming the door in the face of the decent, respectable student have tended to be publicized and have become symbolic of racial prejudice in Britain. These incidents are believed to be traumatic and productive of the greatest amount of anxiety. However, the picture of the bitter, resentful colonial produced by crude and tactless landladies is essentially a false one.

The feelings of rejection by British society are deep but these feelings of rejection would in all probability persist even if there were a considerable lessening of the amount of actual racial discrimination. This is because of the fact that 'colour' rejection becomes symbolic of all the differences to which the colonial student has to adjust. Colour is singled out because it is a highly visible fact and because, of all the rejection, it has the most damaging repercussions on the individual's self-respect. The individual student unaccustomed to table etiquette, or worried about his manner of speech, can usually make some form of adaptation or adjustment which permits him to participate in the host society with some measure of self-respect. The case of colour is somewhat different. This is a biological fact about which the individual can do nothing or very little. The West Indian student arrives in Britain highly sensitive to race and colour discrimination. The fact that he has experienced discrimination before does not render subsequent experience more congenial, although it is unlikely to have any traumatic effect. This does not alter the tremendous emotional significance that colour and race have for the individual and his personality. Even without the experience of overt discrimination, the coloured West Indian carries around with him permanently, always at the threshold of his consciousness, the knowledge of the evaluation of colour current in his society.

The all-pervading character of colour and race in the West Indies and its psychological importance tends to be overlooked. Precisely because colour values are mixed with other social values for a relatively stable system – a great deal of this background of colour is temporarily forgotten. The resident of the West Indies who lives in an area where hotels are not anxious to receive coloured guests or definitely refuses them, tends not to be unduly concerned by this fact. In the world of his everyday experience he does not come in for rebuffs since he knows the rules of the game, and since in his everyday contacts, he shares the common values of colour which make it possible for him to practise or accept shade discrimination. Even so, however, occasional incidents in the West Indies illustrate the explosive force underlying race relations in this relatively peaceful area of the world.

The act of discrimination in England produces an even greater depth of reaction because of the ability to attribute all disaffections to this source. Yet, the number of truly traumatic experiences is extremely small. What really tells upon the personality is the persistence of the situation, the ever present expectancy that an act of discrimination will occur. The creation of the anti-British ideology is a defence against this anxiety. The expectancy of discrimination means that the student is geared to face disappointment and that the absence of discrimination can be experienced positively as a pleasant surprise. The world is painted blacker than it really is in order that the situation may not appear so black after all.

Discrimination is of importance because of the particular context in which it occurs. One of the limitations of the studies of prejudice and discrimination is that attitudes and reactions are often examined in isolation. The particular set of social roles and expectations within which the discrimination occurs is responsible for the nature of the reaction. This can be seen by comparing the reactions of students to discrimination in the UK and in Europe. In the case of the UK, experiences of discrimination were very much more likely to lead to a violent or hostile reaction on the part of the colonial student. The same experience on the Continent would often be retailed as an amusing incident.

At first glance, this phenomenon would appear to be related to levels of expectation and to the status aspirations of the students. This reaction to loss of expected status is certainly important, but the question is a little more complicated than this, for the student who goes to the Continent often goes primarily with a view to achieving status. While there, however, he is free from the complex of attitudes and sentiments which surrounded him in England. His sojourn is even more temporary and with language and other barriers, he takes for granted a certain distance between himself and his continental acquaintances. In the case of the Englishman, there is indeed a greater wish to be loved and respected and consequently, a greater hurt at rejection. There is a certain moral community between Britain and the colonials which renders them both extremely sensitive to rejection by the others. In the case of the British, this is manifested in the expectation of gratitude. The British, in spite of the distance separating the two groups, wished to be loved and respected by the colonials. Indeed, much of the dispute between the groups is not a question of total rejection on either part but of the terms and conditions under which they shall prove mutually acceptable to one another.

This suggestion that the reaction to one group differs to that of another would appear to go counter to the psychological research which has illustrated quite definitely that prejudice tends to be of a generalized nature. It would appear, however, that in the vogue of attitude testing that has occurred, Shands' early definition of the sentiment as an organized system of predispositions or attitudes has tended to be forgotten. Psychologically, these sentiments as expressions of the individual value system, are ranked in some sort of hierarchical order. Inconsistencies of sentiment and attitude may be allowed to persist provided they serve some other value higher in the hierarchy. Thus, in the case of those who react violently to British prejudice and accept it somewhat more easily from continentals, one of the major points is that they can use the contrast of attitudes of continentals as a stick with which to beat the British. In other circumstances, it would no doubt be found that people sensitive to racial slights would tend to react consistently in this manner.

The attempt to evaluate the effects of prejudice as opposed to other factors is due not merely to the fact that colour becomes in so many cases the symbol of all problems, but because prejudice hardly ever occurs in isolation and has a more telling effect because of its association with other factors. Many of the incidents of discrimination are of a minor form but this does not mean that they are not hurtful. These minor acts were more irritating and telling because of the more general wounds to the individual personality caused by loneliness, feelings of unworthiness due to unfamiliarity, etc. The student, for instance, who reported that he had lived for five years in a street without speaking to any one of its residents reacted much more seriously to the little children of the district when they shouted "blackie" than he probably would have if he had lived in a warm, friendly neighbourhood. This problem was naturally most acute in London, but to a certain extent affected the situation everywhere.

The Advantages of Being Coloured

While stress has usually been placed on the disadvantages of being coloured and conspicuous, this was not always the case. In the case of the doctors, special virtue was often attached to this fact, but there were more general factors. The coloured student who did not know his way, or who was in difficulty would frequently arouse attention and attract a sympathy which was not always the case with the white foreigner. One dark-skinned student spoke of how her "wonderful colour" had helped her. On going to see the trooping of the colours, the English spectators had made way for her and made sure that she got a special point of vantage. Occasionally, this factor was abused by the colonial student himself, either in making excessive claims to hospitality or in breaking cinema and other queues in pretended ignorance and the like.

The advantages must be set in perspective. The same student who spoke of her wonderful colour assisting her, was the one who reported extreme loneliness and those who 'used their colour' to their positive advantage often did it vindictively and with a sense of aggression. In any case, the exploitation of this particular situation was hardly moral in character or in any way desirable.

Aggressive Reactions to Discrimination

The reaction to racial discrimination, real and imaginary, was necessarily aggressive. In the interpretation of aggressive behaviour resulting from racial discrimination, there has been a tendency to oversimplify the problem and to use uncritically the 'frustration-aggression' hypothesis. Sometimes, of course, real or imaginary discrimination led to overt action and to direct aggression. Physical and verbal clashes with the host society were few.

Some of this aggression was turned inwards against the self and tended to increase the self-depreciation arising from living in a 'loveless' world in which the individual's primary group relations had been disrupted. Most of it was verbalized subsequent to the incidents complained of.

There also arose a set of beliefs about the West Indies and Britain which the environment had generated. The ways in which aggressive impulses came out were partly through creating a fictionalized picture of the West Indies which compared favourably with the realities of life in Britain. But there were also many factual points which gave semblance to the belief. For instance, some of those points related to the absence of showers, the relative shortage of baths and the stigmatization of the British as dirty and less sanitary than the West Indian. Some students even identified a characteristic English smell which was attributed to their failure to bathe. One student, remembering something more of the West Indian background, found a striking similarity between this 'English' smell and the 'Bouquet d' Afrique' of the lower classes of his home. This question of bathing was the cause of universal jokes. In addition, while the English still used gas for lighting the streets of London, the West Indies had electricity. Even in small shops in the bigger towns of the West Indies, there was neon lighting. There was a relative absence of this in England.

Newly arrived students were often introduced to the *News of the World* newspaper with its fuller coverage of the world of crime and the serious side of Britain. There was pleasure in contemplating this side of life because it showed that the Britishers were not the perfect people that they were believed to be. The 'superior' race had its share of crimes and the peculiar disregard for facts was shown in this sphere as well. It was believed, on the basis of popular newspaper reports, that there was more crime in the UK than in the West Indies. More specifically, there was a belief that more murders were committed in the UK. This belief was the more interesting because one of the few books[16] available that dealt with the West Indies pointed to the high incidence of aggression there.

Here again, we cannot understand the reaction of the West Indian unless we appreciate something of his background. The crimes which the big city threw up were much more colourful than the crimes of the West Indies. Occasionally, there is a startling murder but cases of the order of Heath and Haig were unfamiliar, strange, and quite rightly regarded as pathological.[17] When a lower class man in Jamaica chopped his paramour to death, this was discussed, and unless there were an unusually large number of murders or somebody of significance was attacked it did not strike the public attention. Again, the differences in population were not considered and a 'quantitative' comparison of totals made where percentages should have been compared.

There were also crimes of a sexual nature such as homosexuality which was relatively rare in the West Indies as compared with Britain. Especially when this practice was discovered among upper class people, there was the feeling that the moral depravity of the British, in spite of their pretentious outward appearance, was absolute indeed.

These forms of aggression (that is, aggressive reactions to racial discrimination in Britain) although expressed often were on an individual, informal basis. In the course of time, however, institutionalized means of channelling these aggressive forces developed.

Distortions Arising from the Situation

In spite of the defensive allegation of prejudice, the drive to be accepted by whites was still acute. Even where there was rejection, there was need to salvage some vestige of self-respect. As a result of this drive and this need, there resulted a curious distortion. The memory and image of life in the West Indies was altered in ways which would make them more acceptable in the English environment.

Sometimes there was a conscious attempt to deceive. If students found that the stereotype of the colony, or of their particular position in it happened to be a favourable one, they would let the tedious task of correcting the false impression go by. On other occasions, there was more of a deliberate interest. One student, on lending out his copy of the (Report of the) West India Royal Commission, took care to paste over all the pictures of slum housing in the West Indies for fear that the English borrower might think that he had been brought up under similar conditions. Again, a student engaged to an English girl thought that she was favourably impressed by the West Indians she had met. He was anxious not to disturb this favourable opinion and as far as possible scrupulously avoided all realistic discussions of racial, colour or class issues in the West Indies.

This favourable depiction of the West Indies led in many cases to a form of self-sophistication. Some of it was due to sheer ignorance. Younger students who had come directly from secondary schools in the West Indies were often genuinely ignorant of social life and conditions among the mass of the people there. That there was poverty and colour differences, he was aware, but precisely what they meant in human or social terms he did not know. One girl, for instance, who was an ardent West Indian nationalist, could remember nothing about social conditions except that opposite the convent school which she had attended, there was a series of slum dwellings where poor people dwelt.

The gulf between the middle classes and the mass of the people is immense, and most of the students had a middle class background. Further, the West Indies was an area in which no social survey and investigation of any substantial kind had been carried out. Textbooks in use in the schools did not familiarize the student with his own environment. Under these conditions, it was easy for illusion to flourish. At a public meeting, for instance, one student alleged amid a round of applause from his fellow students that the illegitimacy rates in Britain were higher than those in the West Indies. Others boldly announced that the standard of living or of literacy was higher than in England.

One reason for this was that for the student, 'The West Indies' ceased to be a concrete entity and became a point of reference by which the individual sought to identify himself to the average Englishman. St Vincent, St Lucia, meant nothing, so that the person speaking to Englishmen tended to label himself 'West Indian' as this was intelligible to a much larger number of English people. Intimate knowledge of the individual territory or island was lacking; even more so was knowledge of the larger whole.

'West Indian' came to be a paraphrase for 'what I am' and there was a high degree of identification of the characteristics of the individual with those of the West Indies. The transition to believing that "West Indian is what I am, therefore all West Indians are like me" was easy to make. A fantastic West Indies population with intelligent, cultured and well-bred citizens – such was the picture which many students in all convenience wished to portray to the English public.

The Illusion of Greatness

In spite of this fantastic picture, the student knew and conceived of himself as exceptional. The emergent nationalism which resulted from the personal identification with the West Indies, did not prevent an exaggerated opinion of the social role he would play on his return home. Here again, we have to take into account the factor of ignorance. First, the same factor of ignorance of social conditions in the West Indies and second, the ignorance of the limits and bounds of possible social action. But, besides this, there was need for the illusion of a special role in order to compensate for the position in which the student found himself. The students arrogated to themselves a leadership which they did not possess; they loved to conceive of themselves as ambassadors of their country. Indeed, they were often spoken of by English people in this fashion.

The belief was fostered not only by the need for compensation among West Indians but also by the feelings of guilt among the British as well. There is no field perhaps in which it is so difficult to preserve a sense of balance as in the field of race relations; and liberalism sometimes takes the position of falling over backwards in an effort to be fair and free of prejudice. Many well-intentioned put the coloured student on a pedestal; and then of course fostered the illusions under which they dwelt.

Chapter 4

The Student
and the University

The Experience of the University World

The ideas of university life which are held in the West Indies are nebulous indeed. Insofar as there is a conception of university life at all, it is one of education for professional competence. The idea of research or the independent pursuit of learning are hardly seriously entertained. This does not mean that the stature of the profession is not high. Indeed, the possession of the PhD places the individual in the category of 'one of the most learned men in the world', while a professorship places him among the gods themselves.

Vaguely, the university is thought of as a place of great erudition. The ancient universities of Oxford and Cambridge while enjoying tremendous prestige, especially among those learned in British culture, did not hold pride of place in the majority of minds. The University of London had a special place in the minds and hearts of West Indians. It bore all the prestige of the metropolis in a colonial area, and it must be remembered that in the eyes of many West Indians, the terms London and England were synonymous; people sometimes speak of going to London when they mean going to England. Moreover, the University of London had come to have a special meaning and significance for the mass of aspiring students because of the provision of external degrees. Many of the students had already begun or contemplated doing external London degrees before proceeding to the UK. In a society in which education was regarded primarily as a means of social mobility and of giving social prestige, nice distinctions between residential and nonresidential colleges on the basis of educational value was of little concern. As compared with the systems of Oxford and Cambridge, London University was progressive in that it was extending opportunity to a wider and wider circle of people. In this connection, the LSE, in influencing conceptions about the university as a whole should not be underestimated. The LSE was thought of as being primarily progressive and socialist and identified first of all and above all with the name of Harold Laski. Moreover, the two West Indians best known in academic circles (Dr A. Lewis; Dr R. Capildeo) were at that time connected with the University of London which appeared liberal in its policy of recruitment as well.

People who were struggling in their spare time to cope with the syllabus for the external degree were aware that high standards were demanded and maintained by the examination authorities. So many good students had fallen by the wayside that it was impossible not to consider the external degree worthwhile. This evaluation of the London University was of importance because the bulk of West Indian students were centred in London.

The evaluation of the local colleges in London varied. Some colonial students at King's and the University College of London thought of the LSE as having a superior atmosphere. The students there possessed a reputation for liberality and cosmopolitanism which many students at that institution found it difficult to understand. But by and large, there was not much relationship between the students of the various London colleges. Each tended to regard his college as the university.

The initial reaction of most students to the London University was one of disappointment. The federal structure of the institution – of which Flexner wrote, "it is difficult to see in what sense the University of London can be considered a university" – was not appreciated. The student expected a central collection of impressive buildings. Insofar as anything corresponded to the physical conception of the university, it was the senate house of the University of London.

But once the student had adjusted to the physical condition, there was little complaint with the administration of the university itself. In the case of the Institute of Education, there was the greatest enthusiasm for the university – a fact which the writer believes to be not unconnected with the liberal provision of residential facilities, the fact that students there worked for the most part in small groups and on problems with which they were familiar. It was a student of the Institute of Education who after a bitter attack on the discrimination and prejudice of the British, declared: "The university redeems them all." Few students alleged any discrimination by university teachers and administrators. There were complaints of the impersonality of the system of teaching; of a certain isolation from fellow students, but this was not construed as resulting from a deliberate policy of discrimination.

Those students of the University of London who attended the presentation of certificates and diplomas were appalled. The methods were termed 'mass production' when compared with the highly personalized school presentation to which they had been accustomed. In some cases, this impersonality was linked to the question of colour.

One student described how she had come first in her sessional exams and won her prize. However, although she had been at the college for two years, the lecturers and professors congratulated the other coloured student in the class, not knowing the difference. All they knew was that a coloured West Indian had won the prize; they were unable to distinguish the individual.

There were cases in which the student came into conflict with the university authorities, but in no such case was differential treatment alleged. In matters of housing, those students who made use of university hostels or who sought accommodation at approved addresses encountered no difficulty.

The only case in which anything resembling discrimination was alleged was in the case of coloured students at one of the London colleges. The West Indian students who usually dined together, became friendly with some of the clerks in the administration. These clerks ate in the dining room with the students and some of them were potential students hoping for subsequent admission into the college. The fact that West Indian students became friendly with members of the clerical staff rather than with their fellow students is in itself significant, but does not concern us here. What is of interest is that the girls reported to the West Indian group that the registrar of the college had spoken to them about their friendship with the West Indian students, and had suggested that they should seek to mix with the general body of students themselves.

There was absolutely no clue given as to the motivation of the administrator involved. It might have been that she wished to see her clerical staff mixing more freely and not relegating themselves psychologically to inferior status, or that there was concern with the grouping of West Indian students and she felt that this would force them into closer association with English students.

Whatever doubts there were as to the motivation, the interpretation given to the action was clear and unequivocal. The girls regarded it as a manifestation of prejudice, retailed the story to the students and insisted on asserting their rights to mix freely with coloured girls. The students too accepted this interpretation and were visibly shaken by the incident. The effect of the intervention was merely to cement the alliance between students and clerical staff.

The head of this particular college was noted for the liberality of his views. He had at some time been associated with the development of higher education in the colonies and had made strenuous efforts through the students union to get the colonial students more fully integrated into the general run of student life. Precisely because this fact was known and appreciated by the students, the 'evidence' of discrimination came as a particular shock.

Indeed, the colonial student at the university often found that he came in for special consideration. This can be highlighted in the case of one medical student who failed his examinations and had to be kicked out of medical school. His teachers, however, considered that he was suffering from temporary emotional disturbance and not from any intellectual defect. In fact, the record of colonial students in this particular hospital had been quite high and he was given special opportunities before being finally turned out. Even so, one of his teachers signed documents purporting to show that he had done practical anatomy for the previous six months although in point of fact he had not. Eventually, the student recovered from his temporary disorganization and qualified as a medical practitioner.

The only allegations of discrimination against educational authorities were the suspicions which were held against the Inns of Court by some of the students. There were special circumstances which led to this belief. The attraction of the legal profession was not confined to West Indians. The study of the law attracted the middle class from all the colonial territories. The phenomenon is so widespread that it presumably has a great deal to do with the structure of colonial society, and the nature of its relationships with the metropolitan society. The swarming of the Inns of Court with coloured colonials eventually became a problem to these colonials themselves. There had previously been some official concern with the problem. A circular from the Colonial Office had been sent out to local bar associations suggesting that training in the UK was in some respects undesirable and that alternatives should be considered. One of the reasons advanced was that unfortunate alliances were often made in the UK as a result of such visits. This immediately brought to the fore the question of racial prejudice, and provoked indignation on the part of many West Indian lawyers. It was partly as a result of this that the suggestion was rejected out of hand. More important was the fact that the legal profession was not merely strongly imbued with the intrinsic values of the British legal system but with all the paraphernalia and tradition as well. The Inns of Court had almost a legendary significance for the lawyer and the idea of training in Britain was absolutely necessary for the maintenance of social prestige.

With the intention of wishing to be assimilated in this highly traditional English organization, whose minutest details had been copied in the West Indies, the colonial student found himself mixing in the student union of his chosen Inn predominantly with other colonial students. English law students were in a minority, and it was alleged by the West Indians that they mainly used the students' room on the rare occasions when it was unoccupied. Otherwise, they sought more congenial surroundings. The colonial student, in spite of the fact that he developed a 'nationalism' and a colonial ideology appropriate to the situation in which he found himself, was aware of his high evaluation of the Inns of Court as a *British* institution. He was somewhat worried by the fact that it was in danger of being transferred, outwardly at any rate, into a colonial institution. Fearing this himself, the colonial student was doubly fearful that the British whom he so often accused of prejudice, oppression and so on resented the presence of so many colonials in the place. This predisposed him to believe in action, open or surreptitious, to control the influx of colonials.

This was one reason why it was believed that standards had been raised in the law examinations. In many cases, this belief was transparently a rationalization of failure or a defensive belief against the anxiety of such a possibility, but it was widely entertained nonetheless. The fact that standards universally applied would not handicap colonial students any more than English students did not have the force that one might at first attribute to it. Direct discrimination on racial grounds could not be applied, the counterargument ran, but colonial students lacked facility in English and further were not as well educated as the British student. The latter usually attended a university and contemporarily or subsequently took the examination at the Inns of Court. With such a background, it was impossible for them not to do better than the mass of colonial students. In these subtle ways did the British move.

It was impossible to overrate the cunning and skill of the English lawyer! This opinion was held by West Indians whose position, if the argument had any force at all, would probably have been the least affected by these considerations. If there was a desperate need for this belief in discrimination, the student would sometimes allege that it was possible to differentiate between foreign students and Englishmen on the basis of names. Here again, there was a difficulty for the West Indian since most of them possessed English names, and an Indian from the area with a typical Indian name had recently won first class honours and been placed first in the bar examinations.

The belief in racial discrimination was less marked than the belief in the victimization of colonial students for radical and communist activities. Some students alleged that one of their lecturers had openly used the threat that communists would not be allowed to pass their examinations because the practice of communism and of the learned profession were mutually incompatible. This could easily have been the distortion of a genuinely held point of view. The question of professional compatibility arose again in the case of those students who came to the UK expecting to qualify within a few months. When their funds were exhausted they took whatever jobs they could and some even had to resort to public assistance. It is easy to see how such an individual could accept a radical ideology as a rationalization of his failure. Such a radical position might coincide with some aspect of his behaviour considered to be conduct unworthy of someone called upon to practise a gentlemanly profession. Whether in fact such a situation arose, or how the authorities of these Inns of Court would have dealt with it, the writer has no idea, nor did the law students. The particular form which the rationalization took was significant.

In the case of the legal profession, the failures that resulted were often the most tragic and it was perhaps because of this that the allegations of discrimination developed in the sphere. In the first place, entry to the legal profession was easier than into medicine – the other popular profession. This had always been so but became even more marked during the war when examinations could be taken locally and the period of time necessary for dining at the Inns of Court was cut down to the brief period of six months. Eventually, the period was lengthened, tutorial advisers appointed and greater attention was paid to detail. But in the meantime, many students who were just able to finance the shorter project had taken the plunge. Again, many older people had spent all their savings to achieve somewhat late in life their ambition of being lawyers. The idea that the law examination was easy had also encouraged such students.[18] The whole personality was involved and when failure resulted, it was particularly difficult to take.

Among the West Indians, failure never had any of the pathological results as in some other cases. The belief in discrimination never led to the belief that the *individual* student through some *paranoiac* logic had been singled out as the symbolic object of attack. In the case of one colonial student, the belief led to a representation to the highest authorities, presumably to the individual's ultimate undoing. In another case, failure led to an attack which resulted in death. The most marked case which the writer found in West Indians was that of a student of lower middle class origin. His father owned a small shop and the possibility of his getting a professional education would never have arisen if the Americans had not set up bases in the island. His father had just bought a house for the family after the strenuous efforts to educate his son. Owing to the housing shortage, he was offered a price considerably in excess of the cost of building. Through this windfall, he was persuaded to enter into building on a small scale. When sufficient money had been made the son was sent away to be educated. This proved an unexpectedly long and expensive process. The son struggled through to his finals, but failed. He was about to take the examination for a second time when he was stricken by anxiety. Perhaps he was being failed because he once possessed some socialist literature and was an advocate of socialism. Indeed, students had jokingly stuck up a placard with the hammer and sickle in his room. Perhaps this had been seen by Colonial Office officials and he had been wrongly dubbed communist. Would not the best thing be to approach the examination authorities and explain he was not a communist before the examination? Again, he had heard that ex-servicemen were being given special consideration. He had not seen war service, but he had worked for a short period in a war factory. He had also befriended his landlady who had a son who had been in the army. The son had been killed on the Continent and the student had naturally assisted her in arranging a visit to her son's tomb. Although these things were not exactly war service, were they not sufficiently similar to warrant an approach to the Council of Legal Education? Fortunately, this student was partially successful in his examination – he was referred in one subject – and was then able to weather the storm.

At the university, there was sometimes some evidence of prejudice on the part of the students. In one college, a student reported that he was sitting in the students' lounge when an English student came in, looked at the bunch of coloured students, said in scorn, "I never thought —— would come to this", and walked out in scorn. On the whole, however, such incidents were rare.

Nonetheless, there were little incidents which put the colonial students off from participation in university life. Among these, was the failure of other students to sit near to them in canteens or to engage them in conversation, or as in the case of one institution, there was a cartoon in the students' newspaper showing a well dressed African complete with wing-necked collar, umbrella and bowler hat dictating "Take a letter" to another African who was naked except for loincloth crouched over a drum. Even where there was no ill will, there was still room for misunderstanding. Thus one student at a teachers' college filled a form unthinkingly, indicating that she was interested in dramatics. She was invited by the dramatic club to plan the term's work and only on actual confrontation with practical problems did it dawn on both sides that the colour question was involved. This girl reported extreme embarrassment and a desire to withdraw altogether from the group.

There is one field which calls for special mention and that is the field of sport. Where students were active in sport, they did not find much difficulty in gaining friends. This was partly because the West Indians knew how to play the same sports as the English and there was some familiarity with West Indian cricketers. Sport, however, was considered in the same light as the nursery rhyme "Ten Little Nigger Boys". It would be as silly to object to the nursery rhyme as it would be to the advertisement. Both of them reflected not prejudice, but an affectionate and endearing attitude towards the Negro. Accompanying the letter as evidence of good faith, so that he might see for himself and not be led into misconceptions by second hand reports, was a full-sized cardboard reproduction of the undergrad advertisement!

In a similar vein were the remarks of another student who after recounting his experiences of discrimination stated: "But I must say that we were treated very well by our chemistry professor who used to give special lectures on Saturday mornings just for two of us. I always mention that when people bring up racial prejudice."

Probably the most critical remark on university life was this relatively marked one by a student at a provincial university:

> On the whole, I could say the university has been a relief after quitting the RAF. You find people who are quite decided about coloured peoples and such people just don't seem to penetrate at all. On the other hand, you find some quite indulgent. Yet, I often get the impression that despite some of their friendliness, they have at the back of their minds that *arrogance* which makes them feel we are a class apart. And even if they feel we ought not to be prevented from enjoying the full facilities, yet they don't seem to be in favour of mixing too much.
>
> You may be friendly with a fellow but if he sees you walking out with a girl, which suggests a certain amount of friendliness, he is overwhelmed. He can't accept it as real as what he wants at heart. So that I find you can get along best in colleges with fellows if you don't get too friendly with the girls.

The Older Universities and the Student

The prestige which Oxford and Cambridge share is only rivalled and surpassed by London. Indeed, among the better educated of the West Indians there was a familiarity and pride in the achievement of the older universities. Just as a few of the West Indians followed county cricket and football results in the UK, so did they follow the achievements of Cambridge and Oxford on the sport field. There were some cultured individuals who knew the details of all the colleges.

It was inevitable that the prestige of the older universities should have been transferred to the colonies. Recently, one legislator went on record as requiring that all teachers in the government secondary school of his colony should have first class honours degrees from a residential university. However, this tremendous prestige had to be balanced against the fact that most West Indians receiving higher education were primarily interested in professional education. In terms of medicine and law, the chief professions in which the West Indians were interested, London offered greater attraction than Oxford and Cambridge. Hence the early prestige which the ancient universities enjoyed came to be overlaid by the quicker road to legal training of the Inns of Court, or the more direct road to medical practice of the London Hospital.

The type of education offered at Oxford and Cambridge has always been considered admirable training for the elite of British society. To say this is not in any way to criticize the institutional arrangements at these places. It only means that although the university may be catholic in its appeal to learning, it becomes coloured everywhere by national traditions. These national traditions are not necessarily the best for a student of a different culture, except in so far as they share common traditions.

Perceptive observers believe that many colonial students including West Indians become absorbed with the trivialities and superficialities of life at the ancient universities. The result tends to be the creation of a type of individual unsuited for the social structure. In the past, it was alleged that many colonial students got caught up in the fast and expensive life of the fashionable set but with the widening of opportunity in the postwar period, this allegation was less frequently made. However, it was believed that the student tended to become arrogant, over self-possessed, and lacking in humility. These are allegations which were made before, of *all* West Indian students who had received their education in the UK.

The prestige of the older universities presented peculiar difficulties to the West Indian student. In the first place, he became overawed with tradition and became concerned with adjusting to the wholly alien experience. Secondly, the particular prestige and status which he acquired may have been very sound training but they served to stress the difference of the student from the community from which he came, and his equality with others. The very effectiveness of the educational system in the older universities could be regarded as in some sense a danger to the colonial.

These allegations have more or less disappeared in the case of the general student. They appeared to have some substance in the past since the dominant drive of the individual was that of trying to integrate himself into the host society. The precise emotional results and effects upon the personality were not such as to make adjustment to the society of origin the result which was required or expected. This point raises the whole question of the environment in which the student pursues his higher education and its social effects. It would perhaps be more convenient to discuss this matter at greater length in connection with the establishment of the University College of the West Indies.

The Provincial University and the Colonial Student

In the case of the provincial universities, the reaction of the students was exactly the same as in London. In the smaller places where there was more personal contact, the student was more generally integrated into student life. In the larger places, there were usually groups of students and here, the same conditions of solidarity among colonial students in general and West Indian students in particular manifested themselves.

In the smaller places, friendliness frequently was not an adequate substitute for the feeling of belonging and many students looked forward with anxiety to the period of vacation when they could flee to London, not to see the sights of the city but in order to meet friends from home. The students placed in districts which did not allow relatively easy access to London also felt their loneliness particularly acutely and one girl actually had to abandon her course of study and return home on this account.

Academic Life and the Problem of Adjustment

It is the universal experience of the West Indian student in the UK that his attitude towards learning is different. On the whole, the differences stated are that there is a greater dependence in the West Indies on rote learning, a much more competitive attitude and a much lesser ability to use libraries. The problems involved in correcting these defects, although apparently superficial, are very great. Many students considered that from the point of view of the actual content of their courses, the first year or first few months in the university were largely wasted in adjusting to these problems.

One indication of the attitude of most West Indian students to books was shown in the failure of many scholarship holders to take up the book allowances to which they were entitled. Because of their failure, the allowance was ruled to be unnecessary much to the chagrin of the more enlightened students.

Within the West Indies, the poverty of the place, coupled with the provision of a few open scholarships, led to a fierce competition. This contributed largely to the mechanical examination focused attitude of the student. It also hindered the free sharing and mutual stimulation which should be part of university life.

Thus one student described how he continued keeping his ideas for himself, not disclosing the sources of his information until he was forced to read a paper at a seminar. He then realized the weakness of his position and how much he could learn from criticism by others. Even then, however, he rationalized not sharing his knowledge with others on the grounds that otherwise he would not do well in the final examination. Again, the adequate use of a library is something the student acquires only in the course of his study. Undoubtedly, this is a problem not peculiar to the West Indian student.

In addition, the nonacademic problems which the student had to face affected his academic performance. First comes the preoccupation with the colour problem. For a long time, many students can think of nothing else. One student who had an extremely successful career pointed out in retrospect that in a reply to his headmaster about his progress in Britain, all he did was to post him back a pamphlet dealing with the colour question in Britain. How he managed to find nothing else to comment upon evaded him.

Moreover, there is the failure to participate in seminars or group discussions at the university because of feelings of inferiority. Thus SM stated that for a long time he was unable to participate.

> I think the most important problem the West Indian has to face is the fact that he tends to shut himself up in an island and not go out to meet the outside society. Usually, he confines himself to a little conclave of West Indian friends with the result that he does not benefit from participation in the outside society. I know for myself that whenever I meet an Englishman I just freeze up within. No matter how I may feel theoretically, whenever I am face to face with an Englishman that is my natural reaction. I see it coming on me regularly in class. I never take part in discussions because of this cold feeling, this feeling of sullen resentment in me. I believe it is because I do not want to find myself in a situation in which the Englishman is in any way superior. Feeling inferior, you are afraid to argue with him, to enter into the fray because you will be afraid of being beaten, and on the other hand, by staying outside, you get this feeling of superiority, I have often detected it in myself.
>
> For the first year I was here, it was just torture! [Showing signs of violent emotion] My God! I was literally shut up in a shell. I felt this desire to go out into the English society and to participate in it but on the other hand, whenever I met an Englishman, I could not stand it for longer than five minutes. As a result, I used to spend the greater part of my time locked up in my room. I suppose that it was a good thing because it gave me an opportunity of listening to an immense amount of musical records and to read a lot of art books. I used to spend my time looking

through art books and going to concerts. But I don't think I would like to go through that again (I mean I am speaking to you as I would to a psychologist). Oh no! That was a veritable purgatory. I don't know how it was, I just could not stand an Englishman whether it was a man or woman.

I was not in the least interested in them (girls). I used to go to lectures, take notes, go back to my room and play classical records. There was only one girl who for some peculiar reason insisted on thrusting herself on me. She had come in contact with West Indians and when she learned that I was a West Indian she started speaking to me and being friendly, but I was not interested. I used to do my lectures then back to my room. I *literally* used to live within a shell. Even my wife hasn't made any difference to my attitude to the Englishman. Anyway, she is not really English. All it has done is to enlarge my little circle so that I am more self-sufficient and less isolated. I now have my little circle to fall back on . . .

You see, at first, I never knew whether to mix with West Indians or not. On the one hand, I wanted to have the security of belonging to a West Indian group and had a strong attraction to associate myself with them while on the other hand I felt "By Christ, if I go and do this I will be defeating the whole purpose of my visit to this place", so I sort of fall between two stools. Real problems of a negroid man, eh . . .

Do you think this is my personal problem or is it the general problem of West Indians? I am sorry to be so specific and subjective, but I don't know how it is with other West Indians. As far as I can see, they face the same sort of problem, and many of them are in the same position. Now, I identify myself completely with West Indian society.

One student of economics, when asked how he managed to become interested in economics, replied:

I was not interested, I am not interested even now. It was only the case of a man with a strong inferiority complex who didn't even have to make up his mind on anything and whose parents decided everything for him. I suppose not having any confidence in myself, they decided it would be a good thing if I did economics and if they decided so, well I did economics that was all.

About his teachers, he had this to say:

I think they like me. There are only three of them: Professor Williams, Mr Johnson and Mr Jones. Well you know Professor Johnson, he is famous for his kindness and I get on fairly well with the others. In fact, Jones and I get on very well. He is a good fellow, plays football and all that. Besides that he is interested in colonial problems and always used to give me papers to write upon the West Indians. He knew how to draw me out, with the result that I could increase my self-confidence and take part in the discussions.

It is a common thing. I don't play football or even read about it yet all the people with whom I have got friendly play football. In my class, the only two fellows I can relax with and enjoy their company are two carefree fellows who are interested in football. The rest just get my back up . . .

The students you can class into three groups. There is one group who is very interested in these problems. I mean seriously interested and came and discussed things with you afterwards; and there is the other group who ask questions and show some interest and that is the end of it. The third group are not interested at all (but) definitely hostile. I took care to prepare my paper without attacking the English and being as objective as possible, but right through I came up against the most violent resistance.

In spite of his class friendships, this student states:

I have *never* had a meal with an English student. It is the same question, English students all have this superior sort of air. This keeping aloof because they are considered superior and patronizing, and I can't stand being patronized. Professor Johnson denies that it is so. He tells me that I am completely mistaken, but I am quite sure about it. The attitude is "I am superior to you, but as we know that all men are equals, I grant you equality".

The 'Colonial' Course

The anxieties about the reactions of British students never led to any systematic denigration or disparagement of the university. The only case in which there was evidence of systematic criticism was where a special colonial course was organized primarily but not exclusively for students from the colonies.

Among the students of the social science certificate (colonial), there was much opposition. Part of it sprang from the fact that the course included subjects like physiology. To many of the West Indians and other colonials this smacked of the courses on physiology and hygiene in the lower forms of their secondary schools and teacher training courses. The 'university' subjects of psychology, sociology and economics were what they were anxious to come to grips with. In their ignorance, they did not conceive of physiology as a university subject at all nor did they see its relevance to the jobs for which they were being trained.

Even more important as a source of discontent, however, was the conception of the course as in some sense an inferior one being fobbed off upon colonials. There was the general belief that the English students being trained for social work did a three-year course and received a diploma while the students from the colonies did a two year course and were awarded only a certificate. Recourse to the school calendar should easily have corrected the misunderstanding because both courses were of like duration and for both a school certificate, and not a university diploma was granted. These easily accessible facts were pointed out to the students but the speakers were either not believed or conveniently forgotten. Consequently, they continued to have currency and be relayed to each succeeding wave of students. Two questions were involved. First was the fear of the Greeks and the gifts they were bringing. It was difficult for the students to believe in the genuineness of the scholarships. They were all part of a rising group and there were anxieties both as to their self-sufficiency and as to what would happen when they returned home. They argued that having received proper training (the criticism of the course being conveniently forgotten), they would return home to find that the main jobs were being reserved for Englishmen. The reported story of one of the students that in an interview with a Colonial Office official, a certain post had been referred to as a European post, had wide currency and reinforced these fears.

Second, the idea of a separate course for colonials smacked of segregation. Many of the students lived in colonial hostels – nearly all had received unfortunate experiences in obtaining accommodation. The idea of a separate course with separately organized lectures and reading rooms, awakened all the bitterness provoked by the accommodation problem. The drive for integration into the host society was strong; when the university appeared to be practising segregation these students saw "discrimination everywhere".

The motivation behind the establishment of the course was of course genuine. It represented a serious and thought out policy of adaptation of metropolitan courses to colonial conditions. Facilities for training did not exist within the colonial framework and had to be provided in British universities.

Chapter **5**

The Student and
the Sex Problem

The Adolescent and Sex

The age range of the West Indian students during the period 1945–49 was extremely great. It ranged from students in their fifties doing postgraduate courses to young people just out from secondary schools. The latter faced a somewhat different problem of adjustment. Although a more permissive and freer attitude towards sexual and social relationships between teenagers is spreading in the West Indies, the particular group of students concerned had been little affected by these trends. The fairly strong family system operating in the middle class tends to prolong adolescence. The competition for the limited scholarship facilities and the pressures from social mobility are very great. Consequently, only those students who have been able to concentrate on their studies can be successful. Not all young students, however, are scholarship holders but those who can afford to send their children abroad are usually from a group likely to guard them from sexual experience.

To some of these young students, the problem of sex is seen as one of marriage. Such individuals find themselves often in love and contemplating marriage. Sometimes the inadequacy of their experience leads them into choices which family and friends consider unfortunate. Thus H was friendly with a West Indian girl deeply in love with him. He did not reciprocate but fell madly in love with an English girl several years his senior. She was uneducated, limited in outlook and clearly interested in the money which the student was willing to spend on her. There was even a suspicion of the students' friends being misdirected. All his friends brought whatever pressure they could to dissuade him from the alliance which was leading to marriage. Eventually, the girl was dropped not because of persuasion but because she proved too expensive a proposition.

In another case, a student met a girl and after seeing her two or three times proposed marriage. This was accepted by the girl and a visit paid to her parents. Subsequently, this student went around in bewilderment complaining that he did not know how it had happened but that he had got engaged. Fortunately for him, a relative of his was in England and paid them a visit. Subsequently, this relative explained the position to the girl's parents; marriage could not be contemplated immediately at all, the student was too young, possessed inadequate resources, had acted on impulse without giving the matter due consideration etc. The parents of the girl who had just left school and had only consented to the arrangement because it was a *fait accompli* and because of their lowly social class, readily agreed to the breaking off of the engagement.

Not all such alliances ended on this happy note however. One student in such a situation failed his examinations, was reported to his parents and had his allowance cut off. The 'danger' of marriage, of making an immature alliance without the benefit of any intimate guidance has its obscene side – the danger of promiscuity through the release from external pressures towards conformity.

The Relations between the Sexes and Their Consequences

The interracial marriages in the West Indies have played a special role. In a society in which status and prestige largely derived from ethnic affiliation and in which there was an acceptance of 'white superiority' there was a strong desire to improve the 'colour' characteristics of one's children by marrying someone fairer in complexion.[19]

Hence it was thought desirable in some quarters that the student going abroad should marry an English girl. To many a student, this was also the symbol and badge of success. For a coloured man to be seen in intimate association with a white woman marked him out as exceptional. Since inter-marriage between local whites and local coloured was unusual, it meant automatically that the individual was one of the privileged few who could afford to travel to Europe or that he was an island scholar and therefore of high professional competence.

Before leaving home, this subject of the possibility of marriage was joked about or received more serious consideration. The student was already armed with a definite attitude. There were those who fantasized in their adolescence about marrying Europeans, who fell in love with white girls at a distance and who welcomed the opportunity of making their dreams come true. There were those – in the higher end of the middle class scale – who were specifically enjoined to marry Europeans or it was tacitly understood from the nature of their social contacts that such an alliance would be welcomed by their family. The large majority, however, were intrigued by the question but had the warnings of their compatriots and friends. There was the prestige given to the man who committed the sin of 'hubris' in marrying white but there was also a feeling of self-respect arising from the fact that the best of the land, the scholarship holders, were marrying people of their own kind. At the same time, there was a belief that interracial marriages were doomed to a high rate of mortality. The general belief is that it can't work. The stereotype of the working Englishwoman anxious to marry the West Indian was accepted but so was the belief that once she came out to the West Indies she became corrupted. There were stories circulating in most of the territories of black husbands who drove cars while their European wives drove in the back; of how the lawyer who was carrying his wife's bags was mistaken for a porter; of how hated racial epithets were hurled at the submissive black husband; of the wife attending exclusive clubs while the husband waited outside and so on. Together with these ran reports of frequent lack of faithfulness on the part of the white wife.

The situation was further accentuated by the fact that some of the students who returned with European wives had already had alliances with local girls which had to be broken. This caused a certain amount of resentment. Perhaps because of this resentment, the bitterness of the attack was directed not so much against the West Indian as against the white wife. When people became antagonistic, they were sure to denounce the white girls who were 'barmaids' at home and who now, in the West Indies, were seeking to lord it over coloured folk.

This criticism that many of the English wives were barmaids did not of course hamper the activities of students who were primarily interested in marrying white. The stigma of 'barmaid' status could be easily overcome by marrying someone of some educational and professional competence. Those students who found themselves in alliances with English girls were quick to locate them high up on the social scale. Thus a student married a girl trained in domestic science who was engaged in helping to run a hostel. Friends of his, by stretching their imaginations, were able to denounce the girl as a maid. He on the other hand, was quick to point out that her family background was middle class and her educational standards high. Indeed, all in all, the girl was at least the equal if not the superior of many West Indian students from an educational point of view. This did not, however, prevent the stigma of barmaid from being attached. Other West Indians with English girlfriends who wished to show solidarity with the rest of the West Indian community were quick to use this denunciation.

This question of relationships with European girls came up not only on the departure of the student but in many cases immediately on arrival. Among the older students who had had sexual experience, the questioning of friends and acquaintances on arrival was a matter of course. Among a large section of the students, the question of How soon a girlfriend? or, How soon sexual relations with an English girl? was an immediate obsession. Sometimes the days, weeks, and months would be counted before contact was established.

This urgent need was sometimes responsible for sharp rebuffs. Sometimes students who had heard only of the successes of their fellows, of the strange promiscuity and casualness in sexual matters of the big city, would make brash and imprudent approaches. Others would immediately, on arrival, hasten to public dance halls in the hope of picking up girlfriends. In such cases, the experience of 'discrimination' at so early a period and so contrary to expectation had a telling effect.

The Personality Factor in Interracial Alliances

A certain preoccupation with race and sex existed with all the West Indian students. Yet, not all of them married English girls. It is impossible to give any statistical and accurate assessment of the factors involved in this differential choice. The writer, on little evidence, believes that the personality factor and tendencies operating *before* the student actually left for the UK were the main factors responsible. All students were equally exposed to the problem of sexual adjustment. The adolescent was more inclined to relate the problems of sex and marriage. But it is clear that most of the interracial marriages that took place were not among the younger group. In part, this was a reflection of family control, since financially and emotionally the younger student was still under the influence of the folk at home.

Nor was it merely the inability to distinguish between categories of white people that led to marriage. 'Unfortunate' alliances there were but the student who was in such an alliance might or might not contemplate marriage. Nor was it merely the chance factor of pregnancy. Reactions towards the pregnancy of a girlfriend varied but few looked upon it as automatically requiring marriage. On one occasion, this excuse was used to justify a marriage which was criticized by the student's friends. But by and large, in the permissive sexual atmosphere that existed there was no necessity that marriage should automatically follow pregnancy. In small communities in the West Indies, the pressure of gossip and opinion induced such an association. In the UK, the first thought was how to procure an abortion.

It seems that these individuals were predisposed to marriage, who in the family situations at home had become most preoccupied with race and colour differences and/or who felt that marriage to a European would in some way improve their status in their 'reference groups' back home. In some cases, dark-skinned students who had been discriminated against within the family had become sensitized to colour differences and wished to prove to themselves and their group (family of origin and friends) that they were not rejected on colour grounds. It was in fact a drive for acceptance.

This factor of self-depreciating attitudes coupled with estimates of what the situation could be on their return home seemed extremely important factors. It does not follow, of course, that these individuals were making rational estimates of the situation they would find on their return to the West Indies. Indeed, such individuals were fighting with internal tendencies based on childhood and early experiences, at the very time when the social order in the West Indies was undergoing rapid change. Some students, for instance, who had formed interracial alliances and were contemplating marriage returned home, thus breaking their stay in the UK. On their return, they found friends and parents glad that they had escaped forming unfortunate alliances and received congratulations from their friends for their skill in evading English girls. Some of these changed their minds and broke off their engagements.

It should be borne in mind that not all areas in the West Indies show an equal degree of separation of the races. In some areas, racial barriers are very much more marked and in these areas there was a correspondingly more marked preoccupation with the question of interracial marriage. To some coming from such areas, intimate relations with Europeans became almost a revolutionary act, a form of personal self-assertion. However, among those who contemplated marriage, the question was whether to remain in the UK or whether they enjoyed sufficient social prestige and acceptance (whether through skin colour, professional competence or otherwise) to ensure that the marriage would lead to a greater acceptability at home.

In one area at least, this preoccupation with interracial marriages by the students from that area was most marked. Eventually, a certain proportion of students from these territories formed alliances or tried to form alliances of a permanent nature. In this case, the fact that one person took the initiative and the others knew that there would be interracial couples in their island as a result of their alliances seemed to encourage the tendency. Even here, however, the effect of the primary group of fellow students to which they were attached was to ensure that their adjustment back home would be acceptable and from a social status point of view, successful.

The Psychological Effect of Sexual Relationships with Whites

The experience of intimate relations with a person of the white race undoubtedly has a profound effect on the personalities of colonial students. Thus one student who was later to play a prominent part in one of the colonial territories in fighting against racial discrimination described the extreme stimulation and sense of exhilaration he experienced from finding himself pressed against white women in an underground train. Subsequently, his experiences with a graduate of his university whom he met at a university ball revolutionized both his ideas about their accessibility and his attitude towards them. When he compared the fearful attitude with which he regarded whites in his own homeland, he looked upon the situation in Britain in which he had an Englishwoman actually seeking him out as a prized object, as complete liberation.

In the case of the West Indian student, there was unlikely to be such a dramatic sense of liberation but the achievement of intimate sexual relations with a white person effected an assuaging of feelings of inferiority. Of course, other intimate personal relationships had something of this effect as well, but by and large none had as profound consequences as the sexual relationships. Further, most West Indian men reported greater difficulty in getting friendly with Englishmen than with Englishwomen. Indeed, both working class men as well as students claimed that life would have been intolerable without the sympathetic attitude of the women.

The belief – no doubt justified in the greater promiscuity of those English girls with whom they came in contact – encouraged a split between tenderness and sex in some students. There can be little doubt that some of the reasoning employed in defending the relationship with the English girl was mere rationalization. The 'incest taboo' operated among many West Indians and they were able to release themselves sexually with foreigners to an extent that was not possible with one of their own group. It was not merely that the West Indian girl hoped that friendship would ripen into a permanent alliance but that the male West Indian could only look upon sexual relations with a West Indian as leading to marriage. It was more difficult for him psychologically to have a casual affair with his own countrywomen.

Some of the West Indian men solved the problem by having two girlfriends, an English girl with whom he slept and a West Indian with whom he carried on a somewhat platonic relationship. Such a relationship should not be thought of as universal. Relationships ranged from a nonsexual relationship with one or other ethnic female to one of indiscriminate sexual relationships with every female.

Sometimes, the conflict arose not through the girl's opportuning but through the guilt feelings of the boy. In one case R, a legal student, became friendly with an English girl. There was an understanding that there should be no question of marriage. Nonetheless, they were extremely fond of each other. R expected pressure to be brought to bear on him. However, the girl kept to the agreement. Unknown to R, she became pregnant and would not let him know of this because it might cause him anxiety just at a time when he was taking his final examinations. When these were through, there was a proposal that she should procure an abortion, but in order that this might take place, R had to become heavily indebted. Rather than place him in debt, she attempted at great risk a self-induced abortion. When R was ready to go home, he was besieged by feelings of guilt at his desertion.

In another case, the friendship between a student and an English girl was ripening. The girl hinted gently at home that she was thinking of marrying a coloured man – in this case, it happened to be a professional man of some distinction. Her parents ordered her to leave the home forthwith, not even giving her time to pack her belongings and her sister was forbidden to have anything to do with her. In this situation, the student was forced to give shelter to the girl and eventually the enforced union was legalized.

Where girls have gone through the experience of estrangement from friends and family, it becomes difficult to drop them lightly – particularly when the individual is sensitive to the fate that awaits them. Having become friendly with coloured men, the white girl finds it difficult to be friendly with whites. Several allege this but, in fact, it may be a personality predisposition which has led to the first friendship with a coloured man anyhow. In any case, her fate is usually to be inherited by another colonial student – a process which may continue indefinitely.

Aggression and Sex

We have spoken of the greater release of the West Indians in relations with the Europeans. We find also a release of aggression against the English through sex. Thus some students adopted as their slogan "Love them and leave" and another, the more virulent "None shall escape". The view of sexual relations as conquest and somewhat humiliating to the women was not alien to the West Indian and among the more experienced, it was quite widespread. This release of aggressiveness did not impair but in all probability contributed to the adequacy of sexual performance.

Some students loved to relate stories of their conquest of girls who initially showed prejudice. This did not take the form of legitimate pride in overcoming prejudice through personal charm but in rejecting the rejection through the 'humiliation' of sexual experience. Thus in one instance, the place chosen for intercourse was the public park. In another, the relationship was reduced to a purely sexual one. The West Indian insisted that the girl should continue her engagement with her English fiancé while she was used as a sexual object by him.

Although such attitudes were not universal, there were stories of this kind constantly in circulation. Moreover, among many students, there was the tendency to *count coup* and to look upon their sexual conquests more as a means of satisfying themselves psychologically as to their own adequacy and without consideration as to the consequences for the girl involved.

The Confusion of Categories and Sex

The confusion of class and racial categories so common in the West Indies causes a crisis of reclassification. In the sphere of sexual relations, the equation of white with upper class causes some confusion. H, a student in his thirties of lower middle class origin and a little lower down in the social status than the majority of students, was unable to distinguish between one white person and another. Much to the embarrassment of his fellow students at the colonial hostel where he lived, he gave his telephone number to prostitutes and proudly invited his new conquests to the hostels. On a Sunday, he would parade a girl of dubious character before the assembled gathering to the astonishment of ministers of religion and others who were visiting.

The inability to differentiate was rendered more difficult because of the more democratic nature of the British society. Standards of education were higher and the placing of people in social class terms was not as easy as in the more highly stratified society of the West Indies where class visibility was extremely high. Thus many students found that they could carry on intelligent conversations with people in occupational categories with whom there could only have been a minimum of contact in the Caribbean. This had bearing on that highly emotional problem of the marriage to 'barmaids'.

Racial Discrimination and Sex

The racial discrimination which the students experienced forced them into intimate relations with categories of persons which in terms of the social class could not be described as equal. We must remember that in the West Indies, colour was the main value around which the status system was organized. The evaluation of these friendships brought the different categories of judgement into play. Pride at the possession of English acquaintances had to be tempered by the other 'class' factors. In such a situation, a great deal of rationalization was used by those who had formed alliances and wished to make them permanent.

On the other hand, friendships with lower class girls helped to encourage tendencies to promiscuity. It also awakened some fear as to the desirability of marriage because the casual nature of sex relations conjured up pictures of lack of faithfulness. If more friendships had taken place between social equals, there can be little doubt that pride of possession would have over-ridden many of the obsessional fears of marriage to English girls among some students.

In this situation, friendships with nurses played an important role. In the first place, exchange visits could be made on an institutional basis with the colonial hostels. Second, the nurses rightly or wrongly enjoyed the reputation of being liberal as regards colour questions and relatively permissive in matters of sex. Third, the nurses as a professional group enjoyed a sufficiently high status to obviate the barmaid criticism, while in point of fact their social class origin rendered them favourably disposed to the group.

The Role of Interracial Couples

Because of discrimination, English girls were in short supply. Hence, whenever a friendship ripened the girl tended to be surrounded by a host of friends. Those without girls of their own or whose friendships were not firm cultivated her and sometimes even attempted to trespass upon those friends' preserves or at least to inherit. Where actual marriages took place the married couples tended to form central points around which groups gathered. The tendency to form such groups was not more marked, perhaps, than in the case where there were married students. In both cases, there seemed to be the need to enter into some intimate family-type relationship. It gave the individual, albeit vicariously, a greater stability and a point of reference.

In the case of the interracial couple, there were other consequences because of the preoccupation with the colour question. Here, perhaps, the question should be broadened to include interracial couples not technically of student status but who fitted into the same social class category. In some cases, especially where there were possibilities of passing as white, contacts with the coloured group were shed. More usually the opposite was the case; the woman took the side of the oppressed racial groups. Although no statistical evidence can be deduced to confirm it, a considerable number of the English wives had a bias against the inner circle. Many had one parent who was foreign and others gave evidence of family rejection. In any case, the interracial couple was highly conspicuous and was continually being exposed to the stares and comments of people in the streets and other public places. The marriage of the man was very often due to a drive to integrate with the white group but the interracial situation placed him in a position in which the ultimate rejection was even more apparent. Interracial couples therefore seemed to be a source of strong anti-British sentiment; this in spite of the protest of the man that he could not be anti-British since he possessed an English wife. Thus at one time, the executive of the Caribbean Labour Congress, the radical 'labour' movement of West Indians which relied very heavily on student support, was heavily packed with people belonging to interracial unions.

An elaborate series of compensating beliefs grew up around the relationship with English and more specifically white women. The inadequacy of the Englishman both psychologically and physically in sexual performance was linked with the belief in the generally greater potency of the Negro as a whole. The Negro had a larger penis and the psychology of the West Indian was less inhibited than the Britisher.

These beliefs were inaccessible to reason. Little factual evidence was adduced to support them – and sometimes incompatible beliefs about the sexual life of the English. Whatever factual information there was such as personal experience or the impression of medical students encouraged this belief in the inadequacy of the Englishman.

The great emotional strength with which the views were held came out in the fairly frequent informal discussions of the subject. The evidence more usually adduced was the testimony of the girls concerned. They alleged that they had never experienced such joy as with the West Indian. This may have been a form of flattery or a genuine statement of a personal position. But it was generalized by the student and sometimes by the girls concerned into a general statement of the situation.

We have already noted the split between tenderness and sex in the case of the West Indian students. One of the strongest proponents of this theory was an ex-RAF student who had joined the armed services precisely because of an emotional blockage over sexual expression. Another, an older person, a permanent bachelor, showed difficulty in establishing adequate social relationships with West Indian girls both at home and in the UK. Another had never had sexual relations with any West Indians at all, but strangely enough linked this belief in the biological basis of the superior potency of the West Indian Negro male with the belief in the superior sexual attractiveness and performance of continental women.

It may have been true of both sides that the crossing of racial barriers was linked with the removal of incestuous and other social taboos and permitted both such individuals to experience a depth of feeling which they never knew before. But the proposition was not merely that interracial unions were more satisfying sexually but that Englishwomen as a whole were attracted to the Negro male. The fact that the girls upon whose views the position was maintained were exceptional and socially deviant and could not be regarded as typical was hotly contested. At the same time, these individuals held the belief in the general discrimination of the English people and would give accounts involving discrimination by both sexes.

Tenderness and Sex

Some of the West Indian students wished to marry English girls; a good many more were opposed to it but were anxious to have English girlfriends. At one period, before a certain feeling of West Indian solidarity developed, it was usual for the West Indian girls in London to complain that they were being neglected. The male students did not deny the charge of neglect but rather maintained that it was quite justified. In the first place, they argued, the English girl often paid her way for meals and entertainment. For students on a limited allowance this was of importance.

In the second place, the English girl was less likely to think of marriage than her West Indian counterpart. In point of fact, the question of marriage frequently arose with the English girl. Some insisted on introducing the new acquaintance to the family and awakened the same anxieties as the West Indian girl. More usually, the alliance took place independently of any family connections.

Third, many West Indians felt more at home with English girls than with West Indians. The latter, with a middle class background of a highly stratified society, wished to place every new West Indian male she met and to trace his connections. All those who because of colour or social class origin – and they were many – felt that a negative judgement was likely to be passed upon them, avoided their company. In the later stages, when West Indian girls of more humble circumstances were to be found this did not alter the situation for some, because marriage with someone *higher* on the social scale was a mark of professional success.

The English girls were also believed to be more permissive in their sexual attitudes than the West Indians. Of course, friendship with the English girl even on this casual basis created as many problems as it solved. The girl would often enter into a relationship without a thought of marriage. Indeed, many West Indians in an attempt to be honest would indicate from the onset that marriage would not enter into their consideration. Sometimes for instance, racial considerations would be pointed out as precluding marriage, but as the girl became more intimate, got to know coloured people and felt herself free of prejudice, she would turn to a reconsideration of the 'already settled problem'.

The Position of the West Indian Women

At the start of the period, there were relatively few West Indian girls in London. At first this may appear to have been an advantage, but it was not. The girl in her loneliness turned to the West Indian man around, only to be spurned and to foster the already established view that she was after the man for marriage.

On the whole, the West Indian girl felt herself slighted in favour of the English girl. This provoked attitudes of resignation, defeat, or more usually intense irritation and resentment. There were automatic condemnatory judgments of all interracial marriages and a fear that her boyfriend would eventually leave her to take up with an English girl. This fear was not entirely unjustified. West Indian men frequently used their friendship with their own girls in order to get at English girls. Friendship with a West Indian girl was often the means of entry of English girls into coloured society. Once they had broken the taboo about colour, it was easy to enter into relationships with coloured men. The latter on the other hand, beset with anxieties about rejection by the white girl, looked upon her friendship with the West Indian as at least an indication that the rejection would not solely be on the grounds of colour. The West Indian girl, anxious to ingratiate herself with West Indian men, would introduce him, at his request, to her own intimates – frequently to find herself the ultimately rejected of the three.

Because of her fear of losing out to the English girl, many a West Indian felt that she had to outdo the permissiveness of the English girl, if she were to hold her own. In any case, she faced a crisis in which she had to define her attitude to sex. This involved a rapid process of maturing.

This redefinition of the position became all the more necessary because friendships between white men and coloured girls was much rarer than between coloured men and white girls. There were occasional friendships and marriages – which grew in numbers as time progressed. Such friendships were with outstandingly good-looking West Indian girls of the fair type or with outstandingly shy and on the whole sexually unattractive males.

The position of the sexes in Britain was quite different to what obtained in the West Indies. In those areas, the general movement for the emancipation of women has reinforced certain indigenous features of the social structure to give women a relatively high status. Nonetheless, the emancipation of women has proceeded much further in the UK. We have already commented upon the more permissive attitudes to sex but there were other more general features.

Thus, the shortage of domestic help in the UK has led to men helping out with housework. West Indian women saw in this a further assertion of feminine freedom; it encouraged their femininity but at the price of conflict with their previously well-defined social roles. West Indian men should act like Englishmen in these matters, they asserted. But if West Indian men did in fact act in this fashion, it appeared to rob them of their masculinity.

The conflict between career and femininity was posed for many of the girls. The cases in which the conflict was most acute were among students doing medicine or planning to engage in research. Although academically there was no reason for failing their examination, a few girls consistently failed until they were forced to give up their medical studies. The course was strenuous and the male medical students, jealous of their own dignity, were fond of saying that under no consideration would they marry female doctors.

Chapter 6

The Relationship with
the Colonial Office

While some students of independent means scorned any personal contact with
the colonial students, there necessarily was some contact with the Colonial
Office by practically every student. In the immediate postwar period, all
students attending the universities as well as all nursing students had to pass
through the hands of the Colonial Office. This was a necessary and practicable
arrangement because of the shortage of places in the immediate postwar
period, but it ensured the possibilities of friction over bureaucratic delays and
of such frictions being given a political twist.

The arrangement by which all placement of university students was chan-
nelled through the Colonial Office had the general approval of all university
administrations. But in practice, there was some confusion which served to
show the Colonial Office in a wrong light. Thus students made individual
efforts to bypass the bureaucracy and contacted the university authorities.
They would get what would appear to be unconditional admission into the
university and then discover that the arrangement had to receive the ultimate
sanction of the Colonial Office. The arrangement was the only rational one
in the circumstances because it was clearly impossible for the university to
determine priorities for the limited number of places open to colonials. The
'power of veto' which the Colonial Office possessed was regarded as an evil
instrument placed in evil hands. This point of view was further encouraged

by the fact that one or two individual students did in fact manage to bypass the Colonial Office, or had their acceptance sanctioned while others were turned down.

Thus M, a colonial student, came to the UK in the hope of studying medicine. His educational background was weak and he was placed at a polytechnic institute in the hope of passing his initial examinations. He consistently failed these but blamed his failure on the Colonial Office for not placing him within a proper university. At the same time, he alleged that he knew students with similar backgrounds from his homeland who were in fact placed in medical school. He developed a great suspicion and hatred of the Colonial Office authorities who were perceived as having a 'down' on him personally. Eventually, the student more or less abandoned attempts at passing his examination and obtained clerical employment at the India Office. Shortly after this, Lady Mountbatten visited India House. He poured out his woes to her, alleging discrimination by the Colonial Office. A few months later, he got acceptance into medical school without the sanction of the Colonial Office.

The Colonial Office through its Welfare Department rendered a series of services to the government students and on request, to the private students. Students were greeted on arrival and accommodation arranged for them. Besides admissions, there was the question of transfers and changes of course. There was also the quarterly remittal of living allowances and the payment of fees. Naturally, the Colonial Office was empowered to terminate courses where students were not performing satisfactorily. In spite of the fact that the Colonial Office did not have direct responsibility for the running of special colonial students' hostels, they were held responsible by the students for the policy that was implemented there. It is clear that with such a wide range of student activities coming under their consideration there was every possibility of conflict with the Colonial Office. Quite apart from actual concrete causes of friction, the whole nature of the metropolitan colonial relationship with its background of paternalism and tutelage encouraged the student to think of the Colonial Office as a legitimate target for his complaints and aggressions, and as an organization which existed primarily to look after his personal welfare.

The Problems of the Colonial Office

The fact that the Colonial Office performed these functions led to a misinterpretation of the whole role of that body. The same conflict seemed to rage here that took place in the case of immigrant worker from the West Indies. On the one hand, it was clear that there were special problems posed by the colonial immigration – not least of all by the colour question. On the other, there was a reluctance to give official recognition to the existence of colour prejudice. The legal position was that the colonials were all Britishers and in that sense not in need of being paid any special attention.

Part of the problem was met by shedding the running of the colonial hostels to the Victoria League and eventually the whole problem of accommodation, of receiving visitors and the like was placed in the hands of the British Council. But even before this was done certain concrete steps were taken to minimize the distrust and hatred of the Colonial Office Welfare Department. Thus a liaison officer for West Indian affairs was established and later, an assistant liaison officer appointed. At first, the appointment was not greeted with much favour and in discussing the affairs of the West Indian Students Union (WISU), we shall see the sorts of suspicions that arose. The liaison officer was respected by those who knew him personally but the hostility to the Colonial Office was such that some of it was transferred to their own West Indian representatives. For one thing, it was considered that if they were serious about attending to West Indian affairs the post should have been one of higher status. The appointee was a 'stooge' of the Colonial Office. He had no real power and his opinions would never be given adequate consideration anyway. This was only an attempt to fool the students.

In actual practice, the work of the welfare office came to be well appreciated by the students although there still lingered some of the early suspicions. The sort of work which the colonial welfare officer dealt with was the greeting of students on their arrival.

At first, this might appear to be a matter of minor importance but the impact of London on students accustomed to a rural or smalltown atmosphere was terrific. One student who came from one of the smaller islands had never seen a cinema or a train in his life before passing through Port of Spain, Trinidad on his way to the UK. This was his idea of the big city and he wrote home that he was well prepared for London since he now knew what the big city was like. One student appeared at the Colonial Office with the statement that he had been told that there was likelihood of his obtaining a British Council scholarship on arrival in the UK. He could not remember the name of his informant and a check with the British Council revealed that they had no information on this student. The Colonial Office official then enquired about his present address in England to discover that the student had no idea of where he was staying. He had been taken by a friend to a boarding house, had not taken a note of the address or the telephone number, had found his way by a devious route to the Colonial Office but now had no idea of how to return to his home and his belongings.

Such ineptitude, naivete and simplicity were extreme but a certain amount of lack of sophistication was to be found in nearly all students. There were many students who proceeded to the UK without the slightest idea of entrance requirements. When they reached there they did not know what facilities were available. Other students believed that England was a land of opportunity in which it was relatively easy to earn a living and study.

An accountant with a secondary education became irked by the fact that so many scholarships and opportunities for study were available to his acquaintances while he was being left behind. He decided that he too should have some profession that was respected in the country. He spoke to an Englishman who gave him an introduction to a firm of manufacturers of optical equipment with whose management he was personally acquainted. The hare-brained scheme was adopted of working for this firm while studying to become an optician. Studious habits had been abandoned long ago and the background of this individual was not suited for the contemplated course of action. Yet the idea of being able to be called 'Doctor' as opticians are called in the West Indies caused him to take the plunge. Eventually, he had to abandon the idea of study altogether and seek employment elsewhere.

The task of the Welfare Department of the Colonial Office was particularly difficult because the postwar student population was not purely the young adolescent population that it was in the prewar years. In the first place, there were the students who had been unable to pursue their studies due to the war or who had had the course of their study interrupted. Secondly, there was a wave of students who normally would have proceeded to Britain but who were diverted to the relatively peaceful atmosphere in Canada. For instance, during the war special arrangements were made whereby the examinations of the Inns of Court could be held in the West Indian colonies. This special concession was extended to facilitate those who were going abroad to the University of Toronto. Many law students attended that university and later came to London to complete their studies in law. But these were only part of the general stream of students. Canadian degrees, although considered worthwhile, were not considered as good as degrees gained in the mother country. These students were in a sense almost postgraduate students. They were accustomed to a different university atmosphere, different systems of teaching, different conceptions of student (campus) life. They therefore had a point of view from which they could criticize the British. Wartime hardships persisted on into the postwar period and the general standard of life and the availability of creature comforts seemed primitive, after what they had become accustomed to in Canada. But even more important was the conception of university life which they brought. It corresponded much more to the idea of a residential university than life as they experienced it in London. This gave them a focus for expressing discontent and almost establishing an element of radical leadership among these students.

Some students further thought they could overcome bureaucratic delays. Although all student nurses were supposed to be enrolled through government channels and this fact was advertised in the West Indian press, some would-be nurses made direct contact with hospitals in the UK. When they reached the UK, they discovered that the road to becoming state registered nurses was not open and they had to approach the Colonial Office in order to be properly placed.

The Special Case of the Ex-Servicemen

The ex-servicemen presented a special problem. For the most part, they had joined the armed forces not so much out of patriotic motives as through a desire to see the world and escape from the pressures of the small community. Some thought of it as a means of permanent escape; many others merely as an opportunity to get abroad in order to better themselves in some way they knew not how; others thought of benefits that might be conferred upon them through service – such as preferment in the civil service. Very few thought of actual educational opportunities being created. None conceived of such an opportunity as was opened up by the Further Education Schemes. In this respect, the colonials were treated in exactly the same way as the British. Educational facilities became available to all those whose education had been interrupted by the war. The fiction was that everybody who had matriculated had intended to proceed to the university or some form of further training. Such a conception was a 'fiction' in terms of British society; it was even more so in the case of the West Indians since their society showed considerably more limited opportunity for educational advancement and further training.

The creation of these opportunities, however, magnified the amount of discontent with the Colonial Office. It appeared not as the beneficent arm of the government which distributed these liberal awards but as the negative force denying to many students the courses of their choice. The men in the armed forces had been in the army long enough to absorb the democratic ideology of British society. They found no difficulty in accepting this unparalleled generosity of treatment as a *right* to which they were entitled. In affirming this right, they wished to have freedom of choice. Given freedom of choice, the majority would have wished to become doctors and lawyers. The Colonial Office on the other hand wished to direct them into occupations which were most useful not so much from the point of view of the individual but of the social needs of the area concerned. It is easy to understand how conflict developed in such a situation. The desire for the independent professions was extremely strong and the task of the Colonial Office in determining the needs of the colonial territories extremely difficult. In general, it was known that the colonies could not absorb an indefinite number of lawyers. Nearly all scholarship holders unless specifically directed into other channels went in for law and medicine. Attempts at directing scholars in many of the areas was met with resistance. The general belief was that the learned professions were overcrowded; yet it was felt that there was no alternative for the yearned for independence.

The difficulty of gauging the market can be assessed from the fact that although this general belief in overcrowding is of many years standing, the islands have continued to absorb lawyers and doctors without much difficulty. At the time, however, there appeared to be a flood of lawyers. The enrolment of law students at the Inns of Court had increased enormously. On the other hand, there was a shortage of doctors, not so much in private practice but in the government medical services. However, provisions had already been made through the granting of special scholarships for meeting this deficiency.

The position with regard to the ex-servicemen was rendered more difficult because a considerable number of them did not wish to return home on completion of their courses. Some wished to stay on for further experience in order to ensure adequate placing on their return home; others wished to reside in the UK permanently. The Colonial Office, keeping in mind the needs of the colonial areas, made it a condition of obtaining a grant for further education that the recipient should undertake at the completion of his course to return to his country of origin. Students anxious to obtain grants did not hesitate to sign the document but, a few years later, on completion of the course, they entered into battle with the Colonial Office over this demand that they should leave the UK immediately on completion of their course. Legally, they could be forced to repay the cost of their expenses of training and, on refusing the return passage, it could be forfeited. Even for those planning to return eventually to the West Indies, this forfeiting of a passage had little effect, because a West Indian recruited from the UK usually had his passage paid out to the West Indies and got the right to a return passage. Indeed, it was this right to a return passage to the UK on leave or on completion of their tour of duty which made people anxious to remain in the UK. To return home and be recruited there was financially less rewarding in many cases than staying in the UK and getting placed in the colony through the Colonial Office.

Again, students would demand that planning be carried to its logical conclusion. If they had been directed into studies for which the Colonial Office had assessed the need, it was the responsibility of the Colonial Office to ensure that they be placed in employment on completion of their courses. Of course, many had been trained for occupations for which there was a need but not necessarily a demand. The demand depended upon a coincidence of evaluation between the Colonial Office and the individual island territories and, in many cases, on the creation of posts through governmental machinery over which the British government had no direct control. The student, even if desirous of remaining permanently in the UK, was often able to argue that he was prepared to go home to a job but not prepared to face unemployment for patriotic reasons. Where jobs were actually professed they were sometimes what colonial officials, with their high rating of higher education in Britain, admitted to being not consequential enough. In some cases, students were forced to forfeit their right to a return passage and to undertake to repay their fees and living allowances. But in such cases, the small monthly payments were allowed to lapse. Because of the responsibility of imposing uniformity of treatment, those who found themselves in such a position could allege differential treatment.

Further, the conditions under which the grants were given allowed the ex-servicemen to allege differential treatment as compared with the English students. This was alleged about the administration of the grant itself. Thus one student alleged that his grant had been stopped although he had passed his university examinations. His professor had been asked by the Colonial Office to make comments on this student and apparently it had been reported to them that the professor had not seen him for the term. On this basis, his grant had been stopped by the Colonial Office until he had given appropriate explanations. This student alleged that he knew a great many British ex-servicemen and that no such extrauniversity control was imposed upon them.

These individual complaints, although helping to build up the general ideological hostility to the Colonial Office, were insignificant compared to the more general criticism of the management of the whole scheme. The ideas at the time in the UK were against the allocation of specific scholarships with conditions that the individual should undertake to return to a particular type of employment. The McNair Committee on Teachers and Youth Leaders specifically criticized this manner of recruiting to the teaching profession and in the discussion of the shortages created by the war there was never any attempt to implement the type of control used with colonial ex-service students. Inducement rather than direction was what was urged. The colonial student argued that what was really being enforced was a type of direction of labour. The release from wartime controls and the criticism of totalitarian conditions lent substance to them or served to lend substance to their attack on the totalitarian Colonial Office seeking to give differential treatment to the oppressed colonials. It should be remembered that as in the case of the general student there was a sensitivity over the whole question of remaining in the UK. The ex-service people presented additional problems. They were older, many of them had had experience of Canada and, as in the case of the university students, had a vantage point from which they could criticize the social order. But in addition, the ex-service people who had lived for some time in British society felt more confident about asserting their rights and less fearful of antagonizing Colonial Office officials. Moreover, they suffered from the general malaise and discontent so general in the ex-serviceman.

We have mentioned that the time factor was an important one affecting the type of adjustment the individual made. Length of residence favoured an amicable adjustment to life in Britain; the disruption of the patterned routine of years on demobilization created an attitude very similar to that to be found among those who had newly arrived in the UK.

There was also the specific factor that the uniform sheltered the coloured man from some of the worst forms of prejudice. As long as the coloured man wore a uniform, he could be placed. The use of the uniform to obviate prejudice was even used by coloured officers passing through the USA. Out of uniform, the coloured man was much more difficult to place. Nearly all the ex-servicemen alleged that the attitudes of the British to them visibly changed after demobilization. In place of friendliness and acceptance there was doubt, hostility and rejection. While there can be little doubt of the substantial truth of these assertions, there was an element of rationalization. This could be seen in the contradictory assertions of the serviceman that in the service, he had experienced no discrimination while he would often give concrete descriptions of incidents in which he or his fellowmen were involved. The substantial element led to a resentment at having been used and then rejected; the rationalization served as a form for expressing aggression generated by problems of adjustment that had little to do with race or sex.

The Colonial Office as an Alleged Spy Organization

Many students feared to take part in any political activities or in critical activities of any sort. This was not due to the fear that it would interfere with their studies, or that the students' politics were irrationally based. Rather, it was posited in the belief that the Colonial Office kept a file on every student's political activities. It was believed that evidence of participation could be used to deprive students of scholarships or that they could be in some way victimized. Even with the worst will in the world, it would have been impossible for the Colonial Office to have taken such a dossier of all the students and their activities, or to have taken such drastic action for directly political reasons. Of course, if a student neglected his studies for political activities and failed his examination, the Colonial Office usually had a certain discretionary authority as to whether his scholarship should be continued or not. But the cases which could actually be cited were few and far between.

The area in which the students believed that there was the greatest danger of Colonial Office supervision and intervention was in those courses which were specially run for colonial students. In one case when discontent developed it was known that adverse reports were made about students and their behaviour, and their criticism of the courses run for them. But the fears went much further than could reasonably be expected of the civil servant or trainee hoping for a better job. Those who were training for the independent professions were similarly constrained by the fear of coercion. There is little opportunity of telling what secret controls – if any – operated over the colonial students. It is clear that the students' fears were not based on any factual situation. In fact, it represented the attitude towards governmental authority prevailing in the West Indies. The breath of democracy had not spread through these parts before the bulk of the students had left for the UK. The stereotype of an all-powerful governmental organization accompanied the organization of Crown Colony rule. Further, in many areas of the West Indies, there was not a substantial middle class and many of the people training for professions came from the homes of civil servants and teachers – where the fear of antagonizing those in authority was strongest. In many areas, students knew that the successful practice of a profession, although likely, could not be achieved automatically. With the mounting tide of competition in the professions, students had to bear in mind the cases of several eminent professional people who had been forced to accept governmental employment.

This belief in spy activities by the Colonial Office was a powerful force hindering active political participation. It was greatly diminished with the introduction of more democratic forms in most areas of the West Indies. The students who came later were more convinced of the naturalness and desirability of political activity. However, the fears again arose when the white paper on the suspension of the constitution in British Guiana listed the names of British Guiana students who had engaged in communist activities.

To some extent, the hostility and suspicion directed towards the Colonial Office was offset by the appointment of West Indians in the Welfare Department of the Colonial Office and by the creation of the post (held by West Indians) of liaison officer for West Indian students. This move was, however, only partially successful. In many cases, suspicion, instead of being removed was merely transferred to the West Indians. There was a tendency to suspect them as 'stooges', as hirelings prepared to sell out the students in the interest of their own personal advancement and welfare. The overall effect, however, was a lessening of tension even though the volume of bitter feelings directed towards the Colonial Office remained formidable in proportions.

This reaction of the students to the liaison officer was very similar to that of some of the working groups and RAF personnel (themselves later to become students). During the war, welfare officers had been appointed to smooth out difficulties and aid in the adjustment of the various colonial groups who had come to the UK. Among the tasks which fell to these welfare officers was explaining to the workers some of the behaviour on their part which led to misunderstanding and the worsening of racial relations.

For an Englishman to have made critical comments on matters like these would have immediately rendered him suspect. For a West Indian, the task was easier but still very difficult. The allegations that West Indians frequently did not appreciate that people lived in basements and consequently urinated down them at nights or that they spat openly in the streets – although substantially correct and hence known to members of the group, were strongly resisted. As soon as the student or worker was placed in a position where he was compared unfavourably with the British, he reacted in an emotional fashion no matter who made the comparison. The fundamental problem of so presenting the material that it did not provoke conflict was not a matter involving the race of the person presenting the matter. There was likelihood that a West Indian would understand some of the emotional significance of the problem. But there was no magic in being a West Indian as some people seemed to believe. Elsewhere, in a discussion of leadership within the West Indian group, we shall examine the matter a little more closely.

Chapter 7

Some Consequences
of Education
in Britain

The Evaluation of Changes

Evaluating the changes that have taken place in the students is difficult for several reasons. One has to do with the fact that newly arrived students are usually so preoccupied with personal problems that they are unlikely to report accurately their attitudes on leaving the West Indies. The reports of the students arriving later are also characterized by distortions even though often arising from a different source. Further, students come from the West Indies at a relatively young age at which their ideas and attitudes have not obtained the logical (or psychological) consistency or clarification characteristic of the more mature person.

Moreover, the observed individual changes over a period of time are often so complex and interesting that it is difficult to properly evaluate these changes merely from the individual's own reconstruction. In the highly charged, emotional atmosphere in which the students live, there is distortion not merely by the newcomer of the image of the distant homeland but of their own experiences within the UK. This distortion is partially unconscious but there are large areas of experience, where the individual is sensitive to public opinion and is not prepared to be completely honest in an interview. Thus the student who has been shamed out of shade prejudice by the laughter of his friends will not readily admit this fact but would pose as having always had a liberal attitude in these matters.

As an illustration of the changes that take place over time, we may look at the case of LR who came to England as a relatively mature person. While in the West Indies, he had worked in the civil service. He had an interest in radical politics in the West Indies and had developed an antiwhite attitude. His position brought him into contact with white employers whom he was at pains to treat in the worst possible way. In the interest of pursuing an openly political career, he went to the UK in order to study law.

The initial impact of life in England was to increase his radicalism. He joined and played a leading role in student and other colonial organizations. In spite of this, his attitude towards the British could not be described as consistently antiwhite, for he considered making English friends to be one of the most important consequences of his stay in England.

However, as soon as he was qualified and came face to face with the realities of making a living his views sobered considerably. He became a forthright critic almost overnight, of the very politics which he had been advocating. Before he returned to the West Indies, his views had again swung in the direction of the radical colonial point of view.

Another student, active in British student organizations and Marxist in his politics became completely identified with the values and attitudes of British left-wing politics. In so far as he interested himself in colonial matters, this was in complete conformity to the British point of view. His orientation was towards remaining in the UK and he married a white British girl. Subsequently, as opportunities before undreamt of appeared in the West Indies, the student espoused the nationalist 'West Indian cause' and stressed his urgent desire to return home. As new opportunities appeared in England, however, he veered back to his old attitude. His argument now ran: West Indians were being fobbed off with second-rate institutions, and those who accepted jobs in them were traitors. Only under very special conditions would he consider returning to the West Indies. His position was considered a model for other West Indian intellectuals. The Marxist attitude was shed and indeed there were tendencies to a violent anti-Marxist position. Eventually, as the individual became accommodated to the situation, he developed a more reasonable approach – a sort of consistently ambivalent attitude – to the conflicting attractions of the West Indies. Interviewed at any given period of time, this student would have given his contemporary position as final.

There was also a special difficulty in evaluating the extent of changes in attitude to the British because of the confusion in the minds of students of 'British' with 'white'. Attitudes towards 'British' turned out to be attitudes towards local whites and changes in attitude to the British were reported as changes in attitudes towards whites. This was not purely verbal. The individual suffers from a lack of clarity of thought which only experience serves to clarify, if at all.

Some Psychological Consequences of Education in Britain

One of the most important of the effects of education in Britain is the self-confidence which comes to students. This attainment of self-confidence arises from several sources. There is the general advantage of travel, of coming to see the world as it is viewed by other eyes. As long as the West Indian remained at home, he possessed an exaggerated idea of the importance of the West Indian both in the world at large and in its particular relationship. The visit to England, if we may borrow Marx's phrase, relieved him of 'the idiocy of rural life'. He could no longer hold the naive view of his countrymen that the world revolved around the West Indies. He became aware that the majority of the people in the world were not aware of his own existence. By getting to know the geographical and political insignificance of his country, he obtained a higher perspective.

Second, his education in an alien environment, whatever its disadvantages, meant that he was freer of the narrow and constricting pressures of the small community. In the West Indies, the smallness of the communities, the infrequency of travel, the lack of service opportunity all tend to produce a prolonged adolescence and to limit the emancipation from the family. It was the almost universal experience of West Indians that they tended to overrate the age of their English fellow students. The latter possessed a degree of maturity at an early age. This maturity was not merely a matter of sex or of relations between the sexes but of independence of viewpoint, philosophy of life and so on. Further, the fact that all the foundations of his life were shaken forced the individual to think not only on the large questions of the day, but on matters of everyday moment. The fact that so many situations had to be defined anew may have produced much anxiety; it certainly tended to produce a reflective attitude to life and a workaday philosophy.

Third, the student had an opportunity of competing intellectually with English students. The school system in the West Indies had always been organized on an English basis and the ultimate aim became the passing of examinations as organized by the British educational authorities. For the secondary schools, there has never been any locally organized examinations. When West Indian students started to take these British examinations, it was considered a mark and sign of progress when they were highly placed. Subsequently, this comparison for the purpose of evaluating students and the school system continued to be made.[20]

However, the comparison was not often made by the individual student especially as the system came to be taken for granted. In any case, the comparison of examination performance had a different emotional content to the competition resulting from actual personal contact. Further, this personal comparison had an additional emotional significance for the West Indian student because he found through his contact with other university students that in many respects, the English students were in fact better educated than he had thought they were. This anxiety about his own intellectual adequacy reinforced feelings of inadequacy on racial grounds and led in some cases to an overcompensation and an attempt to derogate the English. Indeed, this competitive pitting of oneself against others tended to produce a nationalist attitude. It reinforced competitive attitudes, which were already well established from school experience in the West Indies.

The development of self-confidence was also based on the fact that the student in England felt that he was part of the stream of everyday life. There was a sort of naive belief that the West Indies was an important area but there was also the fact that all the events of the world that hit the headlines had nothing to do with the West Indies. The students, although they came from a middle class which was not highly literate, were more or less familiar with English journals and periodicals. In many cases, the reading of these journals (*New Statesman, Spectator*) was a means of asserting social status. One was an intellectual and showed a true appreciation of the things of the spirit if one read reviews of books that one never actually read or read reviews of pictures that one never saw. Further, there was an interest in politics which was followed at a distance. To be able to read periodicals that dealt with up to the minute affairs rather than copies that were several weeks old gave a new significance to events. In the West Indies, the budget speech had little interest; in England, it was found that taxation invaded the sphere of everyday life to a considerable extent. The budget speech was of special significance because the degree of popular interest infected the student. The emotional experience of being part of a live democratic community gave a sense of release to most students.

An indication of what this attainment of self-confidence meant in practical terms was illustrated by the case of a journalist who had come to the UK in the hope of improving his education. He found that in the colony from which he came, he had the greatest difficulty in contacting senior officials. On the other hand, in Britain he sought an interview with the colonial secretary and obtained it. This he contrasted with the police cordon surrounding the airport on the arrival of the governor. While in Britain he was able to contact important people in the field of letters who gratuitously gave of their time and advice. On one occasion, he was invited to a press gathering where he had the opportunity of meeting Sir Stafford Cripps and the duke of Edinburgh. These experiences made him wild with enthusiasm and caused him to embark on topics in journalism which he had never before dreamt of attempting. His general reaction in experiencing the freer atmosphere in Britain was to declare, "I can't go back home at all!"

While the incorporation into the general stream of events had powerful effects, they were not all to the good in so far as incorporation into British social and political life took place. It alienated the individual even more from the British environment. In the case of the medical student for instance, the range of attitudes and beliefs surrounding disease in general or of specific complaints existing in the West Indies was a fairy book. Moreover, those who were interested in public health practice took as their standards the system of organization existing in Britain. The 'better', 'superior' system existing in Britain was used as a means of criticizing the organization of the public services as it existed in the area.

One of the most important indirect results of education in Britain is the after-effect of the competitive pitting of the individual against the Englishman. In most underdeveloped areas, the question of expatriation allowances and of differential treatment for foreigners is of crucial importance.

It is clear that in the West Indies, the effect of this has been indirect and masked but, it is of no less importance. The demand of civil servants in the West Indies has been for a West Indianization of the civil service. But this West Indianization has not been conceived as one which will permit of a more efficient administration at less cost or of a more extensive administration at reduced costs due to savings obtained through the employment of natives in the place of expensive importees.

This argument continues to be advanced. Recently, Sir Sidney Caine raised it in connection with the costs of colonial universities. Experience of West Indian conditions holds out little hope of any savings in this direction. The process of equalization of rights and emoluments of West Indians and Englishmen have gone too far to be reversed. Indeed, the number of Europeans now employed in the public service of the West Indies is extremely low. Even before the postwar West Indianization had got under full swing, the secretary of state for the colonies was able to declare that there were fewer than two hundred Englishmen holding senior positions in the civil service in the West Indies.

At the moment, opposition to any reductions in salaries, or to the suggestion that demands for increases should be withheld because of the precarious economic position of the territories, comes from all quarters of the middle class, and not merely from those who had been educated abroad. In its origins, however, the demand for parity of treatment based on parity of personal qualification arose from those who had competitively pitted themselves against Englishmen in colleges abroad. In a sense, this type of education was unable to produce 'good West Indians'. There was too much assimilation, even in antagonism, to the manner and values of the dominant English culture. Naturally, this was not the only factor concerned in setting the relatively high standards of living of West Indians, even if it could be rightly said to be the most important. But it is one that tends to be forgotten precisely because of the general spread of these values.

Radicalism and the Personality Differential

The belief that the colonial students in Britain are in some sense an elite is not entirely without justification. Very much more disputable is the belief that their attitudes towards life and their relationships with the British in general show a uniform character. In the course of our survey, we have seen that although there is a common experience of discrimination, the reactions and evaluations of this discrimination vary considerably. There would appear to be two important factors determining the different reactions to the same experience. One is the conception of the self held by the individual and the particular evaluation he holds of his relations with people fairer than himself and with whites, and the degree of rigidity with which that conception is held.

In very few people is the self-conception incapable of alteration. Indeed, while mechanisms of defence can be called into play to limit the challenge of development to the personality, situations will invariably arise in the experience of being educated away from home, which will tend to alter the individual's perception of himself. In these circumstances, the nature of the individual's intimate relationships would appear to be of great importance. This is one of the reasons why the question of numbers involved and of visibility are important because the development of primary group contacts within the West Indian group rather than the host society is affected thereby.

It would appear that the radicalism of the student springs from two types: those who expect integration to be easy are freed to redefine the situation but their self-concept does not allow them to accept integration on any terms; and those who came with preestablished radical ideas and found easy confirmation of their views. However, there is yet a further problem. It is often supposed that the experiences of discrimination, lack of friendship and so on produce a radicalism which is permanent, enduring and likely to have lasting social consequences. In point of fact, this is not so for several reasons. In the first place, there is the question of student irresponsibility. University students are in a sense relieved of serious responsibilities for a short period of their lives. It may be a good thing that radicalism and unorthodoxy can flourish in such an atmosphere, but it is inevitable that this radicalism should subsequently be tempered by the realities of life. The growth of responsibility after university life is a general phenomenon and not in any way confined to West Indian students. Yet, the process is as visible here as elsewhere. Much of the radicalism of Britain has never been introduced into the West Indies at all. Where the radicalism is a situational response to a loss of status or anxiety over improvement in status, it is easily shed on return to an environment where status is so readily given to the professional who has been educated in the UK.

Nonetheless, there is a hard core of permanent radicalism which survives on return to the West Indies and another hard core which prefers to remain with its radicalism in the unpleasant – as they define it – situation in the UK.

There is also the curious phenomenon of a few individuals who keep away from any radical views in the UK but on return develop a more radical position than they had maintained. This development tended to be among the younger students who concentrated on their studies, eschewed politics and therefore postponed their definitions of serious problems in life. On return home, they find that their views had been influenced in subtle, unconscious ways. Their perception of themselves had been changed in a slow and not traumatic fashion. The changes were nonetheless far reaching and permanent. Their return to radicalism was usually in the same quiet fashion. Just as the radicals of the UK became absorbed in the general stress of life and shed their radicalism almost imperceptibly, so did radicalism creep upon the UK conservatives.

Nothing is more effective as evidence of the hothouse atmosphere in which students receive their education in the UK than the process whereby self-appointed leaders of the people became tame and harmless civil servants and professionals without achieving that personal maturity and insight which allows for an objective reaction to the events of one's life.

In fact, this process of adjustment would appear to be the normal pattern (in a statistical sense). It remains, therefore, to explain why it is that some individuals having become radical in the UK. maintain this radicalism on their return to their homeland. There is some evidence for believing that people end up on the radical-conservative scale in much the same position that they would have been anyway. Those who are predominantly oriented towards an acceptance of authority at home return quietly although somewhat changed to this position. The person with antiauthoritarian tendencies at home finds a situation and an ideology which appeals to him, and returns home with these antiauthority tendencies defined in his own mind. This is a 'clinical' evaluation but is based on an intimate knowledge of many West Indian students and their behaviour on their return home. Verification of this would require a separate investigation but the interpretation is put forward for what it is worth. Since this is a subjective evaluation, it will perhaps be desirable to give illustrations of the process as observed.

(1) In the first case, a student who became radical and defined himself as a Negro socialist later remained in England and became one of the most conservative of West Indians residing there. In another case, a young student attending college was preoccupied with her family relations especially as her brother was also studying in England. Her emotional life was bound up with her family and her studies. Although exposed to radical ideas and influences, she lived a quiet and ultrarespectable life. On return home, she found the family evaluation of the social scene stuffy and undemocratic. She revised her adolescent dream-picture of the family and became emancipated as someone who had travelled abroad.

Again, quiescence must not be confused with acquiescence, and it may be that several UK radicals maintain their radicalism at home but find it inconvenient to advertise the fact. By and large, the educated student is rising in social status and he finds the task of shedding his radicalism much easier than holding a private and a public view of the universe contradictory of one another. Two other cases can be cited:

(1) A student, highly respectable and socially ambitious, became a leader of the radical colonial students. He was always speaking of what he would do when he returned home. However, he was absorbed into the civil service and looked upon these student ambitions and experiences as a pleasant interlude from the more serious business of living.

(2) This can be contrasted with the case of another radical student leader. Before leaving home, he showed definite antiauthoritarian tendencies although these had not taken a markedly political form. In the UK, these tendencies, easily visible in other relations besides the political, achieved a systematic rationalization and a coherent ideology blending socialism and West Indian nationalism. With this, the student returned to the West Indies to carry on a successful anti-British agitation.

Of course there are other factors involved here. For instance, it seems possible that political activity in the West Indies can advertise the aspiring barrister to a clientele. But this is not a sure and certain theory to determine the individual's decision although it is a relevant consideration that is almost invariably examined. Even granting that the lawyers constitute a special case, we still find ourselves faced with the problem that the process of differentiation can be observed among the lawyers as well.

Religion

Life among the middle classes of the West Indies is marked by an increasing secularization. Religious values, while still strong, are on the decline. The process was undoubtedly hastened by the visit of students to England. Persistence of religious beliefs and practices were most marked in the case of women and Roman Catholics. The students, freed from the routine obser-vances which they had practised did not feel any constraint on this score. The majority of churches in Britain appeared to be inactive and the bulk of the population appeared to be hardly Christian. Students found to their surprise that many of their fellow students had not even been inducted into the church by baptism and confirmation. The slip away from the church did not imply that baptism and the Sunday school morality should be shed. On the contrary, their experience was considered as normal and they did not appreciate that they were undergoing a process that apparently had taken place in Britain much further back. The presence of these pockets of agnosticism did not shock them into retreat into the church. Rather, it encouraged the gradual drift away from it.

Among African students, there was much criticism of the British on their lack of religion. Devout students who attended church to find the place of worship relatively deserted reflected upon their experience. In their minds, the superiority of the British was associated with Christianity and the missionaries — at whose schools many of them had been educated. These students were very disillusioned when they came to appreciate the realities of the religious situation in Britain. Some reacted as if they had been deceived and their emergent nationalism seized on the discrepancy between profession and practice. The British had come out as missionaries to deal with the benighted Africans and save them from heathenism but their main activities could with profit be directed towards their own people. Something of this attitude was also to be found among the West Indian students. Their adoption of Christianity was less complete, missionary activity was so long established as to be regarded as an indigenous West Indian institution. Yet, they too were struck with the divergence between the faith and practice of an avowedly Christian nation.

This attitude affected the integration of the students since the Church was one of those bodies with a universalistic appeal and which made efforts in one form or another to reach the colonial student. On the university level, there was the Student Christian Movement (SCM), the London Inter-Faculty Christian Union. On a more popular level, there were the attempts to organize clubs and dances.

Although friendships with English students developed, there was a tendency for such friendships to develop among groups rather than on a purely individual basis. Only those groups which had a strong adherence to a universalistic outlook made a special appeal to the colonials. This was a fact remarked upon not only by the colonial students themselves but by some English students as well. Thus in one college, an English girl who had become friendly with colonials through a coloured English girl was labelled by fellow English students as a Christian belonging to the SCM. This particular girl was dignified and conservative in her bearing. One can easily imagine that had it been otherwise she might be labelled a communist. In some respects therefore, the break away from religion has more profound consequences than are immediately apparent.

Relations between Students and Workers

In some respects, the colour question overrode the question of racial differences at home but always with an element of tension. The loneliness of the big city hit not only the individual student but the businessman or other professional on holiday in the mother country. Those former students usually had idealized pictures of their student days when the pattern and routine of the university gave some meaning to their lives. It is of interest that whatever the problems these people had faced they always spoke in terms of going back to the UK for holidays. On arrival in the UK, however, with time on their hands and few contacts, they were often anxious and willing to mix with people with whom they would have had little intimate contact in the West Indies. The high visibility of the coloured facilitated the easy identification of his countryman. However, there was sometimes resentment – just as in the case of the dark-skinned student against the fair- coloured –among the working class who regarded these advances as not genuine. Hence in one instance, a prominent professional man, on seeing a face he recognized, approached the workman and asked "Didn't I know you in . . .?" "No, Mr . . . ," replied the worker, "you could never know me in the West Indies", to the professional's embarrassment. This story he related to V.

The development of nationalism away from the West Indian environment made it to a large extent an ideological affair. It might appear on first sight that the influx of West Indian students would help to overcome this. In point of fact, there was some identification with the workers. On the whole, however, relationships with West Indian workers tended to show up the hollowness of this nationalism. The reaction of the student to the worker was coloured primarily by the fact that the latter's presence made a difference with regards to the students' adjustment. Considerations of nationalism were secondary.

The organizational relation between the working class organizations and the students union is dealt with elsewhere. Here, we are only concerned with how far the definition of the social situation in Britain was able to eradicate class prejudices which the students brought from home. The new West Indian nationalism drove many to support the labour cause but this was a different matter to entering into due personal relationships with the members of the working class.

In the early period when there was a mass migration of workers, the process of nationalization could proceed with ease. Yet, even then there were some obvious contradictions. Students felt that the coloured members of the working class reduced them in status. As a result, some members tried to differentiate themselves as much as possible from any lower class contacts. The same students who objected because Indian, Arab and other groups sought to differentiate themselves from the Negro in the hope of receiving better treatment acted in exactly the same way towards the working class. "Quashie" (as students from one of the islands called them), violated many of the rules – and he too, was an ambassador for his country.

Whatever the ethics of their standpoint, there can be little doubt that there was substance in the student claim. Britishers did not seem to be able to make distinctions which appeared 'obvious' to the West Indian. There can be little doubt either that the workers' behaviour was more fundamentally different from the English way of life. Even among the students, there were complaints that their fellow students did not know how to behave and therefore gave the coloured group as a whole a bad name. The complaints centred around personal appearance and habits. The students who did not cut their hair regularly and did not pay attention to dress were not thought of in a tolerant light as slightly aberrant individuals, to be excused because of a 'student' or 'intellectual' status but were regarded as demoralized and a threat to the group.

With the workers, this was even more marked. Working class people spoke bad English, swore loudly, spat in public places, were seen as dirty and disorderly. There were rumours that many of them lived on the immoral savings of prostitutes or on public assistance.

Yet, there was one respect in which students approved working class behaviour. It was felt that in spite of the crudity of their behaviour, they had helped in the improvement of race relations. This was particularly true among the students who had been members of the RAF. Students and the RAF people of middle class origin would never resort to violence in a racial situation but members of the RAF ground crew would and did. The majority of students with their aggressive feelings against the British got vicarious satisfaction from the oft repeated jokes and stories in which violence was used against the British. These stories ranged from incidents of common assault, through stories of alleged cannibalism in order to frighten the British, through to the story of the Jamaican who derived his due wages, drew a razor and cut off the protesting official's tie, just as a reminder that he was a wild man who would resort to violence if necessary.

The sole occasion on which there was continuous contact between workers and students was when a special club for colonials was formed. This was at St Martin's-in-the-Fields and membership was open to all colonials. However, it gave parallel but equal facilities. There was very little mixing. Students who wished to use rooms for meetings did so without coming into contact with the workers. There was a dining hall attached to the club but students and workers ate at separate tables unless forced to associate through shortage of space. There was little embarrassment at meeting in this atmosphere because all colonials and the Europeans who worked there were well aware of the social distinctions involved.

This need to differentiate themselves from the workers took several forms. One was to make sure that the individual carried a book or a briefcase as a mark of student status. In one instance, a student insisted on carrying a copy of the *Times* with him and advised other students to do likewise. In other cases, students wore distinctive dress, the rolled umbrella, the striped trousers and dark coat and even the bowler hat was affected by some law students. However, the idea here was only in part to differentiate themselves from the working class. It reflected an incorporation of the ideas of the profession and some of the outward symbols.

Attitudes towards a West Indian University and to the Educated West Indian

Although the idea of a West Indian university had long been projected it never achieved any enthusiastic support from those who had received university education abroad. Indeed, some of the strongest criticism of the projected University College of the West Indies came precisely from those who had been educated abroad. Because of the particularly high evaluation which they attached to education in the best of British universities and the social status which it provided them, they tended to evaluate the setting up of a colonial university as part of a pattern to fob off the West Indian with an inferior type of education. The reaction was exactly the same as that of the lawyers who resisted the idea of training barristers locally instead of at the Inns of Court.

Among the present generation of West Indian students, however, there tended to be a more critical approach to the problem. They too would have been hostile to any attempt to pass off an inferior type of education with their new-found nationalism. Further, with the break of so many students away from law and medicine, there emerged a number of students interested in research who thought in terms of an academic career. The ideas of the students were nebulous and in the extreme and in so far as they got any support from other students, it was from those who were interested in being placed on the staff.[21]

There was a story that a patient in the West Indies refused to have a local anaesthetic and demanded to have the proper foreign stuff. In a sense, this prejudice was to be found among the medical students who were opposed to the idea that they should serve their apprenticeship in the West Indies rather than in the UK.

It was clear that the university was not conceived by the majority as in any way affecting their personal lives. Occasionally, the male student who had engaged in a promiscuous career or was aware of the promotion of promiscuity would declare that he could not send any of his girl children to be educated in London. But by and large, insofar as students conceived of education for their children they thought of sending their children to study in the UK and not at the newly formed, colonial university college.

The failure of students to return home had always been commented upon in the past. This was largely because whole sections of the community looked upon the scholarship holder as the only source of leadership for the community. The loss was not merely material but psychological since it appeared that the best of the land scorned their native land, preferring to live on the superior foreign shore.

Even when students did return, they were faced with the criticism that they were not pulling their weight in the community. Sometimes, their student radicalism was thrown in their face, but more often it was merely that they were apathetic, more interested in advancing their own cause than that of the people.

It is the writer's belief that this criticism had some substance although much of it was illfounded. The critics did not appreciate the difficulties involved in establishing a foothold in a competitive profession. Thus many, instead of taking appropriate action themselves waited for a *deus ex machina,* a leader whom they could hero worship and upon whom they could throw the whole burden of their problems. Further, in the undemocratic atmosphere that flourished in the past it was not always easy to engage in political activity. The mere suspicion of radicalism could, in the case of lawyers for instance, interfere with their clientele. Yet, there was a curious indisposition on the part of the best educated to engage in even the most innocent and nonpolitical of public activities. Caution must be exercised here, for these attitudes were as marked among those who had taken external degrees. It was a man who had taken an external degree who refused to give lectures to a voluntary group because they had not shared in the sacrifice required for his external degree. But the locally educated were usually more hard-pressed economically; it was expected that they would view education and social service in a broad perspective.

The writer believes that this failure to make a significant contribution to the region's public and social life was related to the experience of education abroad. Before the large-scale influx in the postwar period, the numbers of students involved were small. There were limited possibilities of adjustment. There was no large-scale West Indian group to which the individual could turn for emotional support. The drive of the individual was similar to that of the 'adjusted' group in the contemporary situation. We have seen that the basis of this adjustment tended to be the unconditional acceptance of the host society and the negative evaluation of the self and its group. Such a basis of adjustment was possible – as it is possible for a limited number of individuals now – but it was not conducive to that identification with the West Indian group which would spill over into public action. Of course, a certain number of radicals were produced even under the old system but, by and large, the possibilities of mobility through self-denial and acceptance of the values of the group to which entry was desired, reduced this tendency to radicalism to a minimum. This was precisely the type of mobility which was permissible in the social structure of the West Indies. It,is not surprising that people educated under these conditions made use of their experience in the cause of their own advancement.

An additional effect was the loss of a considerable body of the best educated students to the metropolitan area. There were not only the cases of failures, whom, for reasons we have examined, were not anxious to go home. There were the successful students who elected to stay in England. A precise count of the number of students who failed to return home has not been made but the proportion was sufficiently large to give official concern.

The Evaluation of the English: The Stereotype of the Superhuman

One of the most important effects of education in Britain is to give the student a more realistic evaluation of life in England. In the West Indies where contact with the administration and with white persons in authority are perfunctory, 'Britain' and 'The English' became symbolic of a certain set pattern of relationships. This symbolism makes for immaturity both in personal and political thinking. To some extent, the radical student even after his experience of life in England still preserves (and possibly even has reinforced) the symbolism of a colonial society. But by and large, the student comes to have a richer, more realistic picture of life in England, of the attitudes of the English, and hence of the nature of the colonial relationship.

The colonial goes to England with a stereotype of what an Englishman[22] is. In many respects, he has to revive his preconceived notions about British life. And certainly, there are changes in attitudes over time. Nonetheless, there is a remarkable persistence of the stereotype of the Englishman and a remarkable unity of general impressions of the English. This unity of impressions exists in spite of both a positive and negative evaluation. The maintenance of this stereotype would appear to be due to two factors:

(1) Selective perception and interpretation which causes the individual to note or remember only those aspects of the situation which reinforce his preconceived views.

(2) Elements of reality in the situation which gives some semblance of truth to the belief. The stereotypical picture of the Englishman consists of the following:

(a) In contrast to the West Indian, he is cold and unemotional. Typical contrasts of attitude to life are often drawn by comparing the experience of British with West Indian dancing. With an English dance, there is much more formality and the dancing appears to the West Indian to be mechanical and uninspired. By contrast, most English people react to West Indian dancing by becoming violent partisans or more usually denouncing it as a senseless shuffle.

(b) The Englishman is frightfully conservative. This shows itself in the addiction to coal fires, to bowler hats, to ancient bits of history. The West Indian is essentially the 'progressive' who looks upon all change as essentially a mark of progress, and the persistence of the old as essentially a mark of backwardness. In most if not all the islands the bowler hat, the rolled umbrella, the striped trousers, are looked upon as anachronistic survivals, and evidence of an outmoded conservatism.

(c) The Englishman was essentially a 'diplomat' who made the best use of situations; the radical added that he was a hypocrite.

There was common agreement that all British people were not alike and there were important regional differences. It was thought that the people of Scotland, Wales and the north of England were easier and freer in their relations with coloured people. This did not mean that students in these areas did not experience or report discrimination; it meant that there appeared to be a much greater chance of students entering into really intimate relations with members of the host society. Even in London, the West Indian students frequently commented that the more friendly disposed in the city were not native Londoners but immigrants from the Northern provinces.

In the case of the Welsh and Scottish areas, the marked national differences and in some cases the nationalism associated with these made identification and friendship easier. Most coloured students had some hostility to whites generally and sometimes expressed their resentment in terms of antiwhite, racialist sentiment but the dominant feeling was against the Englishman and the stereotypical picture which the colonial carried around with him.

However, the vague anti-English sentiment to be found there (that is, in the Welsh and Scottish areas), found an echo among colonials. Thus one student, on arrival in a Welsh town was greeted by his first acquaintance with the remark that he would find himself at home in Wales because they did not like Englishmen down there. Further, in both Scotland and Wales there were people who spoke English with a distinctive accent. We have already seen how sensitive students were on the language issue, and any deviation from a standard English which was respectable and not identified like the cockney dialect with the lower orders seemed to justify their own position.

The stereotype of 'the Englishman' does, however, get modified. Thus the Englishman as 'hypocrite' and 'diplomat' received some modification. "An understanding of the Englishman's diplomacy and tact" is put by one of the students as one of the main problems. There is some substance in this. The pattern of etiquette and ritual in the UK is perhaps less direct and more elaborately developed than in the West Indies. The failure to appreciate this difference causes angry discussions about the 'hypocrisy' of the Englishman. This would be of relatively little importance if it did not reinforce the stereotype of 'perfidious Albion' in the political sphere. If it were not for such stereotypes there would be an appreciation in the course of time of these differences of ritual and etiquette. But the misunderstanding is conveniently supported by the impression of 'all the world'. Things about which complaints were made by the students were the politely mechanical smile lacking in warmth and the formalities of 'please' and 'thank you' used so often until they appear mere formalities. "Never," said one student, "have I heard the terms 'thank you' and 'please' used so often and mean so little."

Chapter **8**

The West Indian
Students Union

The West Indian Consciousness

Consciousness of belonging to a group called West Indian is something of relatively late development in the West Indies. There has always been some vague consciousness of unity largely caused by the fact that although each individual territory was separately administered by the Colonial Office, it was necessary to treat some matters on a regional basis. Thus, there were various royal commissions on the West Indies as a whole during the nineteenth century, and during the twentieth century Mr Wood, later Lord Halifax, was called upon to report on constitutional development as a whole. Besides this of course, there are certain definite cultural characteristics in common in spite of the variation within a common culture but consciousness of this common culture was limited in the extreme. Again, there were certain common economic interests among the islands due not only to the basic similarity of their economies but to the nature of their economic relations with the mother country.

In the West Indies, the only collective representation which had caught the popular imagination was the West Indian cricket team and a great deal of importance was attached both to the teams abroad and the visiting teams. Nonetheless, even on such occasions the identification of the team with the West Indies was not complete. The term West Indies was sometimes used synonymously with the individual territory. People would sometimes speak of the poor show of the "Jamaican team", the "Trinidad team" and the like, when they were referring to the West Indian side. Conversely, the use of the term West Indian was misleading because it might lead the outsider to think that there was something of a West Indian consciousness while in point of fact the individual was referring to and bearing in mind only the particular territory from which he came.

The absence of West Indian national sentiment was easy to understand. In the growth of modern nations, the importance of a central administration has been shown to be of cardinal importance not merely in imposing administrative unity, but in giving a central focus of attention to the mass of the people and thus permitting common sentiment to emerge. But each island territory had for centuries (in some cases) been administered for the most part as distinct units. Moreover, informal everyday contact did not develop because of poor communication. Until the advent of airplane services, contact was perfunctory and limited. Even now, the high fares still render migration between areas small. Indeed, now (1955) that the territories or the majority of them have become committed to the establishment of a political federation, a subsidized shipping line has been created in order to improve interisland communication.

The lack of awareness of other areas was more marked in some areas than in others. In Trinidad which had been built up largely from immigration from the neighbouring islands and in these islands themselves, there was a greater West Indian consciousness, but even here, the term 'West Indian' as generally used hardly ever included Jamaica, the biggest and most populous of the areas, or British Honduras.

The West Indian student having this background did not have much difficulty in identifying himself as West Indian since the term was already in current use in his homeland. But it tended to have a broader context since its general usage was to identify the larger unit known to the host society rather than the smaller unit of the student's mind.

This identification with the West Indies was not altogether complete. During the war, many of the people from British Guiana (now Guyana) who were serving in the armed forces spoke of and referred to themselves as British South Americans. This practice was taken up by a number of students as well. The motivations for this identification were varied. One reason was a desire to escape from discrimination. Many students, if from the West Indies, found that they were able to escape discrimination in the USA by passing as South American. A knowledge and affectation of Spanish was often able to translate the individual from despised 'Negro' status to 'South American' unsegregated status. Within the UK, segregation was not so marked, discrimination not so real and the need to use such devices not so pressing. There still existed the feeling that in some way identification with South America would bring more prestige. The other South American countries, with the exception of the Guianas, possessed independence and national status and one form of protest against colonial status was to stress the continental destiny of the Guianese. The ideas held of continental destiny by the students were nebulous in the extreme. There was some vague notion of independence, and an even vaguer notion of some sort of absorption into Brazil. The mere physical magnitude of the territory was not sufficient to give the slogan sufficient concrete content. There was a blissful disregard for political and economic considerations. From the students' point of view, however, this disregard was of little importance since the continental destiny was not conceived of as a programme for immediate action but merely as a psychological compensation for loss of status.

By and large, all sections of the British West Indian community in Britain referred to themselves as West Indian, although when formal organizations were considered, terms like Caribbean drew a certain measure of support. This identification as West Indian was also encouraged by those English people who became friendly with West Indians. They soon learnt to distinguish between West Indians and other groups but found themselves quite unable to make the distinction between the various islands and territories. Moreover, much of the insularity that persisted in the new situation was due to the fact that the superficial peculiarities of each group were seized upon by the others. It was easier for a Jamaican to identify idiosyncracies of speech in a Trinidadian than for the Trinidadian himself. Each considered his particular accent as 'natural' and being good English while the others were something degenerate and somewhat comical. It was often only after a few years' residence in the UK that the individual came to recognize his own accent and to appreciate the particular quality of his own insularity. This recognition of the coexistence of common status and problems together with difference hastened the recognition of West Indian 'nationality'.

In spite of the development of West Indian nationalism, there was still a persistence of local loyalties. The smaller the island, the greater likelihood there was of insularity being shed. The groups in which sectional feeling most strongly persisted were Jamaica and British Guiana (BG). Indeed, the latter group even set about the creation of a semiformal association. ABG group was formed which met quite regularly to discuss the social, political and economic problems of that territory. Only BG people were invited to attend although the ruling was not absolute and one other West Indian consistently attended the meetings of the group. In actual content, the discussion proceeded very much along the lines of those that took place within the wider student union with the exception that the frame of reference was BG rather than Caribbean. Higher education, trade and development were considered in purely Guianese terms.

In point of fact, most members of this group were members of West Indian Students Union (WISU) as well and saw no conflict between their loyalties. It seemed to the observer, however, that there was an essential conflict between the two approaches. A similar position adopted by the various groups would lead to an essential duplication of institutions which could on the face of it be much more sensibly organized on a regional basis. It would appear that this group of students privately shared the point of view of the British South American group which envisaged a separate development of British Guiana as a part of Latin America. They were too intelligent, however, not to realize the limitation of their approach. Consequently, there was the same tendency seen in other groups to identify themselves as West Indian. The reason why this particular Guianese loyalty should have been so apparent is difficult to understand.

The question arises as to why this coloured group of West Indian students did not accept the labels 'coloured' and 'colonial' applied to them by the host society. In so far as a 'national' conception entered, they were conceived of as Africans or as 'black foreigners'. Yet, the West Indian students preferred to attach a national label to themselves.

In the first place, it should be noted that the use of the term West Indian and identification of the student as a West Indian was not universal. Indeed, before the great postwar influx of students, the organization which had the greatest appeal for West Indians in the UK was the League of Coloured Peoples headed by Dr Harold Moody. Although not primarily a West Indian or a students' organization, it was heavily West Indian in membership and many students played an effective and important part in its organization. In fact, the formation of the WISU provoked a crisis in the League of Coloured Peoples – a situation which we will examine when we consider the relation of the WISU to other colonial organizations.

In the second place, the conception of a West Indian organization reflected the rise of a new political consciousness in the West Indies itself. Although the majority of students were politically inexperienced and naive, there were a number who had been profoundly influenced by the disturbances of the late 1930s and the subsequent political and social consciousness that had developed.

In the third place, the description of themselves as West Indians was a form of protest against the definition of the host society. The blanket lumping of all 'colonials' and all coloured people together provoked resentment. In a sense, the assertion of West Indians was a form of national identity in a situation where such identity was not considered. Something of the same form of protest – with an even more factual base – occurred in the case of the Indian and Chinese students who found that they too tended to be reduced to colonial status. Indeed, some of the differentiation which landlords practised between fair-skinned and dark-skinned colonials, and between Indians and 'Africans' appears to have been learnt from nationals of India and China.

Again, the classification of West Indians with African groups was strongly resented. At home in the West Indies, students who had come chiefly from the brown middle class despised the black elements of the population and the black members of the middle class shared a great deal of the evaluation. Further, the dominant stereotype was that of the 'African' as a primitive barbarous person – while the West Indian was conceived of as the inhabitant of a rational, progressive, civilized country. After all, West Indians had even gone to Africa as missionaries to help to civilize the backward and the heathen.

The remarkable postwar influx made it possible to conceive of the existence of a separate organization. It is clear that the initial drive came from the older students rather than the younger. In the early stages of an organization, there are usually key people interested in pushing the organization and whose actions make its creation a practical possibility. In the early stages, the individual who most stood out in the drive to create a formal organization was a white West Indian. Before coming to Britain, this particular student had not thought much in nationalist terms. She was primarily interested in the pursuit of her course rather than in devotion to the West Indian cause. In London she contacted the West India Committee. While speaking to one of the attendants there, she found that she had some difficulty in being understood. The English person could not understand her accent and asked (in what appeared to her a contemptuous manner) from what part of the world she came. Thinking of herself as white, British and speaking English, this was somewhat of a shock to her and there and then she identified herself as 'Jamaican', rather than West Indian. This was in itself significant, but identification of oneself as Jamaican did not prevent the identification of Jamaicans with West Indians. One of the first fruits of this encounter was an attempt to organize the WISU.

The Birth of the WISU

The first meeting of the group was held in London where it was decided to elect a small committee to organize a conference of all West Indian students to set up a formal organization. Significantly, the first meeting of this group was at a colonial students' hostel. Eventually, the organizing committee was able to hold a meeting at an independent centre. A good constitution was presented and adopted and an executive committee elected.

The first election that took place, as did many others subsequently held, brought out clearly how the sense of West Indian solidarity was to interplay with the lesser loyalty to the individual group. There was a general persistence of insularity in the new environment and a persistence over the years. One reason for this was that students had experienced or heard of incidents in the RAF in which soon after their arrival in the UK, Jamaicans had attacked other West Indians who were in a minority. Isolated individuals were regularly beaten until other West Indians drew their bayonets and simulated a charge on the Jamaicans. These stories reinforced the general sentiments the individual islander possessed.

The largest single group among the students was the Jamaican group and there was some anxiety on the part of the non-Jamaicans, that they would dominate the group. In actual fact, this did not take place. This was partly as a result of the fact that the organizing committee and its members were in a particularly favourable position for being reelected and partly because in the early stages there was not much opportunity for the Jamaican students to get to know one another and act in solidarity. But there was another reason. The Jamaican who had been most active on the organizing committee and who was the obvious choice for the presidency of the new organization was white. Several among the most prominent members were opposed to the idea that a white person, who lorded it over them in their homeland should now, through the assertion of West Indian nationality in London, continue to lord it over them. Hence it came about that the Jamaican who stood the best chance of being elected lost Jamaican support and a Trinidadian was elected president.

The results of the election were to show a catholicity of choice and, on superficial view, a lack of insularity which was gratifying to the leaders of the students' union. In their printed official reports of the meetings, the place of origin was proudly stated. This was a reflection not merely of the insularity (since the place of origin was obviously a point of identification) but the proud display of West Indian solidarity.

In point of fact, the smaller territories had much less of a sense of unity and were much more anxious to drop the insular identification than were the Jamaican students. In part, this was due to the fact that Jamaica and Jamaican rum were known to a fairly large section of the British public and in practice, it was not so necessary for the Jamaicans to describe themselves as West Indian in order to furnish an acquaintance or point of reference. Again, the Jamaican students were a large enough group to become conscious of themselves as a group. In subsequent elections, some Jamaicans were conscious of having acted as a group and wondered what the reaction of the rest of the students would be, while the latter were blissfully unaware of any block voting. Later, in writing their own lecture, the union executive stated:

> The WISU was formed in December 1946 by a group of enthusiastic students who felt very keenly the need for such an organization, particularly in view of the changing face of the West Indies and the national awakening that was taking place at home and the desire of the students over here that they too might play their part. Realizing that it would be their duty on return home to take an interest in the growth and development of their respective communities and that the ultimate good to which such growth pointed was a unified West Indies, the organizers felt that it was essential to start students over here thinking as West Indians and not merely as Jamaicans, Barbadians, Trinidadians, etc. Further, they realized that the experience gained in learning to organize and run their union, overcoming insular barriers and prejudices of various kinds would be invaluable experience in the West Indies of tomorrow.

Appropriately enough, the first president elected by the members of the newly formed union was a student from Trinidad, that most cosmopolitan island, and also appropriately enough, he was a student of social welfare. At that first meeting, there were students from every one of the West Indian territories and these students had come from all over the UK. Some as far afield as the Bahamas and Bermuda which, from a political point of view, are never included among the British West Indies. The composition of the first and every subsequent executive committee has continued to reflect this wide coverage, but it is important to stress that right from the start, the students were determined not to succumb to insular sentiments and this wide coverage has been entirely spontaneous in character. No attempt has been made by the students from any particular territory to 'capture' the organization, nor has any group of students from any particular territory ever felt that they were not adequately represented. In fact, the West Indian student in England has, on arrival in this country and on joining the WISU, become a *West Indian* merging his island identity into that of the larger unit. The WISU has done much to foster and further the cause of West Indian Federation.

At its first meeting after the usual time-honoured formalities, it was decided that the aims and objects of the Association shall be:
(a) to promote fellowship between WI students in the UK;
(b) to concern itself with the general well-being of West Indian students in the UK;
(c) to stimulate interest in the cultural, political and economic development of the West Indies;
(d) to promote facilities for higher education in the West Indies;
(e) to establish contacts with similar organizations in the UK and other parts of the world.

Membership should be open to professional and academic students.

Associate membership to interested non-West Indians and West Indians studying different courses.

Membership

The Union has had a chequered but on the whole successful career. Although there were students and would-be students numbering something under two thousand, the Union never reached a large proportion of these. When membership reached two hundred, this was regarded as a considerable achievement. In the initial stages, there was some difficulty in contacting students. The organizers of the first conference had to compile lists of students and were able to contact only a fraction of these. Eventually, the welfare department of the Colonial Office and the liaison officers for West Indian students compiled lists of students and their college addresses because the problem became acute. Further, large numbers of the students were relatively poor and their enthusiasm was not of such a high order as to lead them to financial sacrifice.

One of the most important reasons for the lack of a really stable membership was the lack of enthusiasm for a West Indian cause. The emergent nationalism, except in the case of a few, was more of a personal psychological adjustment to the situation than a coherent practical philosophy of action. This sense of nationalism could be satisfied once it achieved articulation through the expression of camaraderie and mutual coupling and sharing of complaints. The WISU found that in order to keep alive it had to fulfil a dual function. It had to serve as a welfare organization serving the 'social needs' of the West Indian student and also as a protest organization. It had in both cases to put up with the rivalry of other organizations. The students welcomed their activity in the field of welfare work, just as they did the similar activities of other organizations. On the part of the student leaders, however, there was an expectation of gratitude that was not forthcoming from the recipients of the benefits. The politically minded leaders of the West Indies were always denouncing those West Indians who asserted their nationality only at dancing time and never attended discussions of a serious nature. A crowd of a few hundred at a dance was a normal occasion; a few dozen at a serious lecture or conference rendered it a success.

One difficulty lay in the fact that WISU had few benefits to offer which could be kept exclusively to members. They had no special club facilities and relied to a considerable extent on the attendances of members at dances in order to finance the organization. Again, when the Union did in fact bring out a newsletter, it was proposed that the circulation be restricted to members in order that they would appear to have some special advantage or return for their annual subscription. At times, however, financial membership fell as low as thirty and to restrict circulation to such small numbers would hardly have been worthwhile. At the same time, it was hoped that nonmembers who became acquainted with the newsletter would become interested in joining the organization. So the newsletter went to all and sundry, actual and potential members.

The Union as a Welfare Organization

Partly through genuine concern for the problems of students and partly as a means of winning supporters for the Union's cause, WISU undertook a number of welfare activities. First, there was the problem of the new student. Everyone – even those with friends in London – knew what a traumatic experience it was to enter into the life of London. The Union obtained notification as far as possible of all newly arrived students and wherever possible made arrangements for greeting them on arrival. Moreover, when the British Council took over responsibility for student accommodation, they arranged for the WISU to help in greeting students on their arrival. New students unable to find accommodation in hostels would be given lists of suitable places to which they could apply. Members were encouraged to help others in finding digs. The British Council agreed to pay the fares of the volunteer students.

The Union over and over described in its newsletter, the problem of discrimination in housing as the most important problem which the students had to face. On this account, they devised a scheme whereby students who were returning home and had accommodation would furnish names and addresses of their landlords, so that new students could be put in touch with bargains or accommodation where the question of prejudice would not arise.

This scheme did not appear to have got any serious support, however noble it was in conception. After the flow of students became sufficiently large, informal arrangements took up most of this accommodation. Sometimes, places were held but not considered good. But more important, the places which did not go to other West Indians by informal arrangement were usually held by people who had few informal contacts with fellow West Indians. They were either people with the drive to be integrated with the host society at the cost of shedding West Indian contacts, or those who in spite of organizational contacts felt that their personal reputations might be tarnished if West Indians of an 'inferior' type took over their lodgings. The Union was therefore unable to make any organizational contribution to the 'basic problem' of the West Indian student.

The Union as a Protest Movement

Although the main core of its popular support came from its welfare activities, the leadership was always more interested in what they considered the *serious* aspect of the Union, that is in its function as a protest organization. Indeed, it was this characteristic which differentiated the Union activity from other types of organizational activity, official and unofficial on behalf of the student. It was felt that the Union could take up issues which were of general student interest. In actual practice, student representation had nothing to do with the university, but centred around the activity of the Welfare Department of the Colonial Office.

Student Allowances

One of the points around which it was thought possible to rally student opinion was the question of students' allowances. There were wide differences in allowances according to the territory from which the scholarship holder came. The larger and more wealthy colonies were much more generous in their allowances than the smaller and poorer areas. Some pressure was brought on the Colonial Office to make representation to the local governments concerned about the inadequacies of the grant. This was a point readily conceded by the Colonial Office which found itself in full agreement with the students and informed the respective governments of this fact.

These cases, however, affected only a small minority of the students and the real core of the Union demand came to be for the upward revision of all students' allowances. In actual practice, the scales of the majority of students were reasonable when viewed in the light of the allowances granted to English students. In the case of the ex-servicemen, the basic allowance was that awarded to the English students *plus* a special allowance which would enable the West Indian student to live over the vacation period. The theory was that the English student could normally fall back on family and friends during this period whereas this was not possible in the case of the West Indian. There would appear to have been little basis for the general agitation that was set up.

Students' allowances were, however, a popular cause that could not be lightly abandoned. Whatever the realities of the situation, the student leaders had to make a case that the allowances were not enough. There were special circumstances in the case of the West Indian which did not operate with the British student. The following arguments were advanced:

(1) West Indian students were exposed to discrimination and had to pay more for comparable lodging than the Britishers.

(2) The West Indian student did not know his way around and therefore the English student was able to live more cheaply. In private, many students objected to being reduced to the impecunious level of the English student. What was good enough for the English student was not necessarily good enough for the West Indian. The latter was accustomed to a high standard of living at home and that standard should be maintained. However widespread these sentiments were it was clearly impolitic to press them in public.

(3) The West Indian student was on a trip to England which might be his last. The treasures of the continent of Europe were always open to the English student. The West Indian student should have that little extra which would allow him to visit the continent. When this argument was not well received, it was argued that special provision should be made to get to know the English people and country better through internal travel.

(4) It was also alleged that due to prejudice West Indian students had always to pay exhorbitant sums for their holidays as they were hardly ever invited into the homes of English people.

(5) Because of this prejudice too, West Indian students were under more psychological strain and tension than the English student. The latter could bear the strain of inadequate allowances but in the case of the West Indian, this was the last straw upon the camel's back.

The core of the organization was built around protest. This was the common culture of the group which made effective action possible, and hence in some way differential treatment had to be alleged. This need led to some strange inconsistencies, not the least noteworthy being that private students who were living in what they regarded as reasonable comfort on small allowances, joined in protest against the inadequacy of government allowances much higher than what they in fact enjoyed.

The problem of student allowance received a 'final' settlement when the advice of the vice chancellors of the respective universities was sought on what they considered reasonable allowances for students. This settlement, by introducing the impartiality of a third party, allowed the Colonial Office to take a firm stand on the question of allowances. However, this settlement created as many new anomalies as those it ironed out.

This settlement and the increase in allowances which followed it deprived the Union of an important rallying point. It was still necessary, however, to maintain its position as a *student* bargaining body, and this would appear to be the reason why the case of loans for allowances came up.

The Union acknowledged that the Colonial Office was hostile to students who came to the UK 'on speculation' hoping that somehow or other they would be able to finance themselves. Such students were particularly irritating to the Colonial Office because they endeavoured to bypass the bureaucratic machinery set up for coping with students' problems and precisely for this reason had to fall back on this same bureaucracy. The Colonial Office wished to dissuade these adventurers who more often than not had no opportunities open to them. The Union claimed that the fact that these students had taken the initiative of coming to the UK showed that they were serious students with enthusiasm and grit and therefore should be encouraged. They proposed that a system of loans for students be adopted and that the needy students should benefit from the scheme whether or not their visit had been officially sponsored.

The idea of loans for students was never seriously considered although a precedent had been established in the case of those studying in the USA and Canada. In those countries, several students were placed in a serious position due to devaluation and West Indian governments had undertaken to provide loans for bona fide students in need.

In the case of the West Indian students, those in need of loans in the UK were either scholarship holders who had failed their examinations and whose allowances had been suspended, or private students who had difficulty in passing their examinations or whose allowances from home had been stopped, for these or some other reason not connected with finance (for example, unfortunate alliances). In the circumstances, the Union was unable to do anything more than make a brave show of representing students' interests.

Wherever the occasion arose the Union was in the forefront of battle. An unkind critic would say that it found it necessary to create issues where they did not exist. For instance one newsletter stated:

HEALTH OF WEST INDIAN STUDENTS

The Union regrets to have to report that two residents of one of the largest of the colonial students' hostels, one of them a West African and the other a West Indian and a member of the Union,' have recently been rushed off [*sic*]) to hospital and are lying critically ill suffering from tuberculosis. The executive takes a very serious view of this matter, and immediately decided to take action to prevent further occurrences of this kind. A letter was immediately sent off to the Director of Colonial Scholars and another to the Secretary of State for the Colonies.

The Union pointed out that colonial students, particularly those resident in hostels are not very conversant with the National Health Scheme, and that most are not registered with doctors as very often they do not know to whom to go. We recommended that facilities for *mass X-Ray tests* should immediately be made available at hostels for the benefit of residents and also of other students living in digs who can attend the hostel for this purpose. This facility is a matter of common form at several colleges of London University (for example, LSE) and all students should be encouraged to take it.

We also recommended that information re the health scheme should be circulated to all colonial students, and further that the hostels should have a doctor whose special responsibility should be the health of the residents, and perhaps that there should be a specially appointed doctor to whom students could go for registration under the Health Scheme if they are unable to make other arrangements.

Despite our stress on the urgency of getting the mass X-ray tests carried out, the Union has not to date of writing received a reply from the Welfare Department. We are sending another reminder to spur the Department into action. The menace of TB in this country to people who feel the climate as we do is too grave to be lightly treated.

PS: Since the above was written we have had an acknowledgement of our letter to the Welfare Department, but no indication of action they propose to undertake if any.

In choosing this case, the Union acted wisely. It was possible to link tuberculosis with the climate – a constant source of complaint – and the obsessive West Indian fear of draughts. Further, tuberculosis is a disease with special emotional connotation in the West Indies. There is no disease more wrapped around with secrecy or more encompassed with fear. Further, the fact that the victims were residents in a hostel made the possibility of infection more strikingly alarming to students.

Yet, it is difficult to see how the Union could shift responsibility in this matter to the Colonial Office. Nor does the sense of urgency of which the Union speaks appear to be very intelligible in the light of circumstances. There were in London several West Indian doctors willing and in some cases anxious to have West Indian students as patients. This fact could easily have been made known. But the Union, in making this belated protest, was confessing the inadequacy of its own welfare programme. The tone of the quotation gives some idea of the need of the Union for issues upon which it could stage a fight. Perhaps it was the difficulty posed in 'proving' cases of discrimination that contributed to the adoption of other issues.

If the Union had a difficulty in finding special West Indian students' grievances, it was always possible to get general 'colonial' or 'racial' issues upon which to protest.

In the same issue of the newsletter, there was the following item:

II. Posters in the underground etc. caricaturing the coloured people:
(a) Food Office, Golders Green. On the representation of the Union the Minister of Food, Mr Strachey, has arranged for a set of posters over children's canteen (the term Little Nigger Boys of the nursery rhyme) to be withdrawn.
(b) Advertisement re "Nigger Dates", Eucryl Tooth Paste and Spa tooth brushes.

The Commercial Advertisement Officer of the British Transport Commission received and discussed this matter with a deputation of three executive committee members. We pointed out that we resented the concept of racial superiority which lay behind those advertisements, and that in the absence of any real quantity of straight advertising, the average English person received a completely misleading picture of coloured people. On his side, he stated that he fully appreciated our point of view and that he would give orders that any future advertisement on this theme or of this type should be submitted to him personally for his scrutiny. As regards the ads complained of, he said that he had not the authority to order their withdrawal or order that their contracts be not renewed. British transport was being critically watched, and on an issue of such importance as this he felt that he must wait for directions from the Minister of Transport himself and that the executive will soon be considering further action, and securing the aid of kindred organizations to air the matter in appropriate quarters. Perhaps a campaign to educate cabinet ministers on this subject might be fruitful.

There was also reported the case of R. Simms of the Caribbean Labour Congress.

THE CASE OF R. SIMMS

A case of perhaps close interest to members of WISU since it involved a member of WISU was the recent trial and conviction of R. Simms on a charge of *obstructing the highway* and of *obstructing the police in the execution of their duty*. Readers of the last Newsletter will remember that the *Union's President stood bail for Mr Simms* who had been 'locked up' overnight at Brixton. Representatives of the Union also attended the subsequent trial at *Bow Street* before the Magistrates Court when *Mr Simms* and another young West African student (who had been bailed out of Brixton by popular West Indies doctor David Pitt) were each fined £30.

At the invitation of the Executive Committee, Mr Simms attended a meeting and gave an outline of the story. Shortly put, he and several others were taking part in a demonstration ('Peaceful-picketing') outside South Africa House on the Strand, being aware that Dr Donges, the South African Minister of the Interior and the person largely responsible for its racial legislation, was due to visit South Africa House that afternoon and desiring to express their views of the Malan policy, they picketed by walking slowly in procession, carrying banners, round South Africa House, or rather the block containing it.

Acting under Legal Advice which subsequently seemed to have proved incorrect or inadequate, the demonstrators were careful to keep at a distance of 30 yards apart so as to see that they did not constitute a procession (now illegal without prior consent of the Metropolitan Police or Home Secretary). The police arrived on the scene and advised the demonstrators to move on. Mr Simms, acting on his legal advice, argued the point with the police who thereupon arrested him and another student from West Africa. He was taken to Bow Street, and efforts to find bail and contact friends for this purpose having failed, he was conveyed to Brixton and detained overnight till next morning when WISU who had been contacted overnight bailed him out.

At the subsequent trial, he was legally represented, and his solicitor argued unsuccessfully that no obstruction of the Highway had in fact occurred and that also carrying a bill board at about the same spot was a man advertising Railway Lost Property Sales. The magistrate found as a fact that an obstruction to the highway had been caused, and that even if there had been no obstruction at that time, the police were reasonable in expecting an obstruction to occur and were acting within their discretion in advising the 'picketers' to move on. He fined Mr Simms and his colleague £30 each.

The Union does not seek to question the correctness of this decision but it does echo the feeling expressed in the *Observer*, that the law needs clarification. It should be possible for intending demonstrators to find out *before* what their legal position is, and insofar as the police had a discretion in the matter, it seems unfortunate that its exercise in this case should lend colour to charges of being proMalan and in favour of the discrimination of the Malan Government. No doubt it is the duty of the police to protect from hostile demonstrations visiting diplomats, etc. whose policies and views are unpopular, but how far does that duty go and was this really a case calling for action of this nature?

The Union hopes to pursue some of these questions in the appropriate place and manner. It also will have to make some arrangements for a more precise kind re bailing out WI students who have the misfortune to be picked up by the police.

Another item deals with allegations of discrimination against West Indians in hospitals.

DISCRIMINATORY TREATMENT OF NURSES IN HOSPITALS

Two West Indian nurses, one of whom has since given up the profession, have recently complained to WISU of being the victims of discriminatory treatment in their respective hospitals. Their complaints indicate that they feel that they are being given the 'dirty work' to do far more than their English comrades, and that this is because the Sisters (or whoever is responsible for them) are prejudiced against them on racial grounds. They complain too of not being allowed to handle the patients, and one states that in her entire period of service, she was kept continuously operating the 'sluice' and in her six to nine months never even took a patient's temperature until the day after she handed in her notice to quit.

These are serious allegations, and the Union proposes to examine them most carefully, and if it finds them proven, to take it up with the Ministry of Health and the Colonial Office with a view to seeing that no more West Indian Students (WIS) are sent to hospitals guilty of such treatment. On the other hand, it must be realized that such charges are extremely difficult both to investigate and to prove. The individual nurse (not that we have any reason for saying so in these two cases) may herself have been at fault. She might have been misled by the glamour of the Dr Kildare movie pictures etc., into overlooking the terrific amount of 'dirty work' that all nurses have to do. Nursing is a 'vocation' and it might be that she had not really a sense of calling. Again, even nurses from this country find the training so hard and rigorous that many quit under the conditions and never complete their training. Further, it not seldom happens that individual Sisters etc. get grudges, or that individual nurses are considered by the Sister 'insubordinate' or 'rude'. Whatever be the case here, WISU will investigate it and at the same time would welcome views from other WI nurses on the treatment received in training here.

Other Sources of Protest

Another favourite source of protests were cases of 'victimization' of students in colonial hostels. But this aspect of the matter will be more fully treated in the discussion of the problems of accommodation. Yet another type of protest which was sure to awaken a protest for the West Indian student was cases involving the Negro question in the USA or the treatment of natives in the Union of South Africa. Thus any apparent miscarriage of justice in any of these areas which were taken up as popular issues by communists and radicals found an echo. Thus in the same issue of the newsletter in which the two cases are cited, reference was made to the Martinville case:

> Some members will have seen press reports on the Martinville case. The facts of the case are far from clear. Some seven American Negroes were charged with and convicted of the rape of a white woman. The woman had been in mental institutions before the trial and is in one today. (Some sources allege that she had been incarcerated to prevent her subsequent revocation of her testimony becoming known). The seven were tried by an all-white jury and convicted in May 1949. They were sentenced to *death*. They appealed to the Virginian Supreme Court and to the US Supreme Court and lost their appeals. They were sentenced in early February of this year despite appeals made by organizations in the USA and all over the world. Alastair Cooke of the Manchester Guardian, a usually reliable paper and a usually reliable writer, states that in the evidence the men appear to have been guilty of the offence charged, and even so reputable a body as the National Association for the Advancement of the League of Coloured People seem to agree with him, for their protest and campaign has been against *the sentence* and not *the verdict*. Their point is that no Negro ought to be executed for a crime for which no white man has ever been sentenced to death in the state of Virginia. The laws of that state do prescribe death as a penalty for rape, but this penalty has never in the history of the state been imposed on any white man convicted of rape. *The West Indian Students Union* has supported the appeal against the execution of the Martinsville Seven.
>
> Speaking at a public meeting held at Holbon Hall on the 30th January, the President of WISU expressed the union's views in a similar manner.

Such a state of affairs (as existed in the USA) was calculated to provoke the danger of racial wars and he pointed out the incompatibility of racial discrimination with the aim of the West Indian people and WISU to achieve racial integration.

The crop of incidents reported in this particular newsletter were not everyday occurrences but there was always an issue of some sort to be dealt with. Where of course a West Indian was involved or where a leaflet announced something dramatically, the emotion generated was high as illustrated in the following:

West Indian Seaman Murdered By South African Police Protest Against Malan's Racial Policy.

It should be pointed out, however, that the Union never of its own accord took the lead in any of these agitations. It never itself summoned protest meetings or organized protest marches. Its position was one of giving general support to the 'progressive' cause. Although its aims and objectives stated nothing about aiding the worldwide fight against racial discrimination, sentiment on this point was so strong that the Union executive invariably supported the good cause without raising constitutional quibbles.

The only occasion within the first few years of the Union's activities when the irrelevance of these activities to the Union's specific aims arose was when a West Indian from outside the ranks of the Union took it to task. This was on the occasion when the students gave general support to what they considered the progressive cause in East Africa by protesting against the dissolution of the African Union in Kenya by the authorities there. The burden of the argument of the West Indian lecturer who spoke on this matter was that the action of the Union was unconstitutional. In spite of his protest however, the Union showed full solidarity with the 'progressive' cause.

There were one or two serious problems of student life in which the WISU was able to function as a protest organization. We have already spoken of the problem of students who were seeking to obtain entry into medical school. This was an issue on which the Union could make protest and ask that adequate provision be made for the placing of colonial students. At the time, it was believed that entry into medical school was by quota but continuation depended upon passing the MB (Bachelor of Medicine). The chances of passing were here limited to the number of places actually available in medical school. It was the general feeling that the British government and British universities owed a special responsibility to the colonies since adequate university facilities had not been provided on the spot and students had been encouraged to proceed to the UK instead. The needs of the British had to be given consideration but this special responsibility to the colonies could not be overlooked.

As the first batch of postwar students graduated, the question of the 'market for college graduates' arose. The anxieties of many students led to the demand for an appointments officer and for special information about vacancies in the West Indies. There was a tendency to put the blame for any unemployment or threat of unemployment upon the Colonial Office. It was clear however that that organization could only influence appointments within the government service. The whole range of employment in private industry was not answerable to any action except inducement by good example.

The liaison officer did in fact bring to the attention of the WISU advertisements for jobs for graduates in the West Indies. There does not appear however to have been any special need for such an arrangement. Most posts were in fact publicly advertised when there was the need for recruiting new people. This information was as readily available to the West Indian student as it was to the English applicant who, however, was conceived as receiving special treatment. In the anxiety producing situation, the response was to attempt to put blame on the Colonial Office. Again, the constitutional position of the Colonial Office precluded any dictate of appointments but students preferred to believe that the wishes of the Colonial Office were the only ones which came in for any consideration. Another area in which 'legitimate protest' could be played was in implementing the plans for the establishment of a university college within the area. As this point is of some interest, we will examine the overall concept of a university as it emerged in the period 1945–49.

The Concept of a University for the West Indies

The first step towards the formation of an organized opinion in the university came from outside the Union. However, many people later to be prominent in the leadership of the Union were introduced into pressing for implementation of a university college at this stage. The initiative came from a West Indian for a long time resident in West Africa who was vitally interested in the development of higher education both in the West Indies and Africa. Hence the early demands were for a joint committee urging the implementation of certain aspects of the Report on Higher Education in the colonies.

This committee called itself the Association of West Indian and West African Graduates and Students in Great Britain and forwarded a memorandum to the Right Honourable George Henry Hall, MP, His Majesty's principal secretary of state for the colonies.

In spite of its title, this association was not a formal one but an *ad hoc* committee. It wished to act as a pressure group but because of the tenuous nature of the Association, it had to proceed in a more cautious fashion than the subsequently formed WISU which was able to express itself in a more truculent manner. The leadership of this *ad hoc* committee expressed 'profound gratitude' to the members of the Association. With regard to the Commission on Higher Education in the West Indies, they more or less expressed agreement with the report but also made some concrete suggestions. One point which did not figure much in later discussions was the question of salaries. On this point, there was unanimity of opinion. The memorandum stated:

> With regard to the question of salaries, we are absolutely opposed to any differentiation between the salaries paid to staff recruited locally and to staff recruited overseas when the persons concerned hold posts of equal responsibility and possess the same qualifications.
>
> We have examined very carefully the case for the payment of extra remuneration to staff recruited from overseas as compensation for their being uprooted from their own environment. We think any necessary compensation for their being uprooted can be met by the provision of expatriation allowances as suggested in the report. But the allowance should be quite distinct from the salary attached to a post. The salary for each post should be determined by the responsibility which the post involves and anybody qualified for the post when appointed to it should receive the salary irrespective of his or her social and economic background.
>
> The argument that it would be inequitable to ask the taxpayers to contribute for the payment of high salaries to a small class of professional men in the community with a low general income level, and that the existence of such a class would be socially and financially disturbing is quite intolerable for it rests on a fallacious assumption.

In the first place, locally recruited staff who could hold such posts would be persons of exceptional ability and we see nothing unsuitable in rewarding exceptional merit.

Secondly, nowhere in the Colonial Empire do we find the lives of highly educated and capable professional men approximating to those of the masses of the community. The standard of living of such men is quite different from the masses. As a rule, they do not live more cheaply than persons from overseas of the same status resident in the community, as is generally but wrongly assumed by superficial observers. Moreover, a university teacher will be expected to maintain a standard of living corresponding to that of his overseas colleagues with whom he will have to associate in the social life of the university.

Any differentiation, it was held, should be personal to an individual if difficulties cropped up in the initial phases of recruitment. This and other requirements noticed above could be met without the introduction of the dangerous practice of differential salaries. A differential salary scheme in a university was bound to create a feeling of dissatisfaction and disharmony such as existed within the colonial service itself. Staff recruited from overseas and paid on a differential scale would mentally develop a feeling of superiority and a *Herrenvolk* attitude toward their less fortunate fellow workers. This it will be agreed is the last thing to which a university should lend its support.

These arguments are interesting for several reasons. First, the question had cropped up in the case of the Committee on Higher Education in the Colonies. On the whole, formal differential scales of pay have not been enforced in the West Indies. The suggestion brought about a cleavage of opinion within the committee; the West Indian members (who were later to be appointed to key posts in the administration) came out strongly in opposition to any form of expatriation allowances. This point of view was shared by all the students concerned.

Second, the suggestion showed the conception of the student leaders themselves as essentially middle class, sharing in all the current standard values and prejudices of that group. In view of their rationalization of their position as one of protesting in favour of the masses, this open avowal of middle class status and attitudes as soon as it affected an issue in which they were personally involved, was as typical as it was revealing. Their conception of a grandiose role for the student on returning home as a leader of thought and opinion and the masses never seriously interfered with the conception of themselves as essentially middle class persons entitled as of right to certain standards of living. The Medical students for instance would be found to be highly critical of the inadequate staffing of the medical services in the West Indies and very conscious of the responsibilities of their governments for adequate provision of such services. Yet, except in the case of those thinking in terms of a university career, there was a general desire to escape as soon as possible from the government service to which some were committed on bond (an attachment mentally onerous) because of the more lucrative opportunities in private practice. The service of the masses was not to interfere with their incomes. It was the same in the case of the teachers, social workers and civil servants.

Third, the reaction to differentiation between English and Europeans was particularly galling to students fostering resentments against the British and alleging inequality of treatment in their own homeland. It is clear that the hostility to differential salaries was not at all confined to West Indian students or those West Indians who had been educated in Britain. It would appear, however, that the strength of sentiment was much more marked among those who had been educated abroad as compared with those educated within the local environment.

Informal representation on a general basis soon gave way to more specifically West Indian formulations of their own problems. The newly organized WISU found itself making representations of its own. On 13 July 1946 a deputation waited on the secretary of state for the colonies. They pointed out that "among the aims of the Union was the promotion of higher education in the West Indies". The Union, as representing the largest body of West Indian opinion abroad, felt that in view of their presence there, where plans and policies were being shaped, it was their responsibility to the West Indies to try and obtain information on what was happening with regard to the university. This was necessary because in the fifteen months since the release of the Irvine Report, the complete lack of information was aggravating "the feeling of disappointment and frustration" referred to by the report. The deputation then proceeded to raise specific points on which information was desired.

The deputation asked whether the report had been accepted as it stood or whether any alternative schemes were now being taken with regard to the following:

(a) The medical school in Trinidad and the offer of McGill University re same.

(b) The question of extramural studies.

(c) The creation of the Guild of Graduates.

(d) The steps being taken to secure the cooperation of local teachers and the need for revision of the curricula of the secondary schools to suit the requirements of London University exams.

In view of the fact that the university was intended to revitalize all sections of West Indian life, its opening to women would be particularly important and the Secretary of State was asked whether the proposed ratio of men to women would be revised. He was next asked if there was at present any UK representation on the Inter-University Council and the desirability of being represented on this body was stressed. The deputation enquired what steps had been taken so far to recruit staff and if an assurance could be given that qualified West Indians would be appointed if available. This would be very desirable in view of the fact that the university would be completely autonomous and as the governing body, the Senate recommended the new appointment for it would be all too easy for the University to become a little English community around it. He was also asked to make a statement on the question of site and building plans, possibilities for legal education and the approaches so far made to the local governments on the score of financial support for the university.

Finally, the important question of academic freedom for the university was raised, and the desirability of block grants for a fixed period of time was suggested as the best means of securing not only this but also a certain measure of financial permanence and stability for the university which would then be unembarrassed by the annual necessity of passing estimates in the local legislatures.

The Secretary of State for the Colonies was able to furnish satisfactory replies to all the points made. Indeed, there were no controversial matters raised as the Union was merely acting as a pressure group seeking to implement a report which had already been accepted in principle. The only deviation from the official report was the question raised of the facilities for legal education. The university continued to be a focus of interest. When the principal of the University College was appointed he was entertained and lively discussion took place.

Fears were expressed that the majority of the staff of the university would initially be from abroad. To remedy this, several speeches favoured awarding scholarships to promising West Indian graduates who, having obtained higher degrees, would subsequently be drafted in to the staff. While he did not altogether approve of the scholarship scheme, Dr Taylor thought that young West Indian graduates, being inexperienced, could be appointed to junior posts which would otherwise be difficult to fill. He was endeavouring without prejudice to select the men and women best suited for the posts from the many applicants from all parts of the world. As evidence of his good intention, he referred to the two appointments that had been made.

Those two appointments were of the registrar and the director of extramural studies. In spite of the universal popularity of these two appointments, there was still some suspicion. Somehow, it was felt that these two individuals would be used as 'front men', would be given undue publicity so evident of a liberal policy while in fact, Englishmen remained in the saddle relegating West Indians to perpetual junior posts. Those fears continued to be expressed and questions were asked of the principal as to whether he would appoint W. Arthur Lewis (then a lecturer at the LSE) or Dr Eric Williams to junior positions. When the principal indicated that they would be appointed to readerships there was some satisfaction but when Arthur Lewis was appointed to a professorship at an English university some time later, the suggestion of a readership was reinterpreted as a slight upon a West Indian.

Although the agitation was for the implementation of the Irvine Report, the debates and discussions around the university showed some divergent viewpoints. Although the question of facilities for legal students was raised in the initial interview with the secretary of state for the colonies, there was a predisposition to accept the view of the first principal that there was no need for a law school because there were too many lawyers in the West Indies.

The type of statement which received general approval was one in which the university was seen as a revolutionary force. There was a great stress by the majority on the importance of utilitarian education. Unable to develop positive criticism of their own of the concept of the university college, the leaders of the students had to fall back on the criticism of Dr Eric Williams in which this aspect of higher education was stressed. Their experience of university life precluded them from accepting the whole of his thesis, but on this particular point there was a tendency to go along with him.

Whatever the enthusiasm for useful education, however, even the most radical utilitarian held that the university should serve the cause of West Indian nationalism and a focus for West Indian culture. Thus, in a debate on university policy, one advocate of utilitarianism stated that

> He did not think we should support learning for the sake of learning. Knowledge should be sought for the sake of the community. Our need was for a university

that would lay the stress on practical problems. There should be a strong faculty of agricultural science, since our economy was mainly agriculture. The university should teach people how to grow grasses, how to irrigate the soil. Again, he felt that medicine should be made practical. The time had passed when our would-be doctors had to go to England to hear a lot of guess work about tropical diseases dished up at second or third hand. He felt that in research, we should concentrate on work of particular importance for the community.

But he also affirmed that

We did not want in the West Indies a university which was a copy of British universities. We did not want to be any one's little brother. We wanted to be free to choose the best and to leave out what we did not want of the British or any other system.

In spite of the need of a 'realistic approach', he believed that the university had terrific potential in the sphere of culture. He would have a good language faculty concentrating on English, Spanish, French. He hoped that the Cuban, Puerto Rican and British West Indian universities would get together. The importance of a sense of oneness with non-English-speaking peoples of the Caribbean must be stressed, for once we formed a close cultural link with them, we should find a new cultural life born of this contact, not British, French or Spanish but truly West Indian.

While there was a range of opinions in these early days about the exact 'cultural' and 'utilitarian' roles of the university, there was hardly a member of the organization who would have disagreed with the view of another union leader that the West Indian university should be free, that in a colony, one of the principal objects of a university should be to help its people to rise above colonial status and the university would have to regenerate both itself and the West Indies. No dominating power in possession of colonies could wish to see a university working to throw off its power. In these early days, there was even talk of the university being made the centre of direct political action. In all these discussions, the distinction between a university college and a university was never borne in mind. The term university was always used in discussion and correspondence. This would at first glance seem to indicate an impractical approach, but the extreme nationalism of the WISU leadership was coupled with a sense of realism. However, while there was stress on the need for a university serving the area and molded to suit the people's will, there was never any doubt as to the advisability of starting off with London degrees.

There was a curious blend of nationalism with the demand that the university be set up out of British funds. In the interview with the secretary of state for the colonies, it was he and not the West Indians who pointed out that a great deal of the details would be shaped not by his decision but the pressure of local opinion.

The financial dependence of the West Indies inevitably led to a dilemma, always posing itself for West Indian nationalism, of how to achieve a viable independence for a poverty stricken country while accepting aid from the metropolitan power. In the debate on the university, there was the inevitable discussion of the desired autonomy and the necessary dependence.

An English visitor asked whether it would not be possible for a West Indian university to be started without the consent of the Colonial Office. It was explained that this idea had occurred to West Indians, but had to be scrapped because of its impracticability. Financial assistance was indispensable. The university had to build up prestige and could not do so unless it had an efficient staff and adequate equipment.

Miss —— said that she considered we might do worse than start a university on our own. "At present, we had no voice in fixing the curricula of our schools. How could we guarantee that we would have greater influence on the foundation of the university. We did not want a lot of talk and no action. We ought to make the university an investment and take shares in it."

There was no response to this call to self-help. The nationalism of the students did not go this far. Autonomy was not to be purchased at any price. In spite of the ideological outpourings, there was a realistic appreciation of the financial situation.

The General Radical Ideology of the Student Population

The relation of the WISU to the communist organization is a special problem of such interest that it will be treated separately. Here, we propose to touch a problem of some relevance to that one, that is the general radical ideology of the student population. This ideology has strong Marxist and even revolutionary overtones and these elements were never recognized as such.

On the political level, the Union took the extreme democratic stand. Consistently during its existence, whenever it expressed an opinion it came out for complete, total, unadulterated, self-government. Thus at its general conference on 5 and 6 January 1950, in London, there was a "report of the commission which considered the political scene in the West Indies". This stated that WISU supported the basic principle that all people have the right of self determination *as to island governments*. In addition, it was revealed that:

(1) WISU supports the immediate introduction of unqualified adult suffrage in all British West Indian areas.

(2) WISU agrees that fully responsible governments should be simultaneously granted in all the above areas.

(3) WISU agrees that fully responsible governments should be organized on a single chamber basis consisting entirely of popularly elected members and that this chamber should be the sole source of legislation for the area.

(4) WISU agrees that a cabinet of ministers fully responsible to the popular chamber and elected from that chamber should be the final source of executive authority.

(5) WISU agrees that the chairman of such a cabinet should be elected from the popular chamber, and that whereas the governor of such island should remain as titular head of the state, he should be free to act only on the advice of the chairman of the cabinet.

(6) As to the federal government, WISU urges that the self-governing units suggested in section (a) above should immediately appoint delegations from the popular chambers so formed to a convention to draft a federal constitution for the BWI.

(7) WISU agrees that the federal constitution should centre on a single chamber legislature based on direct popular election and that a system of sliding scale representation should be used to constitute the chamber which shall be organized on the same basis as in section (a) 3, 4 and 5.

(8) WISU agrees that a federal constitution should seek such a range of powers as to create a strong central government to deal with all matters of national concern while leaving all matters of purely local concern to the legislatures of the constituent areas.

(9) WISU agrees that to secure this end, the constitution should be simple in its provisions and easy of amendment by a majority of the central legislature to be ratified by majorities in each of the island legislatures.

(10) WISU agreed that residual powers should be deemed to accrue to the central government but that local governments should be free to experiment beyond their constitutional mandate subject only to a vote by the central government.

The subsequent reports and discussions of the political scene and developments in the West Indies showed an unswerving attachment to the cause of complete and total self-government. Thus on 11 August 1950, recent changes in favour of adult suffrage are noted with gratification:

The WISU has presumably accepted the principle of federation of the West Indies. We could not properly call ourselves West Indians if we did not. Further, by our acceptance of the principles of the right to self-determination, we have committed ourselves to the liquidation of colonialism. Any federal constitution which we support must reflect the acceptance of these principles.

On these grounds, the Commission on Political Problems:

Regrets that the report of the Standing Closer Association Committee makes no attempt to end the colonial status of the peoples of the Caribbean area.

Regrets that the report recommends the retention of official and nominated members in the legislature and executive bodies and the setting up of a bicameral legislature.

Regrets that the proposed constitution does not contain proposals for a strong internal government.

Regrets that some West Indian legislators on the eve of constitutional changes, wished to deliberate on and adopt the Standing Closer Association Committee's report and urges that the report should be reconsidered by the new legislatures partly elected by legislative suffrage.

However, although there was something negativistic and obstructionist in the political conception of development, this was not entirely so. We find that this same commission recommends that the students equip themselves for discharging their political duties when they return. They therefore urged the introduction of civics in the curriculum in all grades of the education system; that all students for professions should acquire a basic knowledge of social and economic affairs; and that the executive committee be requested to arrange courses or classes with this in mind.

One of the most important effects of the education abroad of the West Indian elite is the fact that their political and social notions develop in a void or more accurately, that they develop within an environment altogether different to that in which the students will pass the greater part of their lives.

The democratic atmosphere affects them, but it becomes associated with a particular content. Students get a point of vantage from which to criticize their countries at home. But this is not necessarily all gain, since the 'superiority' of the alien system is taken for granted. The notion that 'what is British is best' ceases to be merely part of the equipment of the expatriate administrator who brings his experience and knowledge of one society to bear on the practical problems with which he is faced. The notion becomes introduced in the West Indies by West Indians themselves.

Thus, in an effort to educate the West Indian student population in the health services, a special course was designed on Health Services and the Welfare State. It was directed primarily at nursing and medical students and to all those interested in social affairs. It was given by the staff tutor of the British Council and the outline of the course was:

> The National Health Service considered in detail; the reconciliation of professional interests and national policy; finance and administration; the hospital and specialist services; the family practitioner services and the local government services; present problems and possible development.
>
> An examination of the history and political implications of the social services with particular reference to the health service but with some consideration of social insurance, housing and other services.

Small wonder that an enthusiasm developed among some students for the introduction of social services on the same level as in Britain into the West Indies.

The whole programme for practical reform put forward by the students took on a somewhat unrealistic form because the ideas and attitudes were divorced from the realities with which they were supposed to deal. Further, the ideology of protest against 'colonialism' which developed through education in the UK even led to some ideological resistance to thinking in any realistic terms. When an eminent economist (that is, Arthur Lewis) who had made a study of industrialization in the West Indies addressed the group and pointed out the difficulties involved in industrialization and the necessity for dependence on foreign capital, there were many who felt that despite his authoritative statement, the money could be raised locally. Study groups organized under the academic leadership of West Indians in Britain helped to bring an element of realism into the picture and one of the better students of economics was able to transcend the narrow ideological confines and come to grips with some aspects of the problem. Nonetheless, the overall tone of suggested solutions for problems of economic and social policy were affected not at all by the application of general principles to concrete facts. Thus the question of local food production was discussed on the basis of the speaker saying that "he thought we could feed ourselves". What resources could be required to achieve this end and how this could interfere with the allocation of resources for export crops, what consequences it would have for the general standard of living of the population, were not considered.

The speaker who raised this point (in 1951) on the role of science in West Indian national development suggested, in contradiction to what Professor Lewis had urged earlier in an address to them, that the West Indies should concentrate on industrial chemistry (stressing the high capital low labour ratio) on the local market (Professor Lewis had stressed the branch firm).

The idea of boundless wealth was still accepted. The oilfields in Trinidad were producing more than before in spite of the protestations of many years before that the supply would be soon exhausted. Turning to the field of industry, the speaker commented on the fact that although 'experts' had been predicting for years that Trinidad's oilfields would be exhausted, production of oil had increased three times over the 1928 figure. In the Pitch Lake, the West Indies had a source of industrial byproducts which had not even been scratched. Today, asphalt was used mainly for road surfacing but from it could be extracted fuel gases, bezine, tricolene, graphite, several industrial acids, disinfectants, plastics and even food. Exploitation of the asphalt would not call for any very vast capital outlay, and it was a challenge to the West Indies to develop this resource instead of letting it go to waste. Again, both British Guiana and Jamaica had large bauxite resources and plants could be set up on the sites to produce aluminium. Power for such plants and other industries could be got by hydroelectric schemes. Other local industries which could be set up would be small plants to make housing materials, exgypsum cement etc. He thought that the West Indies should aim at creating light industries first to produce materials for local consumption; heavy industries, if possible would come later.

This programme, unrelated to economics, was more in line with general West Indian student thinking than those of professional economists who had investigated the problem. Indeed, speakers went further and urged not only that it was a feasible programme but that it could only be implemented through political change. Questions after the lecture dealt primarily with the nature of the relationship between scientific investigation and political change. Thus, there were:

> Those questioners who did not see how it would be possible for the West Indies to develop itself successfully along any of the lines mentioned by the speaker until it had settled its political problems first and won dominion status, self-government or national independence etc. They thought that investigation into and application of science to WI problems would have to await the solution of the political problem. The role of science was secondary in relation to political development.

The Commission on Scientific Agriculture in the West Indies which was held at this conference followed on the lines of the main speaker and shows that his point of view was not merely a personal observation. It recommended a complete land use survey and the appointment of a Federal Agricultural Commission with regional or island agricultural commissions:

> . . . and to each region should be allocated the growing of specified crops etc. In order to arrive at such allocations of crops, the federal commission should consider:
>
> (a) suitability of soil for crop;
> (b) disposition of existing labour force;
> (c) circulating of capital resources for the development of new crops in each area and allocate these crops after full consultation with each island or regional government.

The conception here is of a planning authority paying no regard to the concrete economic circumstances in which the West Indies were placed. This disregard for economic factors was again to be found in the mere discussions about the sugar industry.

At the same conference, the Commission on Production, Prices and Population emphasized the need for planning with stress on food production to eliminate the need for the importation of food. This nationalistic desire for self-sufficiency led to controversy over the question of foreign capital. When at an earlier meeting this problem had been raised by Professor W.A. Lewis, one speaker had refused to accept the dependence on foreign capital for an industrialization programme; he stated that the money could be raised cooperatively and that he had been informed of a similar successful scheme by a friend in Nigeria. A few years later, by the time of the conference under discussion, emotions were coming to grips with some of the facts but finding them no less unpleasant.

The commission stated:

> As to the *financing of the industrialization programme,* some £130,000 would be needed. Some capital could be raised locally, some by taxation of such existing industries as oil. There would have to be a *West Indies Development Corporation* and a West Indies Government Bank. Foreign capital must be encouraged to come in, but it would have to come in terms of or designed so as to *protect the West Indies people from foreign exploitation.*

Within the commission, there was a good deal of discussion as to the wisdom of inviting in foreign capital at all. Some members were completely against it, feeling no safeguard could be adequate, short of total exclusion. Others thought we needed money and more important still the 'know how' to get industry organized and suitable safeguards could be devised.

In the discussion that followed, most stress was laid on the question of *foreign capital.* Some speakers felt that the foreign capitalist could not be trusted not to prefer their own private interests and that no safeguard which could be derived would be effective. Further, that there were sufficient resources for that development in the West Indies itself if we looked at the £2,000,000 made by Trinidad Leaseholds last year, and also at the profits made by Tate and Lyle. In reply, others pointed out that the programme would need at least £180,000,000 and sources like Tate and Lyle had a limited amount only. Industry once started would generate itself, but to start it we needed the money and the technical knowledge neither of which we had in the West Indies today. It was agreed on all sides that political change was a prerequisite to industrialization and also that foreign *technicians* would be necessary at the start to get industry organized and growing. On the voting in the report, a majority of members in the rough proportion of two to one carried the section of the report saying that foreign investment with suitable safeguards was necessary. An amendment providing for the nationalization of every industry in the West Indies was defeated by a narrower margin. And after a very long and at times heated discussion, the report presented by the commission was adopted by the conference.

The strong nationalistic and antiforeign bias coupled with a plan with a total disregard for the limits of possible action, were displayed again in the Commission on West Indian Transport:

For external transport the most important problem was getting *Sea Transport* on a sound basis. This should be a No. 1 priority. Less reliance should be placed on foreign owned shipping and greater efforts be made to develop BWI shipping. This might be done by nationalizing all WI transport, placing it under the control of the WI Federal Government and having a special Minister of Transport to control WI external transport. The Commission noted the need for trained WI personnel to take part in the development and control of WI transport.

As if these were not unrealistic, they proposed that all main roads in the islands be wide enough to take two lane traffic.

The commissions in which there were the highest degree of realism were those on domestic service and on education, and research in technical development in the West Indies. This was probably due to the professional training and experience of the people involved. Even here however, there was still something of a stress on unrealistic copybook planning and the distrust of big business invaded even this sphere. The need for technical education and for technical research in helping to raise the productivity of the area was pointed out. One member of the commission also recommended that 'big business' should be encouraged to endow chairs and so on at the university and possibly to develop their own research laboratories. This position was heretical but did not bring any dire harmful results for we are further told that

In the discussion on the report some members were very sceptical of the wisdom of inviting 'big business' to set up research laboratories etc. but it was pointed out that it was proper for a commission report to mention a minority opinion and a motion to delete the clause in question from the commission report was defeated by a large majority.

Nationalization of Sugar

In the attitudes towards the sugar industry, there was a certain amount of realism but even here, one got the impression of theorizing in the void and the uncritical taking over of slogans meaningful perhaps in terms of British experience but lacking in wisdom in terms of West Indian conditions. Here is the Union statement of the case:

The only present solution for the WI sugar market was to find a guaranteed market, unless they could so *improve and increase the efficiency of their production* as to be able not only to compete on the world market but to compete against preferred producers in markets like the American.

The sugar industry was the largest employer of labour but in view of the above, it would clearly be unwise to expand the sugar industry especially when we consider our weak economic bargaining position vis-à-vis the United Kingdom.

Our hopes for political independence would be further jeopardized if we became even more dependent on the UK market.

The relevant commission recommended further the specialization of sugar in low cost producing areas. It they were unable to solve the problem, at least there was a clear realization of the dilemma. However, the commission went further and recommended the nationalization of sugar. It pointed out that "the sugar industry was almost in effect already government controlled". The argument used in favour of nationalization was clearly taken over from 'British experience':

It was a public utility and should be brought under public ownership and control. The government now negotiated its prices and interested itself in its wage disputes. Nationalization would take this to the logical conclusion. The industry took no risks while on the other hand, the profits of its owners through ownership was incommensurate with any service that they rendered the community.

The method of nationalization indicated a blend of British experience with a clear preference for Marxist expropriation if this were only possible.

"Should the industry's owners be compensated in the event of nationalization?" The commission did not answer the question but explained some of the arguments pro and con. It was not only an internal problem. One had also to consider the effects on the world markets, particularly the UK market, of nationalization without compensation. Compensation could be given in bonds. High death duties would of course have the effect of bringing back much of the compensation to the state.

The argument about death duties of course made sense where the capital was owned internally but where, as in the case of the West Indies most of it was foreign in origin, nationalization would have no such effects as the death duties would accrue to the UK state and not the West Indian government. At a time of shortage of capital, the proposal really amounted to one of repatriating foreign capital already in the West Indies. At a time when this fact was increasingly becoming apparent in the West Indian territories themselves and legislation was being passed seeking to induce foreign capitalists to come in and establish pioneer industries, the hothouse atmosphere of the individual in the alien community committed the student to an adherence to the outmoded and unrealistic ideology.

West Indian Culture

The nationalism of the West Indian had little to fall back on. It became tedious to be always seeking to show the British that the way of life of the West Indies was the same as in England, that West Indians wore 'British' dress, ate 'British' food, spoke English and so on. Such an admission frequently put the individual at a disadvantage because there were in fact differences. These differences usually were extremely irritating to the West Indian who resented the claim of the British that their way of doing things was best. It smacked of superiority and he was forced to concede the claim once he accepted the fact that West Indian 'culture' was a derivative. The difficulty of the situation is illustrated in the instance at a students' hostel when one of the leaders of the West Indians thanked the management (who had gone to great pains to produce a typical English Christmas dinner) for giving them exactly the type of dinner they were accustomed to at home – a truly West Indian dinner. There was great displeasure at realizing the derivative character of the 'truly West Indian'. Students were always under attack by the radicals for 'imitating Englishmen' and not being truly West Indian. Yet, so often the 'truly West Indian' of the radical turned out to be merely something obtained some generations before from the UK.

Because of this there was a frantic search for something different, which could become symbolic of West Indian identity. The assertion of Caribbean solidarity – as in the case of the West Indian university – was one means of attempting to make up the deficiency and of identifying the West Indians as non-British. The Union placed the development of their cultural life as sufficiently important to warrant the appointment of a commission. In this search for difference, the WISU took up all aspects of cultural life in the West Indies; West Indian dramatics, dances, the steel-band – all found a special response. It even led to an assertion of solidarity with Africa. Interest was shown in African music and dance, African speakers were invited to give addresses and one African intellectual was asked to prepare a select list of books on West African history for circulation to members of the Union.

The most explicit statement of the beliefs of the students on the cultural aspects of things was given at the WISU general conference of 11 August 1950 in the "Report of the Commission on Cultural Factors in the West Indies". The group began by defining culture as "the synthesis of all the creative efforts and attainments of a people which spring from and are fired with that people's basic natural characteristics". There were in addition "some members (who) felt that racial as well as national characteristics played an important part in the growth of a culture. In short, culture was a way of life which embraced everything that was believed or practised by any given community." Having accepted this definition, the group set out to discover what were in fact the basic national (and racial) characteristics.

> It was considered necessary for obvious reasons to confine our discussions to the British West Indies but the group felt there were strong arguments for thinking of the whole Caribbean region as a simple cultural unit and deplored the lack of social intercourse with our non-British neighbours due to international barriers set up by the metropolitan governments.

The basic ingredients, then, of a West Indian way of life were found to fall roughly into the following categories:

(i) Religious beliefs and superstitions, for example, the shango and shouter cults, obeah, pocomania and the like.

(ii) Manners, habits and customs which stem from religious beliefs and folk activities, for example, the practice of holiday 'wakes', the notable instance of nine-nights, types of West Indies cooking customs and so on.

(iii) Folklore, music, songs and dances, proverbs, games, dialect and so on. In this group, the West Indies were richly endowed with folk material most of which was inextricably interwoven in the foregoing sections. Examples too numerous to be detailed fully include:

Folklore: Anancy stories, traced back to the Ashanti stories of the Gold Coast.

Music: The calypso, steel band.

Songs: Jamaican folk songs, the calypso, the gayap, work songs, sankey and shouter hymns.

Dances: Bolo, bongo, calinda, a bel air dance, limbo and the like.

Leadership and the WISU

Although the WISU membership comprised only a small proportion of eligible students, and although the bulk of its membership was concentrated in London, there can be little doubt that the organization could truly be taken as representing in an appropriate fashion the majority of West Indian students.

Because of the nature of the situation, the students who make successful adjustment to the host society do so on an individual, personal basis. Leadership of the West Indian group as a group therefore, had to come largely on the basis of protest rather than welfare, or to put it more accurately, the welfare had to be largely conceived in terms of protest.

Whatever the nature of the dispute, the solidarity of the students, whether expressed through the Colonial Hostels Students Association or through the WISU, made it quite impossible to assess any claim on its merits. Thus on one occasion, it became possible for a student guilty of gross misconduct with one of the maids to maintain that he was the object of victimization and to enrol the whole weight of student opinion behind his "just cause". Similarly, delinquencies on the part of members of colonial organizations were kept quiet. In one of the most outstanding cases, the secretary of the Colonial Organization was attacked as fraudulently claiming to possess certain degrees. To some of the English visitors present at the meeting, this was an allegation of such consequence that they felt that the organization faced a moral crisis. However, many present felt that the exposure of such a delinquency would only hold the coloured men and their organizations up to ridicule. Consequently, they were prepared to consider the matter of slight consequence. It was felt that if the allegations were true, they should be considered in the light of the service rendered to the colonial cause.

One interesting feature of student leadership is that in spite of the high proportion of private to public students, it is clear that the scholarship holders play a much more active part in setting the tone of the West Indians as a group. This was because the scholarship students had issues that they could raise. They could afford to be unrealistic and demanding while the private student found that he had to be economical and realistic.

There may have been an additional factor at work as well. Many of the cases of people on public scholarships had won them in open competition of a quite fierce nature. Having won an open scholarship, they were cast in the public eye as playing a special role. Not only did the community hope that the individual would return to give it some leadership, but it felt that such leadership should fall to by right. In any case, if no public leadership was forthcoming, the community still obtained positive satisfaction by identifying itself with the independent professional. The scholarship holder was not uninfluenced by this evaluation in the community. Indeed, it was usually family pressure based on the acceptance of these values which had goaded him to give his utmost in preparation for the examination. Finding himself in a situation which called for leadership of protest against governmental organization, the scholarship holder was often not unprepared for the role.

Of course, there were many private students, particularly among the lawyers, who conceived of themselves as playing leadership roles on their return home. More usually, public activity was conceived as aiding the private professional career. The money spent on private education was an investment which, to be worthwhile, should pay dividends not merely in prestige but in cash. Private students were therefore more prone to accept the narrowly conceived social prestige which went to the accomplished professional and to allow the public student to take the lead in the espousal of the radical colonial cause.

Another aspect of leadership that is of interest was the problem so often found in radical groups of maintaining radicalism while rising to the responsibilities of mature leadership. This was a problem not confined to the WISU but affected all colonial student organizations and the leadership of the colonial hostels in particular. It was not only in the hothouse atmosphere of international conferences that accusations of treachery could develop, although they might on such occasions take on a peculiarly bitter form. Any advocacy of moderation led the leader to be suspect. So good were personal intimate relations within the group of people who led the WISU over the years that no one seriously considered that the more conservative individuals were seeking purely personal advancement in adopting their point of view. What is interesting is that the accusation should have been made at all precisely because in most cases, the good faith of the 'traitor' was not seriously questioned. It is more an indication of the need for release of aggression against the host society than of hostility against the individual. His condemnation was purely because his standpoint interfered with the rationalizing and challenging of aggression.

It indicates at the same time that the need, although powerful, does not in the usual case serve a dominant or central value for the individual, since it is contained within bonds which allow for the continuance of good interpersonal relationships.

A Note on the West African Students Union

The West African Students Union (WASU) was founded in 1924 even after separate Gold Coast and Nigerian student groups had been formed. Mr Philip Garique,[23] writing about these developments in his article "The West African Students in Africa", seemed to assume that the development of a West African nationalism was a natural response and corresponded to the geographical unity of the area. This is surprising for it is an elementary commonplace of sociology that social life does not reflect the geographical in a direct fashion at all. Indeed, in the light of later developments, it would appear that the conception of a West African nationalism was a temporary aberration which reflected the fact that the 'nationalism' of West Africa was then confined to a relatively small group of educated people and had not achieved any mass support. On Mr Garique's own evidence, there was the competition of both narrower (Gold Coast, Nigeria) nationalisms and the broader 'African' nationalism. This nationalism may in fact, as he alleges, have been a reaction to colour prejudice and discrimination but the specific form which the 'nationalism' took still remains to be explained. Colour discrimination could indeed have also taken (as it did in many instances of other colonials) the even wider form of expressing solidarity between all coloured peoples. It seems most likely that the educated progressive Africans, relatively few in number had their self-confidence increased by the larger 'West African' concept. Moreover, the concept to a certain extent corresponded to an administrative political division which made some sense.

For a period at any rate, the concept of West African nationalism overrode the narrower national and tribal loyalties which have latterly shown their strength. When the organization was formed, it was a wholly independent organization and sought its finances from voluntary sources. The initial sum for its establishment came from the voluntary subscription raised in Africa. Eventually, however, shortly before the outbreak of World War II, the WASU received a grant from the Colonial Office for its work.

This problem of the independence of the WASU was and is still a matter of some urgency. The WASU was able to acquire a hostel and to maintain it adequately only through the support which the Union obtained from powerful private British patronage as well as from the Colonial Office. This support has led to some formal genuflection before the spirit of brotherhood and cooperation but on the whole, there was the same predominance of the radical ideology which we have seen operative in the case of the West Indians.

Roughly the same process of accommodation in practice to the authorities while affirming ideological independence took place. The grants to the WASU increased steadily in size at the very moment when nationalism in the colonial areas was increasing sharply. Indeed, in defence, it appears that the WASU was forced to assume a radical pose in order to demonstrate publicly that they had not in fact sold their souls.

In the light of subsequent development, the contrast between the early struggles between the WASU and the Colonial Office and the later ones between advocates of different policies in the WISU are interesting. In the early period when the Colonial Office set about the establishment of Aggrey House, the officials of the WASU agitated against the project alleging that this was a countermove to keep students under the control of the Colonial Office.

Although such allegations about the Colonial Office by no means ceased, the grounds of objection took a different form. The postwar influx of colonial students led to a totally different evaluation of the hostel problem of colonials. Pressure for accommodation became so acute that the protests were directed against the Colonial Office for *not providing* suitable accommodation and more colonial hostels. It was clear that the concept of a cultural centre or home for any of the national colonial areas could not in any way conflict with the establishment of hostels.

The pattern of agreement between the Colonial Office and the WASU which eventually emerged appears to be the direction in which the WISU is moving now that a West Indian Students' Centre financed by the local governments has been set up.

Chapter 9

Relations between the WISU and Other Organizations

The self-identification of the West Indian student – even of the most militant – was only partial. To some extent, the colonial identification remained. Both as a result and as a consequence of this, the WISU found itself in constant contact with a series of colonial organizations, and with many British organizations concerned with the colonial cause. The most important of these was the League of Coloured Peoples.

The League of Coloured Peoples had a grandiose name and on the face of it embraced all the non-European peoples of the globe. In point of fact, it tended to become a colonial and more specifically a West Indian organization. Moreover, in the greater part of its existence it centred around the personality of its founder and president for many years, Dr Moodie, who was a West Indian medical practitioner domiciled in the UK.

The organization was largely supported by permanent or semipermanent residents in the UK. Student activity therefore was only a relatively minor part of its activities. The organization was largely Christian in inspiration and held out the ideals of cooperation among peoples rather than conflict. Opponents of Dr Moodie often alleged that the leaders of the movement were all his puppets and that the organization instead of fighting for the rights of coloured people used the discontent of the mass in order to further Moodie's own individual cause. There can be little doubt that Dr Moodie conceived of the League of Coloured Peoples as an 'accommodating' rather than a conflict group, as a welfare rather than a political organization. As such, the organization naturally came in for recognition in a variety of official ways. This appeared to lend some substance to the radical claim.

When the decision to start the WISU was made, there was some misgiving as to the desirability of such a move on the part of the leaders of the League of Coloured Peoples. It was thought that some arrangement could be made to have a student wing within the League. The students, however, were very conscious of themselves *as students*. They tended to be impatient of already established authority and the decision was made without much heartburning or difficulty to start a separate organization. Throughout the period of their existence, the question of cooperation and the consequent mutual accusations of lack of cooperation from the two organizations were ever present.

The situation was rendered more complicated because the League of Coloured Peoples at the time that the student organization was formed, was pursuing an objective which the WISU itself was to come to consider one of the main aims and objects of its activity. The president of the League of Coloured Peoples had just returned from a tour of the West Indies seeking to collect funds from governments and individuals for the establishment of a West Indian cultural centre in London.

Further, the League of Coloured Peoples during the first few years of the life of WISU was passing through a great organizational crisis. Other organizations besides the WISU catering for the growing West Indian population were being founded. There was the Caribbean Labour Congress which sought to attract the workers and the radical pro-labour section of the intelligentsia. Again, within the League itself the postwar discontent brought a desire on the part of the radical element to transfer the organization from a 'welfare' into a conflict organization.

Thus, when the president of the League returned from the West Indies after his partially successful effort to raise funds, he found that the radical element in the organization had laid plans for the capture of the organization in order to put an end to his lifetime presidency. On the eve of the threatened deposition, Dr Moodie died, and the radical element took over control of the organization. Thereafter, whenever conflicts took place within the League, attempts were made to make use of student opinion. Eventually, the League accepted the fact of the WISU's existence and the relationship became cordial if not close. Members of the WISU executive actually served on that of the League. This was facilitated by the fact that for a period, the League became more of a general colonial protest organization and therefore came more into conflict with the similarly oriented Caribbean Labour Congress than with the student organization. After this brief period of radicalism, however, the League became once more and is at present more of a welfare organization. Periodically, however, there is an eruption of the radical element.

The idea of dances, socials, job placement, the working of responsible representations, the creation of a cultural centre — became the paramount features of the League's activities. These activities did not appear as fruitful of possible conflict as they did in the earlier stages because the students from the West Indies ceased to be the most significant (numerically) element in the coloured population of London. The new working class immigration from the West Indies got under way a few years after the war and the League was able to cater for these people. It is interesting to see how it developed roughly the same activities and the same ideology as the WISU. Clearly, the position of all coloured persons was the same and led to precisely the same types of reaction. The definition of the people from the West Indies as coloured did not in fact serve to override the social class differences in the West Indies. The dances, socials and so on of the League developed on quite different lines and in quite a different atmosphere from those of the WISU.

The League of Coloured Peoples was only one of a series of organizations interested in the coloured and colonial problem. The range of these organizations was wide. Their effect upon the rank and file of the Union was not direct but very great. The leadership, having defined the situation in a radical fashion, was reinforced in their interpretation by the existence of other organizations and leaders more or less in agreement with their point of view.

Of special interest because of our discussion of the general relations between the West Indian and the African was the WASU. There was profound admiration among the West Indians for the achievements of the WASU. The name WISU was indeed fashioned after the model and the objective of acquiring a home of its own derived largely from a desire to emulate the older and better isolated organization.

Cooperation was not however as easy to achieve as it appeared at first. Although there was the 'colonial solidarity', there was the fact that most West Indians including the leadership never felt socially at home with the West Africans. The marks of goodwill such as the sending of complimentary tickets for dances and official functions to the officers of the WISU often went unattended. Again, the 'common colonial problem' around which the organizations sought to achieve some measure of unity, apart from that of accommodation, broke down into a series of discrete problems. This was to a certain extent recognized by those who strove for a common colonial solidarity. Yet, in some vague way, it was felt that 'coloured' and 'colonial' solidarity would overcome all the difficulties.

Thus for instance, we find that the WASU invited the WISU to "a meeting of commonwealth students organizations in this country for the purpose of creating a broad organization to meet our common needs and common problems". They felt that "such a body would fulfil a very useful purpose in providing a means of making our joint view felt on common problems such as welfare, accommodation in Britain and the combating of any form of racialism and discrimination and the promotion and coordination of cultural activities". Such a body might also present a more effective and united viewpoint in relation to the British National Union of Students and Scottish Union of Students.

The imputation pointed out that it was realized that the Commonwealth students' organizations in Britain were all of different structures, with different aims, but it was felt that on common problems there was room for such a coordinating body which could support "joint activity on questions where there is unanimous agreement between us".

In practice, there were few points upon which WISU ever made representations to the British Students' Organizations. Indeed, one of the mainstays of the organization, the agitation for increased allowances never found favour with the British students who tended to think of the colonial allowances as being generous as compared to the British. Their approach to the problem was rather different. They regarded the 'special' treatment accorded the West Indian and colonial as a point through which pressure could be exercised for the levelling up of British students' allowances. In the other fields mentioned, there seemed little that could be achieved with a new organization that could not be achieved through more informal methods of collaboration. The desire for a new organization was more an expression of the sentiment of 'colonial unity' rather than of any practical need. It was a reaction to the common status given the colonial in the host society.

Occasionally, this desire for colonial sentiment so far from helping a practical cause was more of a hindrance and a source of embarrassment. Thus after the hurricane of 1951 in Jamaica, the WISU busied itself in doing some sort of relief work – in raising funds, soliciting aid and so on. They were so close to the disaster that they adopted attitudes of responsibility and were duly grateful for aid of any sort that was forthcoming. To others less deeply involved, the matter was an opportunity for political action. Thus the *African League* whose motto was "Freedom for Africa" called a protest meeting in September 1951 against

> the totally inadequate amount of monetary aid offered the inhabitants of Jamaica who have suffered most cruelly from the recent tragic hurricane disaster, by the British Government. This approach to the economic problems of that territory, and for that matter all subjugated territories is all the more repugnant when consideration is applied to the official estimate of £50,000,000 as being required to rehabilitate the devastated area.

The WISU was asked to undertake kindly to interest as many of their members as possible, "since the issues involved are such as to be capable of arousing the utmost indignation of all oppressed persons".

Again, we find this same organization appealing for support for another 'colonial', subjugated peoples' cause (26 July 1951).

> I am instructed by the executive council of the African League to draw your attention to the clandestine attempt of the British Government to withhold passports of 'subject' peoples thereby restricting them from travelling abroad. The recent debate in the House of Commons is a classic evidence in point, and it is desirable that all 'colonial' organizations in Britain must join issues to combat the implementation of such a vicious treat.
>
> I would explain that prior to the debate mentioned above the African League has been receiving reports dealing with the British Government's refusal to issue passports to intending 'colonial' travellers and that the League undertook to interest both the UK Government as well as local governments in the matter. Strangely enough, the reply from the UK Government shifted responsibility on local governments, some of whom denied any intention to meddle in the liberty of movement of 'colonial' applicants.

From the foregoing, it would appear that the authorities are well cognizant of the growing resentment of 'colonials' against any form of control of movement, but as usual the British Government intends to proceed with imposing its will on those concerned. Quite apart from this disgraceful intrigue, there seems to be a great measure of connivancy by the USA Government, and the confiscation of Robinbson's passport lends additional weight to the League's contention.

Perhaps your organization will support the League's protest against such highly nefarious practice, for if those who are known for their notoriety are allowed to proceed unchecked, the impact will be more far reaching on succeeding generations, and it is in this light therefore that the League seeks to solicit your immediate support.

Another organization of some influence was the Congress of Peoples against Imperialism, even though members of the WISU who attended meetings found that sometimes great difficulty was experienced in drawing a quorum. However, the grandiose title of the organization coupled with its general, anticolonial nature meant that it could function as a sponsoring organization for visiting speakers from the colonies. In this manner and by taking up various causes which would never have come to the ears of the separate organization, the Congress of Peoples against Imperialism helped to develop the general feeling of colonial solidarity. The fact that a member of Parliament (Fenner Brockway) was associated with the Congress also gave it a certain amount of prestige and respectability. One African student has stated that if there were a popular selection for the presidency of a United States of Africa the most likely candidate would be Fenner Brockway. The special position he enjoyed was due both to the fact that this organization tackled all 'anti-imperial' sources, while the position as a member of parliament gave him prestige and an opportunity to air grievances.

As an example of the type of problem with which the Congress of Peoples against Imperialism concerned itself, we may mention an invitation to the executive of the WISU to send a delegation to a meeting at a committee room in the House of Commons "to plan a campaign on the arrest of Ignatius Musazi, President of the Uganda Farmers' Union, who was arrested on his return to Uganda". The facts about his case were enclosed; the WISU was also asked to formulate a resolution of protest to be sent to the secretary of state for the colonies and the governor of Uganda.

Finally, because of the emotional importance attached to the South African issue, we may use as an example of 'colonial' contact the appeal of the London secretariat of the South African Indian Congress.

This is to bring to your attention the arrival of Dr Donges, the Member of Interior in the cabinet of the Malan Government to this country within the next week.

You may no doubt be aware that Dr Douges is the one directly responsible for the recent series of anti-European laws to be added to the already stringent race measures on the statute books of South Africa.

We are sure in the belief that the policies of racial discrimination and segregation and the oppression of the non-European that goes with it, which is the kernel of the member state policy, is odious to the deep seated sentiments and contrary to these cherished beliefs of democratic people in general and your organization in particular.

Our organization is planning to utilize the visit of an important member of the Malan Government to this country as an occasion for registering a protest under a broadly representative sponsorship whereby the attitudes and feelings of the people in this country are brought to the attention of the South African Authorities.

The WISU was accordingly asked to sign a letter of protest to be handed in at South Africa House. The letter read as follows:

We the undersigned deeply conscious of the proposed duty resting on each and every civilized being to foster racial tolerance and for the cause of world peace and human happiness, and being aware that racial oppression and the suppression of the will and the desire of nationalities for self-expression and progress must foster, as between peoples and nations deep and powerful conflicts that are wasteful of human resources must condemn the conscious state policy of race and colour discrimination or 'apartheid' as practised in the Union of South Africa, with particular regard to:

(a) The Group Areas Act, whereby all people in the Union of South Africa, shall henceforth be segregated in predetermined and scheduled racial areas.

(b) The Mixed Marriages Act and the Immorality Act which makes unprecedented inroads into the personal liberty of the individual.

(c) The Suppression of Communism Act, whereby all organizations and individuals demanding the extension of democracy to all inhabitants of the country stand the threat of being suppressed.

(d) The Population Registration Act, whereby the individual's economic social and political status in life shall be determined primarily on the grounds of racial origin, as inconsistent with the civilized way of life and repugnant to the maintenance of amity and peace between nations.

Of course, the colonial organizations were not the only ones to woo West Indian students, nor was the colonial point of view the only one with which the Union was inundated. The special case of the appeal of the communist organization will be examined in detail later, but here some consideration will be given to the appeal of other parties and groups to win the political support of West Indian and other colonial students.

The Conservative Party had no appeal to the mass of the West Indian people at all. It was identified with all the worst traits of the British. The general conservativism of the British was something quite incomprehensible to the West Indian. Because it was the conventional thing to do, because of their symbolic significance with regard to status in the West Indies, there were certain ceremonies which were attended, for example, a debate in Parliament, the changing of the guard. By and large, however, any ceremony which showed an addiction to ancient custom was an additional illustration of old-fogeyism to the West Indian. In these respects, the West Indian had come to a large extent under the influence of American ideas. Change was, ipso facto, a good thing; the 'progressive', 'modern' attitude to life was emphasized and conservativism was the opposite of progress.

Moreover, the ideology of the Empire and the Commonwealth as presented by the Conservative Party was not acceptable. Its symbolism was outmoded and hence could easily be labelled reactionary. Although the majority of West Indians shared the belief of most colonials in England that the party differences in colonial policy were small, negligible or nonexistent, this did not render the Conservative Party as acceptable as the Labour Party.

Indeed, this allegation of identity of outlook usually developed as a criticism of the Labour Party and as an answer to its more emotionally satisfying appeal to colonials. The accusation levelled at labour being pseudoradical and really conservative at heart was merely another way of saying that they were as bad as the worst. "All Britishers are the same."

The only occasion on which any enthusiasm for the conservative cause was shown was when it became personally profitable for the individual. It is true that one West Indian student was actually discovered to be the secretary of a local conservative party organization. But when students went to the polls in country and general elections, there can be little doubt that they voted heavily in favor of the non-conservative parties.

Thus, when the Conservative Overseas Bureau organized a special conference for discussing colonial affairs, there was some difficulty in getting most West Indians to attend even though scholarships were offered. Many of the leaders of the WISU felt that it was their duty to try and educate the English public as regards the colonies and the colour issue. Any legitimate platform was seized upon – even the conservatives. This was a patriotic duty and had nothing to do with the internal political division of the British people. From their point of view of the 'national interest', the British were all one. The Labour Party was in fact as bad as the Conservatives, if it served the cause of raising the status of the West Indian politically. On the other hand, there were those who took a friendly exploitative attitude towards conservative interest in the colonies. They would speak of their colonies on Empire Day or attend a Conservative Party summer school provided they got a fee or had their expenses paid.

The concern of the Conservative Party with contacts in the colonies and with the problems of colonials in England is of recent origin. At the time of the foundation of the WISU, no special organization existed for tackling such problems but a few years later the Conservative Overseas Bureau was formed which set about actively tackling these problems.

On the other hand, in the case of the Labour Party the concern with the colonial problem was of long standing. People from the West Indies were well aware of the names of Creech Jones, Fenner Brockway and others who were interested in the colonial cause. Moreover, Dr Hyacinth Morgan, a Grenadian who did not deny her West Indian origin was a member of the Labour Party and was actively in touch with many persons and organizations in the West Indies. Moreover, the Labour Party had been for many years in the wilderness and the tone of its criticism, whether due to the irresponsibility of the opposition or not, was much more congenial to public opinion.

Moreover, there was an organization, the Fabian Colonial Bureau, of many years' standing which showed an interest in colonial problems. Indeed, one of the problems of the Fabian Colonial Bureau was the explanation to angry colonial students of its position and role within the Labour Party. The bureau was so consciously identified with socialist policies that the contradiction between expression of opinion by members of the bureau and official party policy was a source of confusion and acute embarrassment. The situation was even more complicated because in the initial postwar period, the Labour government was in power. When Creech Jones became secretary of state for the colonies, he was strongly abused in colonial student circles. First, there was the distinction between his responsible actions as a minister of state, and his agitational role in parliament when as champion of colonial issues, he was ready to use any legitimate stick with which to beat the government. Defenders of British colonial policy at the time were fond of pointing out that the colonial student did not appreciate the true function of an opposition, and that it was wrong to expect a detailed correspondence between opposition, criticism and governmental policy. This defence did not dispense with the difficulty, however. Colonial students who were quite aware of the political process resented the charge of ignorance. Rather, they thought that the leaders of the Fabian Colonial Bureau did not appreciate the nature of the metropolitan-colonial relationship. To take the colonial issue and make use of it as a matter of purely internal (UK) party political interest was not giving it the attention it deserved. It smacked of 'using' the colonial question without regard to colonial sentiment. It was this exploitation of the colonial issue as a party matter and not misunderstanding of the British constitution that caused offence.

Colonial students found that supporters of the British Labour Party were usually just as ignorant of colonial problems as the rank and file of the Conservative Party. Thus one Negro West Indian found himself being congratulated at a May Day gathering. On further questioning, he discovered that it was on having achieved independence. This was shortly after the grant of independent status to India and he had been mistaken for an Indian.

The realities of official policy were often brought dramatically to the attention of the student leadership. Thus, a colonial student speaking on behalf of the League of Coloured Peoples in a Fabian Congress on The Democratic Future of the British Empire found that one of the speakers was unable to attend the Congress (Mr Bottomley), because he was attending the United Nations meeting in New York, where he defended the Union of South Africa against the unwanted intervention of the United Nations. In his speech which was read and in all the other speeches, it became clear that the 'democratic future' of the British Empire was conceived as the development of collaboration between the already established dominions. The colonial empire was conceived as remaining, in the immediate future at any rate, in a stage of tutelage.

In actual practice, the support of the Union of South Africa did more to alienate West Indian students from the Labour Party than any other single source. The thinking of the student was stereotyped. He did not appreciate the complexities of the situation. Bombarded by news items and correspondence which stressed the race issue in terms of black and white, and preoccupied with the problems of racial discrimination himself, he was satisfied with nothing short of complete and total denunciation of South Africa.

The other issue of colonial policy with which the West Indian student felt most involved was the issue of Kenya. The complexities of constitutional development in the Gold Coast and Nigeria interested him, but not so greatly as the idea of the white settler. The West Indies was an area of the white dominance at home. Stories of white oppression in Kenya or of the dangers of South African policy spreading northwards aroused his worst fears. This fear of white settlers was also very apparent in the reactions to the Evans Commission Report (1948). This report, which dealt with the possibilities of West Indian as well as European Refugees settlement in British Guiana and British Honduras, recommended that the hinterland of British Guiana should be opened up to European settlement. This suggestion met with the bitterest of responses. The WISU wrote: "In British Guiana, however, the commission considers it possible to settle at least 20,000 Europeans, as compared with 22,400 West Indian immigrants. This is referred to somewhat ambiguously in the circumstances as relatively limited European settlement." Further:

> The question of European settlement especially is a critical one, and the Commission has not lessened its difficulty by proposing peasant-collective settlement for Europeans as against plantation settlement for West Indians. To propose different patterns of social and economic organization for these two different groups is to emphasize rather than lessen the gap which in the present state of evolution divides the white and coloured people. If it were decided, which is a matter of some considerable doubt, that European settlement on a large scale within the predominantly coloured areas of the Caribbean was an undertaking acceptable to the present inhabitants, it would surely be the wisest policy to ensure equality of status and of opportunity by submitting all immigrants to a similar plan of settlement.

The commission itself had declared, in words which have the ring of truth, that

The Colonies of British Guiana and British Honduras are, and must remain too small to afford without serious prejudice, the distractions of artificial division into self-segregated majority and minority Communities based on racial or geographical origin.

Yet, what else could be the result of the plan proposed by the commission to introduce into British Guiana, for instance, a strongly organized racial, religious and social minority group of Europeans, placed at a strategic point of penetration, as indeed the commission itself points out, for the colonization of large tracts of the colony's area? "After all," they remark, with reference to the proposed area of white settlement, "this area must be the centre from which population of the future interior will spread, if at all."

We call the attention of all West Indians to these remarks because we feel that they contain tremendous implications for the future of British Guiana and the future of the West Indies as a whole. In terms of mere numbers, the West Indies are predominantly a coloured area. Yet it is hardly necessary for us to point out that even now, when European predominance seems to be on the wane as a result of the growth in political power and economic importance of the coloured populations, it might still be possible for a European group colonizing systematically the interior areas of British Guiana, seriously to disturb the present figures of the coloured peoples of the West Indian area toward self-government. The possibility is not precluded. The example of Africa alone offers ominous warning.

Where any serious efforts were made to tackle nonpolitically the political question of the relationship of the colonies to the mother country, the difficulty was encountered that except in the case of organizations like the Fabian Colonial Bureau, there was a group of people with an intimate knowledge of the colonial empire, who could be readily called upon. Indeed, some students felt superior because of their own knowledge of their homeland. Colonial Office officials who had never visited the areas with whose administration they were concerned, sometimes spoke to knowledgeable students in order to get a better background on contemporary events, and officials going out to the West Indies frequently showed a desire to meet students from the relevant colony. This placed the student in a position where his superiority was manifest and this did not make for easy acceptance of a British definition of the colonial problem.

One of the ways in which the aggressive feelings of the West Indian were expressed was through taking advantage of the ignorance of colonial conditions. Among the stories which received general circulation and approval were those in which anthropologists interested in 'native' life had been easily misled by fabrications about native life. And the fact that someone training social workers told West Indies welfare trainees that in doing their work in the villages they should make sure that they contacted their village headman, was frequently adduced as proof of the English academic's ignorance of life as it was lived in the West Indies.

The shortage of knowledgeable people and the development of such attitudes did not render special courses directed towards colonials very acceptable. Special courses were designed but these had to ignore completely the individual differences in the colonies which were so important to the West Indian group. In so far as there was a common colonial ideology, it was an ideology of protest and any attempt to deal with 'colonial' issues awakened these sentiments of protest.

The course which had most bearing on the colonial problem was a series Parliament and the Colonies Today. The brochure describing the course ran as follows:

PARLIAMENT AND THE COLONIES TODAY

A series of discussions under this general heading had been arranged at No. 1 Hans Crescent during this term. The series is intended to demonstrate the machinery of central government in this country, illustrated, as far as possible, from colonial issues in parliament.

Through the cooperation of the Colonial Office and of the three political parties in parliament, we have been fortunate enough to secure highly qualified speakers to lead these discussions.

A large number of the residents at Hans Crescent will be attending the discussions but we would also welcome as many colonial students, who are not limited so that admission will be by ticket.

In each case the meeting would begin at 8:15 pm. The talks would be followed by an interval during which refreshments would be served and the members of the audience would break up into groups which would formulate questions which the speaker would be asked to deal with.

The following meetings have been arranged:
- April 23 Discussion led by a representative of the Colonial Office; Sir Charles Jeffries, KCMC, OBE, Joint Deputy Under-Secretary of State, Colonial Office.

- April 30 Discussion led by a representative of the Government: The Parliamentary Under-Secretary of State for the Colonies, Mr. J.F. Cock, MP.
- May 7 Discussion led by a representative of the Conservative Party: Mr. Alan Lennox-Boyd, MP (Formerly Parliamentary Secretary, Ministry of Labour; Parliamentary Secretary, Ministry of Home Security; Parliamentary Secretary, Ministry of Aircraft Production).
- May 24 Discussion led by a representative of the Liberal Party; Mr R. Hopkin Morris, KC, MP Member of Parliamentary Delegation to East Africa, 1928; Member of Palestine Commission, 1929.

May 28 Forum.
Hugh Paget
Director, Hans Crescent.

The fact that all parties presented the case, was not likely to lead to a better appreciation of the role of parliament and the organization of parties. Rather, it led to a further reinforcement of the belief that all the parties were really identical as regards policy. The presentation of a 'national front' by the British awakened a united 'colonial' response. Any systematic bonds between the British and the colonial lay paradoxically through radicalism and 'anti-British' sentiment.

Chapter 10

The Communists
and the Colonials

The general position of the West Indian was similar to that of most colonials: a heightened self-consciousness was coupled with strong feelings of hostility and resentment towards their immediate environment. Thus with the rise of the Mau Mau movement in Kenya, there was strong emotional identification with Mau Mau as opposed to the forces of law and order. Here, as in other cases, there was no desire to examine the case on its merits and the simple 'colonialist' ideology of 'British' exploiters oppressing the colonial, even to the extent of waging war and using armed forces, sufficed for explaining the situation. The issue was clearly one of 'imperialism' versus 'the people'.

In keeping with this emotional identification with any radical movement in the colonies, there was a corresponding distrust of anyone who in any way showed disagreement with the particular form of opposition which colonial unrest took. Such an individual was likely to be described as a traitor. Thus the term 'loyal Kikuyu' came to be used as a term of abuse for anyone who criticized in any way the radical colonial cause.

This term itself naturally arose after the development of the Mau Mau movement but before this, there were similar terms used. Thus the term 'mission-trained', directed chiefly but not exclusively against Africans, carried much the same emotional connotation.

As a result of this attitude, the support of anticolonial causes was unequivocal and unswerving. The complexities surrounding the issues notwithstanding, the majority of students interpreted the issue in Kenya, as elsewhere, as a straight fight between blacks claiming freedom, with the whites reimposing oppression with the aid of a few lick spittles or 'loyal Kikuyus'. The same position was adopted in the case of the suspension of the British Guiana constitution. A few students, Catholics, taking issue with the general body of opinion, supported the British government. But by and large, the students were opposed to the suspension of the constitution and the introduction of troops – whether they happened to argue with an Englishman or amongst themselves.

The reaction at the meetings called by the students to hear the radicals Jagan and Burnham on the one hand and the conservative opposition which supported the British government was most marked. In one case there was a sympathetic, in the other a very hostile crowd.

This tendency which we have noted on the part of the West Indian to denounce opponents in the field of politics as traitors and stooges is not of course something confined to the West Indian student. It is often to be found within the ranks of the radical movement in the West Indies itself. It bears very many similarities to the communist denunciation of 'Trotskyite traitors' and 'fascists'. In the case of the West Indies, the sources of this suspicion of deviation are twofold. In the first place, there is among all West Indians a more or less strong desire to obtain integration with British society. As we have seen, much of the radicalism of the student springs from the rejection of this desire for assimilation. Although there is sometimes a defensive denial by West Indians, these facts are well known to all and sundry. The suspicion of the willingness of West Indians to change sides is therefore not without some rational grounding. The indiscriminate way in which any moderate is attacked as "falling over backwards", or "seeking a job with the Colonial Office" indicates that more is involved than a critical assessment of tendencies to assimilation.

The real root of these attacks of 'treachery' would appear to be based upon certain psychological tendencies within the self. The attacker is fighting not merely against tendencies to assimilation in other persons but against similar tendencies within himself. The dark-skinned nationalist and revolutionary whose favourite song was "The Girl that I Marry Has Got to Be as Soft and as Pink as a Nursery", and who proudly displayed his English girlfriends, was not unaware of the potency of the attractions to abandon his position. His attacks were all the more bitter on that account. It not only discredited an opponent, but also proved to the world and himself how genuine a radical he was.

Moreover, the situation of the student in the UK produced many hostile impulses. One way – and for most persons the most effective way – of dealing with those impulses was to see the situation in terms of simple black and white. This 'simple sociology', this categorization of the English/British as essentially alien, hostile and aggressive, justified the other stereotype of the radical colonial as oppressed, victimized, struggling on behalf of a righteous cause. Any attempt at rational or careful assessment of the situation appeared to the radical remote from the realities of life as he knew them. As soon as they made any impact on his thinking, he had to face the alternative of either rejecting them out of hand, or changing his basic pattern of thought. To some extent, he found himself placed in the same situation of coloured students from the USA who, accustomed to thinking in terms of simple black-white dichotomy, were forced to face up to the complex colour situation in Britain. Like so many of these students, he could not easily abandon a simple, moral, legitimate outlet for his aggression. Nor is the reaction difficult to understand. It was unlikely that the feelings of hostility created by his environment would cease. Without a legitimate target for aggression, they might have to be turned against the self with the result of even deeper wounds to his self-esteem. Recognition, identification and proper evaluation of the source of aggressive feelings implied a degree of personal maturity hardly to be found among a young group facing serious problems in an alien land.

Moreover, these attacks were never productive of much harm. The accusation of being a 'Colonial Office stooge' while hurtful, was usually interpreted as being more an expression of resentment against the British than against the person attacked. The individual concerned usually hastened to show, in one form or another, his genuine 'colonialism'. Only on one occasion did any such accusation have any far reaching consequences. In the case of attacks on the Colonial Office itself, the attackers were likewise exempt. In spite of the belief in spies, in victimization and so on, the students were aware that they did in fact possess a large measure of freedom. The Colonial Office was in itself subject to the pressure of democratic opinion. Moreover, the framework of values within which it operated permitted freedom of speech. Indeed, the establishment of the Welfare Department so far from reflecting vindictiveness showed a protective attitude towards the colonial student. Students were not unaware of these facts even if they did not influence greatly their expressions of opinion.

Early Contact with the Communists

The first contacts which the communists had with members of the WISU were informal ones. In the individual colleges, the communist societies and the communists within the Socialist Society (or Soc-Soc as it was popularly called) tried to draw in as many colonial students as possible into their ranks. However, West Indians found that their area was not particularly rewarding for protest movements. Nearly all the delegations of West Indian politicians which came to the UK, came cap in hand asking for some economic relief, which included either dealing with the 'capitalist' problems in alliance with capitalists, or bargaining better prices for West Indian produce. In addition, they often came with some constitutional issue not capable of dramatic presentation. For this reason, the communists found other colonial areas much richer material to exploit. West Indians got dragged into attending meetings of these organizations or into the organizations themselves, on general 'colonial' issues and not through the advocacy of special West Indian causes.

However, the return of some British communist ex-servicemen from the West Indies led to a much more specific attempt to recruit West Indians into the communist movement. The first attempt that the writer is aware of was that of starting an informal group among the leaders of the WISU. A small group was invited to meet a communist ex-serviceman just back from Jamaica and proposals were then made for the starting of a West Indian study group which would study West Indian conditions in the light of Marxist theory. It soon became clear in the course of the discussions that what was envisaged was not a purely academic exercise. The facts were not to be studied impartially, but were to be selected in such a way that they would bolster the Marxist interpretations. Anything, no matter how important, was to be neglected if it did not fit into that scheme of things. The material thus collected was to be disseminated among the West Indian students in the hope of converting them to the cause. Even among students with some tendencies to accept the Marxist interpretation, this approach was unsuccessful. Straight political denunciation would perhaps have been effective, but for students not yet committed to the acceptance of Marxism as the final truth this was a blunder of the first magnitude. The idea of a study group brought their academic background into play; and the attempt to select facts not on the basis of their relevance but on their ideological convenience struck at their pride as university students.

This approach was attempted on another occasion but both of these failed. In so far as West Indian students became affected by the communist movement it was not through the study group approach. With regard to the London students, the approach which indirectly affected the students most was not through the British but through the appeal to solidarity with Caribbean labour.

Although there had been some talk of organizing West Indian workmen in London, and though many individual residents were sympathetic to the labour cause, there was no effective movement until the return of Dr Lewis from the West Indies. Having lived in the area and taken part in the labour movement in the West Indies, he was much more knowledgeable about the best manner of approaching the problem of organization. The students and colonial workers in London were organized on a specifically anticoloured basis. The attempt was made not to bring the West Indians into British labour organizations, but to use the colonial and nationalist discontent and swing it into line as a 'labour movement'. In order to achieve this end, a Caribbean Labour Congress (CLC) was formed to be the London branch of the larger CLC that had been set up in the British West Indies. Eventually, the latter organization was to split completely on an issue which showed the difference between the climate of 'radical labour' West Indian opinion in the UK and that in the West Indies.

This split occurred over the speech made by the Barbadian leader Grantley Adams at the session of the General Assembly of the United Nations in Paris. Adams was selected as a member of the British delegation and as such made a speech which achieved wide publicity. The newspapers and weekly periodicals as well as the BBC gave full reports on it. This sudden attention paid to the colonial speaker on a colonial issue awakened the suspicions of the majority of West Indians – and apparently of coloured people – in London. It was thought that the whole speech and the publicity attendant upon it had been so arranged as to put forward British colonial policy by a colonial speaker in a good light.

On this account, there were many who were prepared to denounce Adams as a stooge being used by the Colonial Office against colonials. There were allegations that Adams had had nothing to do with the preparation of the speech and that he had merely been handed a printed document on the day of the speech which he proceeded to read out. Such stories accentuated the picture of Adams as a colonial puppet moved at will by his imperialist masters.

The speech was a forthright denouncement of Russian expansionist tendencies, and a recounting of the political advances that had recently taken place in various parts of the colonial empire. In other words, it was a counter on the international plane to the Russian propaganda of imperialist exploitation. The sections of the speech which angered West Indian students were those which appeared to give an unconditional, blanket approval of British colonial policy generally, and the sections which dealt with the 'slavery' which the Russians were seeking to impose upon others. The first point, although irritating to West Indians, was not as irksome as the second. Adams had compared the new slavery (Russian) with the old slavery as experienced by the West Indies, and speaking as a descendant of the slave group declared that Russian domination would introduce them into a slavery worse than anything they had ever known. This latter reference was particularly galling because the question of slavery had always been the cause of much embarrassment among West Indians. Living in an age when freedom is highly prized, the West Indian looks back with a certain degree of shame at a past of slavery. However, this identification of his history with that of a slave past is not all loss because it legitimizes (as well as causes) hatred and aggressive feelings towards the British. In point of fact, the details of the history of the slave period of West Indian history were not known even among the best informed of the students. The popular stereotype was that of a completely brutal, heartless regime, in which the slaves, ever willing to revolt and unwilling to work, were broken into subservience by the whip and the lash. The remarks made by Adams seemed to the radical West Indian contrary to fact. Only a diabolical British plot working on an innocent – or perhaps not so innocent – colonial could have produced such a speech.

While in Barbados, Grantley Adams was acclaimed a hero for having represented Britain at the United Nations; the leftist element in the CLC in the West Indies led by Richard Hart denounced him as a traitor. This led to a split with the critics being left in a minority. On the other hand, in the UK itself, the whole of the CLC and West Indian student opinion were critical of the Barbadian labour leader and his speech.[24]

During the early life of the London branch of the CLC, however, there were no such incidents to mar the smooth working of the organization. At its early meetings, labour, communist and nationalist spoke on a common platform in the cause of West Indian labour. It was an unofficial popular front – until the communist element sought to capture absolute control of the organization for its own ends.

The bulk of its membership in its early stages consisted of students and their friends though there were some West Indians, more or less permanent residents of the UK, who played an active part. Most of those in the leadership at any rate were married to Englishwomen and much of their politics appeared to spring from the difficult psychological situation in which the man in an interracial marriage found himself.

The basis of student support for the organization was partly the result of the new found self identification of the student as a West Indian which led him to the support of all 'West Indian causes'. It was also a result of the more democratic ideas and values imbibed from the host society. Students who knew nothing or cared nothing about labour found in this atmosphere a capacity for supporting labour which no one would have suspected. Frequently, there were feelings of guilt, particularly about the exploitation of domestic servants since these tended to be the only lower class people that middle class folk came into prolonged contact with, so great were the gaps dividing the different social strata in the West Indies. In all cases there was an idealization of labour, based partly on ignorance of the working class and the problems in the West Indies, and partly on the fact that support for the labour cause sprang not from human sympathy arising from actual contact but from the psychological needs of the students themselves. Radical socialist ideology was congenial and support for labour stemmed largely from the acceptance of such ideology. How great was this lack of contact with labour was shown when the predominantly middle class leadership of the CLC started concerning itself with the problems of West Indian workers coming to Britain. Elaborate preparations were made for meeting one immigrant ship and a special meeting called to welcome and indoctrinate the newcomers. When the time for the meeting arrived there were only a number of students and their friends present and no workers were to be seen, far less newcomers for the speakers to address. Hurried attempts had to be made to collect odd workers from nearby pubs in order to save face and keep on the appearance of being a purely labour organization.

This shipload was in the 1940s before the new emigration from the West Indies really got under way. In the course of time, the number of workers in the UK grew so appreciably that there was really room for two organizations, the WISU and the CLC. The latter came completely under communist leadership and although communist students continued to give it their support, many more workers were drawn into its activities. At the beginning, the reliance on student support would have led to a crisis were it not that some of the British trade unions – under leftist influences – gave the CLC some support.

While the main organizational drive behind the Caribbean Labour Congress was communist, it should not be thought that this was recognized by the mass of the students or that membership in the CLC implied communist affiliation or any sympathy with communist views. From the point of view of rallying the mass of West Indian opinion behind the 'progressive' cause, the organization was effective, but there was very little opportunity at this stage for drawing students into straight communist organizations. In any case, so much of the fervour that went into the movement was innocent and unsuspecting nationalism, that the discovery that the organization was of communist inspiration and had remote communist control would have driven most of the members away. The CLC, in its early stages at any rate, functioned more as a 'front' organization rallying support for a general cause rather than as a recruiting ground for potential communists.

Nonetheless, there were some students who became communists. On the whole, those were students who were directly approached by British organizations rather than those contacted through colonial ones. The allegation that communists recruit workers and maintain contacts and supervision through the use of female agents has often been made. It is not necessary to believe in the more lurid of these stories to appreciate the fact that friendships offered by communists were welcome to lonely students. It was not that the communists were merely doing a party duty. Among some who deliberately set out to organize colonials, there was much calculation and attempts at manipulation. But by and large, the communists showed a greater facility for entering into personal relationships. One student declared that he found the British and particularly the men, unfriendly. "Whenever I get friendly with an Englishman," he stated, "he turns out to be a communist or a homosexual." The communist movement had its strength in London and the suggestion has been made that this is because the loneliness of the big city lends the movement a certain attractiveness not apparent elsewhere. Certainly in the case of the colonial students, this factor was of importance. With the communists there was no colour bar, no liberalism which (in the popular phraseology attributed by the students to G.E.M. Joad) accepted the student as a brother but would not accept him as a brother-in-law.

There were other reasons besides those of loneliness and the absence of a colour bar which gave the communist movement some sort of appeal. Communism appeared to some of the students under the guise of science. This appeal of scientific socialism was not confined to coloured students. But to a population without any highly literate background, and greatly interested in advancement through education, this scientific aspect had a special appeal. It had the appeal on the 'intellectual' level that 'metaphysics', Rosicrucianism and other esoteric cults had on somewhat lower levels in the West Indies. It was a simple explanation in the sense that its main categories fitted in with their naive assessment of the world around them; it had all the appearance of 'science' because of its difficult, incomprehensible phrases which gave it something of the appearance of scholarship.

Again, Marxism appeared as a 'world view', seeming to have all the answers to all the questions. Deviant beliefs in the West Indies have tended to be religiously based. The adoption of such ideologies was not possible for the sophisticated and educated West Indian who was rapidly shedding religious beliefs. By appearing scientific, it permitted the belief that the adherent was 'progressive'; by its all-embracing philosophy, it provided the security hitherto provided by religion.

More important than all these things was the fact that psychologically, Marxism made sense. The West Indian student loaded with aggressive feelings had the strong desire to see things in black and white. Marxism presented him with a philosophy which illustrated how rational and correct it was to think in terms of a simple dichotomy. Marxism too was a mixture of nationalism and internationalism comprehensible to the West Indian. It had the prestige of being the official philosophy of a white power. It sanctioned 'antiimperialist' and antiwhite feelings, yet it gave a ready answer to the charges of racialism because of its international connections. The idea of a culture or a movement "rational in form but socialist in content" although explicitly expounded by only a few, was readily comprehensible and emotionally satisfying to many students.

The avowedly 'Marxist' group was always a small minority but the Marxist way of thinking influenced more students than were aware of its influence. The Marxist group ranged from the student who got hold of a stray pamphlet and henceforth abused in his misunderstanding all those who did not accept his viewpoint as members of 'the artisan class' to those who drifted into Marxism through political activity. Among all who professed Marxism there was the acceptance of the slogan rather than the comprehension of the philosophic creed.

Relationship with the WISU

The communist group in England sought to win support by fighting for the colonial cause; by the cultivation of individual friendships with students; by taking up colonial students' hostels issues; and by means of cultivating the leaders of the WISU and the CLC. In the course of time, as a few of the students became imbued with Marxism, there was the opportunity for working directly from within these organizations as well as from outside.

The Communist Party eventually developed a West Indian section which made continuous appeal to both student and worker alike. Eventually, a brochure was brought out and the usual party line attached to the interpretation of West Indian affairs.

However, in so far as the WISU came at all under communist influence, it was not so much through the efforts of British communists as through its international student affiliations. Because the communist ideology fitted in so neatly with the emotional predisposition of the radical West Indian, the communist line on the international plane was able to win active support from students, who rightly denied any communist affiliations or desire and intention of ever becoming communists, but who in all innocence and seriousness found themselves in fact advocates of communist policies. A most interesting aspect of this came out in the crisis in the WISU arising from attendance at the Budapest World Conference in 1949. When the WISU was founded, it was decided that it should be a nonpolitical organization. The reasons for this were:

1. Some students would be scared away from joining through its political affiliations – the majority of students, it must be remembered, were government students.

2. It was also felt that as a group the West Indies would have to look for support from the opposition and not the government in power. If the Conservatives were prepared to take up a West Indian cause in order to embarrass the Labour government, the WISU should not hesitate to make such an alliance. A party political affiliation would lead to ideological commitment and reduce the possibility of manoeuvre.
3. The whole tone of the new West Indian nationalism was to stress unity and to minimize differences. Sectarian influences should not be allowed to interfere with the common West Indian cause. The Union should therefore be broad enough to encompass all political shades of opinion.

As can be seen from the activities of the Union, WISU's nonpolitical status was interpreted broadly as not engaging in party political activities; the more general aspects of political activity were not excluded. Consequently, when the question of affiliation to the International Union of Students (IUS) and the World Youth Congress arose, there was no opposition on the part of any one to the WISU joining those organizations and taking part in their activities. In the immediate postwar world, the split in the World Youth organizations had not occurred, so that there was even less room for hesitation about participation.

The secretary published an account of her attendance at the first World Congress and her report gives some indication of the way the congress was regarded by the organization as a whole.

Two hundred and ninety-eight students from 38 countries registered for the Congress and on this historic occasion pledged themselves to build a better world desirous of liberty, peace and progress and to take that place in the vanguard of the youth of the world which students have held so often before in the course of history and for which purpose the Congress set up a new organization, the International Union of Students. This organization considers that the unity of all democratic forces which work for progress and base their activities upon the principles of the United Nations is an indispensable condition for the realization of a just and lasting peace, and the equality of all peoples. Its main aim is to defend the rights and interests of students and to promote improvement in their welfare and standard of education and to prepare them for their tasks as democratic citizens in a democratic world.

The West Indian Students Union . . . is now a member of the International Union of Students, and is represented on its council, and it is our duty to supply information about student activities in the West Indies. Surprise was expressed by many delegates at the Congress that there was as yet no university in the British West Indies, and above all, that in many colonial areas there was no compulsory primary education. The need for obtaining factual information from all colonial and semicolonial countries was particularly stressed and the international student press planned to disseminate this knowledge by devoting sections of *World Student News* to articles based on reports from colonial student organizations.

Finally, I should like to say how grateful I am to have had this opportunity of taking part in this International Student Congress. It has been for me a great experience. I have come to know and make friends with students from all parts of the world, and above all to realize what a vital part can be played by an International Union of Students which offers opportunity to meet and work together to create a better world based on the equality of peoples.

To those acquainted with communist literature, it would not be difficult to identify the mark of the beast, but the author of this document was completely innocent of any such association.

In subsequent years, the WISU took part in the IUS. The annual congress afforded, among other things, a means of obtaining a cheap holiday and a trip to the Continent – itself a status giving factor. But there can be no doubt of the general, even if vague, sympathy felt by the organization and its members for the 'progressive international cause'.

The loose attachment to the IUS continued even after the split between the 'East' and the 'West' developed within the World Youth Movement. In a sense, the WISU did not feel itself involved. This was largely through lack of awareness of the principles involved and their implications, but also because the ideology of the IUS with its emotional overtones of antiimperialism were appealing. The split movement seemed to follow different political camps and the majority of WISU members, if they were not forced to a point where they would have to make a decision, would have agreed with a formulation (similar to Mr Nehru's more recent formulation) of "neither East nor West". They were not communists but to declare an open break with an organization to which they were affiliated in order to join another dominated by Britain and by her western imperialist allies, smacked too much of the 'stooge' behaviour which West Indians were so quick to identify and to condemn.

On one occasion, however, the WISU was forced temporarily at any rate to make its position clear. When the International Youth Festival Committee announced plans for the celebration of a festival in Budapest under the joint sponsorship of the World Federation of Democratic Youth and the IUS, WISU showed little official interest. It announced the festival in the newsletters chiefly as a means of bringing the opportunities of a relatively cheap holiday in Europe to the notice of its members. No policy was outlined and when free places were announced, these were allocated to those who had originally expressed a desire to participate in the festival. The delegation that went to the festival as the official delegation was not a delegation of leaders although some members of the executive committee were members of it.

The neutral disinterested attitude towards the conference was adopted in spite of the fact that the split in the youth movement between the 'Western-democratic' and the communist wings was in full progress. The politics of the matter was of little concern either to the intended participants or the mass of students, although there were rumours before the delegation left that the Colonial Office was frowning upon colonial students attending the festival.

This caused little concern, however, and it was only on the return of the delegation from Budapest that even this story received its full significance. Immediately upon the return of the delegation, a scandal broke out among the students. It was widely reported as established fact that the secretary of the Union who was head of the West Indian delegation had betrayed the Union and the cause of the West Indies. The mere word from the Colonial Office that they frowned upon participation had been sufficient threat to make him disgrace himself and the Union. Through fear, he had become a Colonial Office stooge. News of the 'sell out' became a major topic of conversation among all West Indians, although it was difficult to discover what were the specific acts of treachery.

Eventually, the executive committee had to consider the matter. After hearing reports from the 'treacherous' general secretary and the majority group of West Indians, it passed a resolution which sought to heal the split between the two groups. The resolution ran:

> The executive committee regrets the incidents which took place in Budapest, reaffirms its general confidence in the Secretary of the WISU and head of the delegation and that the executive takes to itself the blame for not having specifically defined the policy he should have carried out at the festival, and while disagreeing with the action taken in dissolving the group (by the majority members) is aware that those who took this action were motivated by what they considered were the best interests of the West Indian Students Union.

In spite of the fact that the executive committee had given a full hearing to both sides, the majority group remained dissatisfied. Only a forthright condemnation of the secretary and leader of the delegation would satisfy them. At their insistence, the matter was carried to a general meeting where the position of the executive was upheld and their position strongly endorsed.

The Case Against the General Secretary

They reported that on 11 August the group met in Paris and proceeded to Budapest, and that on 24 August a meeting was summoned. At this meeting:

The chairman announced to the secretary on behalf of the group that this group had decided to repudiate his leadership and rather than function with him as a leader, to dissolve itself. The blame for this action was placed upon the shoulders of the general secretary.

The dissolution of the group on the afternoon of 24 August may seem to have been sudden and dramatic. It was indeed a disappointment not to be anticipated, a depressing climax to the hopes we entertained of our group's ability to work in unity on a unique occasion. The sole blame for the dissolution of the group lies in our opinion in the conduct of our leader (the general secretary). He met us in Paris and told us that about three hours before he set out from London, he had heard privately that the Colonial Office would take a dim view, to use his own words, of colonial students and civil servants who travelled to Budapest as all of us were then doing. He seemed considerably shaken by this bit of hearsay and his entire subsequent conduct appeared to us not uninfluenced by a fear of official reprisal. This fear perhaps dictated the ideas and opinions he expressed, possibly intended to accumulate in his own future self-defense.

From the start, it began to be evident that the peculiar complex created by the secretary's political suspicions and personal fears might lead ultimately to the disintegration of the group. En route, he put forward the view that the singing of calypsos by our group would be embarrassing, since they seemed to him culturally second rate and morally degenerate. To our surprise he declared that statistics with which he had dealt disproved the existence of exploitation in the West Indies by any large imperialistic interest. Although some members of the group protested he continued irresponsibly to make offensive criticisms of other people, all too similar to those stereotyped representations of coloured peoples, against which the Union recently decided to remonstrate. He labelled as being too 'pro-communist' for his liking, views which would be commonplace assumptions in any WISU discussion, and we do not think that the WISU has at any time considered itself as a communist organization.

Further, the general secretary had vetoed the use of a banner engraved with the message *Greetings, West Indies*. At the opening day ceremony, he appeared completely panic stricken, and for all practical purposes may be said to have ceased to function as leader of the group. There had been a dispute as to where the group should march. The group, under the secretary's leadership, had gathered behind the British delegation.

In accordance with his instructions, we took up our place behind the British. The Africans behind us, who were also marching with the British, suddenly moved off before the gathering of the whole delegation was completed. The WI group began to wonder whether the instructions had been changed, and as the general secretary said nothing and did not seem inclined to act promptly and inquire, one member of our group pursued the Africans to find out what was being done.

In the meantime a Hungarian interpreter arrived and informed the remainder of the group that another place had been allocated for all colonial groups. Our group moved off, followed by the interpreter and eventually found itself with other colonial groups and away from the British delegation. At this point two other members of our group went in search of the member who had pursued the Africans. They found her in our original position behind the British delegation and brought her over to the place which the group was now occupying. A violent altercation now arose about the question of the new position. The secretary who so far had seemed completely paralysed in his role as leader of the group suddenly revealed that he had special information which he had kept from the group. He disclaimed all responsibility in the matter, charged the individual who had originally left in search of the Africans with the sole responsibility and finally declared that the whole question of the position of colonial groups had been a matter of contention between the British delegation's leadership and the organizing committee.

As a result of the confusion, the group marched with the other colonials. On the following day, a meeting was held and the group called upon the general secretary to share his information with them and constituted themselves a consultation committee. The group defined its attitude and policy in four points:

(1) That they were West Indians and concerned primarily with the West Indies and generally the colonial problem.

(2) That none of them were communists.[25]

(3) That they were not concerned with any particular European ideology.

(4) That they had come to the festival as young people and as human beings to meet young people, other human beings from all parts of the world, to build ties of friendship with them and to support peace.

In spite of the general agreement on these points, a bitter controversy ensued. The secretary wished the delegation to use a simple identifying banner engraved *West Indies*. The majority group wished to have *Greetings West Indies*. The secretary maintained his position. The majority group "could see no fundamental difference between the two banners" and

> could only look upon the secretary's final·decision as escapist. We could but feel that his continued opposition to the majority decision of the group reflected either a convinced disbelief in the sincerity of our statement of policy or a desire to escape responsibility for any controversial action taken by our group.

There was further, the whole question of the relationship between the colonial and UK delegation. Rumour had spread that the members of the British delegation were not one with their leader who had declared on the opening day of the conference that British youth were in favour of colonial independence. There was agreement among the West Indian and West African groups on the need for the formulation of a policy, and for a clarification of the position of the UK delegation.

There was further confusion as the communists sought to use this urge for the expression of a separate colonial point of view for their own purposes. The view of the majority of the WISU group was expressed then: "That we were colonials and concerned primarily with the colonial problems; that the colonial problem was absolutely valid in itself; and that regardless of the sympathy and support of noncolonials, we felt most strongly that the responsibility for solving this was entirely our own."

As a result of this, the colonial delegations met with the British delegation and the colonial students presented their cause. This led to renewed conflict, since the points raised by the secretary as leader of the delegation were not acceptable to the majority group. They described them as follows:

> (1) That politically as far as he knew there was no demand for national independence in the West Indies. National independence was embodied in no political programme. The riots in 1937 had nothing to do with a movement for national independence, they were only for higher wages.
>
> (2) The islands were so tremendously isolated and divided that he knew less of the Trinidadian, Barbadian, etc. than of the Englishman.

(3) Federation was improbable. Perhaps it would be at some future time and perhaps a federal government might work.

(4) Economically, the West Indies may have been worthwhile to England two hundred years ago; but they were now "useless to anybody" (his exact words). They were of no use to England as they were not dollar saving areas. The West Indies had no products which the dollar countries could not provide for themselves.

(5) There was no exploitation in the West Indies, and he found himself unable to follow the line of other speakers. Statistics he dealt with showed that the revenue entering Jamaica was larger than that which left Jamaica, partly because of remittances made by Jamaican workers abroad.

(6) Even so the black exploiter was "far worse" (his own words) than any white exploiter. (This statement drew a burst of cheers from his audience).

(7) He was unaware of the flight of any vast profits from the West Indies to absentee capitalists.

(8) The West Indies, however, had large scale unemployment and Jamaica had perhaps the highest percentage in the world.

This was the use to which the general secretary put the single greatest opportunity in the whole of the festival. He was the last colonial speaker from the platform, and the statements were thereafter closed. R, however, asked the chairman to be allowed to speak, and to clear up the most unfortunate impression of the West Indian problem which had been created by the secretary's speech. The chair was unwilling to concede the request, but it was pointed out that the secretary had not, in his presentation, paid any regard to the views of the majority of our group, a majority of at least 5–1. The audience then forced the chairman to grant the request. The speaker for the majority group then submitted that

(1) The secretary had given a distorted view of West Indian facts, of which he was perfectly aware and which were contained in the published reports of every Royal Commission to the West Indies.

(2) The secretary with his experience ought to have been more serious and responsible in representing his country to a completely British audience who by their very presence had shown both interest and a sense of responsibility.

(3) That even a remarkably sincere *Daily Express* correspondent (whom a previous delegate had quoted) had represented the 1937 riots throughout the West Indies as arising from a demand for a greater measure of political responsibility as well as for economic justice.

(4)   With reference to the question of political independence, did the secretary not know that the Montego Bay conference in Jamaica in 1947 was called to discuss that very question, and that a Closer Association committee was even then supposed to be preparing a new federal constitution?

(5)   How did the secretary reconcile his statements that there was no exploitation and that Jamaica had a favourable balance with the huge percentage of unemployment which he himself had mentioned for Jamaica and with the slum conditions throughout the West Indies?

(6)   Had the secretary read in Eric Williams' *Negro in the Caribbean*, a statistical statement that Tate and Lyle invested £10,000,000 in WI sugar and in five years made a profit of £11,000,000 declaring a dividend of 13½%?

(7)   There was no greater difference between the Jamaican and Trinidadian than exists between the northerner and southerner in England. The differences were often artificially created.

(8)   The whole WI was a unit with a common historical and social background, common social structure and economic problems, and the majority of the population throughout the islands were coloured peoples.

(9)   On the political side, the problem was one of instituting universal adult suffrage as in Jamaica, and of facing the changes attendant on that step.

(10)   On the economic side, the major problems were those of large scale ownership of land and other capital by vested interests, of absentee ownership, export of profits, of inadequate wage payments to the masses of the people who depended upon sugar, and all the welfare problems arising out of low wages, dependence upon monoculture with its concomitant disadvantages and the need to revivify and diversify agriculture and to establish new industries from the resources available in the Caribbean area.

The speaker was sorry that he could only very rapidly sketch in the outlines of the problem, but he reinforced his arguments by brief comparisons pointing out that Switzerland, and Ceylon (i.e., Sri Lanka) were both poorer in natural resources and smaller than say British Guiana, yet they had become independent and prosperous. Japan, Indonesia, and the British Isles, all collections of islands, had despite this fact formed self determining units.'

It was following this that the West Indian group held their meeting. At this meeting, the secretary was told that he had brought the group into disrepute, that he had selfishly ignored the known views of the group of which he was the leader and that "in view of his disregard of his fellow West Indians and for the cause of the West Indies itself", the group had decided to dissociate themselves from him. This was particularly necessary since the secretary was attending committee meetings daily without any check.

The secretary, in turn, presented a report which did not appear to differ greatly in material particulars but certainly in emphasis and interpretation. His position was that the WISU was unpolitical and the conference was decidedly political. He was able to quote from the official documents of the conference that it was directed as "a great blow against the war-mongers, the Anglo-American reactionaries and their accomplices", and in defence of the Soviet Union. His interpretation of the conference was one in which the WISU was going to be used in the 'colonial cause' against the imperialists. With regard to the demonstration he wrote:

> As I had anticipated, the idea was to spotlight the colonials. We were greeted by a battery of newsreel cameramen who took not only ordinary pictures of the group (West Africans, West Indians and Malayan) but requested special shots of the group showing the clenched fist and shouting slogans. At least one West Indian who refused to show the clenched fist was asked to leave the photograph.

He had subsequently explained his position and his interpretation to the group, but this had not been accepted and he had even been called a blackmailer and a spy. His report continued:

> Bearing those facts in mind I began by stating that I would only mention such matters as I considered to be in some measure new items of information. I would not mention matters like poor housing and health conditions with which an audience of this type would already be familiar. I had limited time, 20 minutes. I then proceeded to give a statement on the position regarding unemployment, pointing out that in at least one of the territories the unemployment rate of 20% was one of the highest in the world. I set out the figures of the cost of living index to show how this had risen in comparison with the index of wages, the result being a steady deterioration in the standard of living. In all these matters I relied for confirmation on the published official statistics. The remainder of my talk was largely in this strain but I should mention three other points made by me which I believe provoked criticisms from the West Indian group. I stated that so far as I could judge, there was no widespread mass demand for national independence (meaning by this term complete political and economic severance from the Empire as distinct from the common demand for Dominion status). None of the major political parties in the West Indies had national independence high up in their programmes, and some indeed would not even consider it. So far as political

advancement was concerned the drive was for Federation (and the achievement of Dominion Status). At political meetings national independence was not one of the burning questions discussed, and the absence of its mass demand had its effect in the absence of a popular press unlike the position in Nigeria and the Gold Coast. I said further that thinking people in the West Indies realized that the mere granting of national independence meant little if it meant merely a changing of black masters for white. As a matter of fact, there are cases where black exploiters treat their own people worse than white exploiters. It was a question then of ensuring that the local people who take over were honest in their desire to achieve the best for our country. On the question of exploitation I stated that the net profits drained out of the West Indies to foreign investors were not so large that their retention would make an appreciable difference to the standard of living of the people. I instanced the case of Jamaica where the latest balance of payment figures show that not only were the net profits remitted abroad small (£182,000) in comparison with the national income (£60,000,000) but that the profits remitted to Jamaica in respect of investments abroad held by Jamaicans was in excess of this figure. In the matter of dollars we were not in the position of Malaya and the Gold Coast of supplying a net flow of dollars into the sterling dollar pool. From the official figures to instance the case of Jamaica again, this territory spent $36,000,000 more dollars than she earned in 1947. The wealth of the West Indies had been largely drained away in the past. Much was not being taken out now. The wrong being done to us was that our affairs were being grossly mismanaged and our remedy lay in having our own people equipping themselves to take over our administration and to maximize the use of the resources which we still possessed. Of course other matters were dealt with in my talk but I have singled out these as the passages which offended. I should state that the object of the talks was not so much to put over the political philosophy of the speaker, but rather to give as objective a statement as possible of the political and economic situation. So that by stating that he could not observe any conspicuous mass movement for independence was not proof that the speaker approved or disapproved of this state of affairs.

The report has been given in full because it illustrates a great deal of the viewpoint of the radical element in the WISU. There can be little doubt that the accusations of the majority group found a sympathetic echo in the minds of West Indians. Their forthright condemnation of the secretary was not accepted, but many students believed that there was much substance in their charge. It is not difficult to imagine another group of West Indians acting in precisely this fashion.

The interpretation which fits in best with the facts was that the emotional atmosphere of the conference aroused a great many of the complexes and emotional predisposition of West Indians:

(1) As predominantly coloured folk[26] in a white society, there was a desire for integration with white groups which was hindered by the barrier of racial prejudice. Among many students in the UK the problem was solved by becoming friendly with other European foreigners in the UK. The trip to the foreign country provided the opportunity of establishing European contacts freed of the taint of race, as well as another vantage point from which the British could be criticized. Just as American and Canadian experience was frequently used to belittle the English, so the superiority of one or other European country in one or other trait could be used by the discontented student. It is interesting to note that many students who had travelled in Europe repeated as humorous incidents, occurrences which would have given grave offence in the UK. Such for instance were the touching of the black person for luck, or the pointing and laughing of children and so on. This was not invariably the case and much of the same sensitivities to race was apparent in Europe. Nonetheless, students seemed on the whole more relaxed, less emotionally involved and there-fore more tolerant in Europe than in the UK. Because of this predisposi-tion to be friendly with the foreigner, there was a consequent sensitivity to criticism of them by the British. Hence the interpretation of slurs on other peoples and the identification with the oppressed as similar to those passed upon West Indian and colonial peoples.

(2) In this atmosphere, the national identity of the West Indians became important. They were furnished with a heaven sent opportunity to assert their national identity to the world. It was precisely at such an international gathering that the question of national status became of supreme impor-tance. Here, if anywhere, there was the need to assert (an unkind person would say exaggerate) and stress the 'national' strivings of West Indians. On this account, the suggestion that the delegation should march behind the British and between the English and Scottish delegations was unat-tractive; and the alternative of a separate and independent demonstration – even if it implied some collaboration with the communists – eagerly seized upon.

(3) This sensitivity to international status also led to the resentment of points made in the secretary's speech. In particular, there was profound resentment at the reference to 'black exploiters'. The most offended of the majority group declared in explanation that he was not concerned with the truth or falsity of the secretary's position. It was wrong in principle for a black man to criticize other black men before a white audience.

(4) The whole tone of the secretary's speech went against the grain of current West Indian ideology. It was not merely that he showed the West Indies in a poor light as regards social conditions. In this context a depiction of the deplorable state of affairs was in order provided somebody could be blamed. Here again, although no one explicitly stated it (one delegate came pretty close with the statement that "statistics usually hide more than they disclose") the facts were of less importance than the need to assert a progressive and revolutionary ideology. The picture presented by the general secretary was substantially correct. In the place of his facts, there were counter assertions.

(5) Of special interest is the charge of blackmailer and spy. The intervention by the Colonial Office succeeded in provoking precisely the opposite reaction to that which it is presumed was desired. Colonial Office intervention awakened dormant fears and appeared as a challenge to the delegation to which there could be only one answer. The more moderate person was placed in a different position because no matter what the sincerity of his position, it was always possible for the radicals to project their own fears and anxieties upon him.

The acceptance of the challenge to oppose the dictation of policy from the Colonial Office quite overshadowed everything else. In more general terms, the emotional preoccupation with 'colonial status', racial questions and the like permitted the communist to exploit the situation. In a sense, the majority group was a party of innocents abroad not appreciating the international significance of the conference in which they were taking part. To talk about the "colonial problem as being valid in itself" as if a discussion of such a problem does not immediately involve metropolitan relationships, and the whole balance of power on the world stage, betrayed an incredible naivete which not even the subsequent return to the more settled atmosphere of London sufficed to cure.

The need to believe in the myth of the West Indian subject to imperialist exploitation was not confined to West Indian students or West Indian radicals only. It fitted in neatly with the whole communist theory of imperialism. It had sufficient foundation in fact to make it plausible. The largest concerns in the West Indies were in fact foreign enterprises. In so far as any large scale profits were ever made in the West Indies, they were made by these foreign firms. These facts were highly visible ones and the simple theory of exploitation was almost a naturally developed ideology of people low in status to those highly visible facts. The common 'facts' were so inextricably intertwined with the ideology that the ideology itself and its interpretation became so well established that no one had ever questioned it. This ideology was in part due to the fact that West Indians had never in fact been responsible for their own affairs. One writer in the WISU newsletter had indeed pointed out that one of the important reasons for establishing study groups was to make students well acquainted with the facts of life about the West Indies. The irresponsibility which flourished through ignorance was thus to be combatted.

These study groups, however, had not had sufficient influence to interfere with the generally accepted ideology. It must be remembered that the majority of students were engaged in professional study and very few in research. Perhaps it was not pure coincidence that the general secretary of the Union who modified his ideology to suit the facts was a student of economics fairly advanced in his course. The simple popular political ideology of the West Indies did not receive a new formulation from the hands of its intellectuals. Indeed, it received a fantastic elaboration because of the particular emotional atmosphere in which they were being educated.

In spite of the public airing of the grievances, WISU continued to remain affiliated to the IUS. It was felt that the principle of international solidarity should be affirmed unless that organization became completely communist. There was even a widespread feeling that the IUS had only become unrepresentative of international student youth because of the breakaway of the other democratic youth body. It was the latter organization and not the IUS that was partisan. Here again, the West Indian student organization was acting in all innocence. There was the quite admirable point of view that anything that could be done to heal the split on the world political level be attempted. At the same time, there was the naive assumption that the international organizations were run without any sort of concern or attempts at group domination and control, and a consequent belief in the possibility of solving major political problems by the expression of sweet good will.

Participation in the IUS did not alter the group's sense of identity. Thus, when following the controversy between Tito and Stalin the Yugoslavia Youth Organization was expelled from the IUS, the WISU took the stand that an injustice appeared to have been done and called for an impartial investigation by a committee composed of representatives of countries not party to the dispute.

However, the WISU did learn the lesson that delegations could not be sent to international conferences without adequate preparation. Thus we find a WISU directive instructing its delegates to take the following lines:

> The executive had appointed one delegate, Mr Leigh Brandt and one observer, Mr B. Shackleford, to the congress, and sought the approval of the general conference on the directions it had given to the delegate. These included inter alia:
>
> Atomic Bomb: The delegate could support resolutions of a general nature re the abolition of the bomb as a weapon of war.
>
> Korea: WISU hoped for a peaceful settlement and the success of the United Nations negotiations, and the establishment of a democratic government in Korea.
>
> Formosa: WISU felt that the American action in Formosa was provocative and should be condemned and that the Chinese Republic (new) should be represented at the United Nations Organization (UNO).
>
> South Africa and South West Africa: We asked that the South African flouting of the UN resolutions and the Court of International Justice's decision re incorporation of South West Africa be treated by UNO in the same way as the Korean issue. The racialist policy of Malan should be condemned and there should be a removal of all disabilities and discrimination on grounds of race. The United Nations Human Rights Charter should be enforced in South Africa and the British Government should also apply it in the colonies of Kenya, Tanganyika, Uganda and Rhodesia (now Zimbabwe).
>
> Seretse Khama: WISU once again deplored the actions of the British Government in refusing to recognize and accept the decision of the Bamanguata people who wanted Seretse as their chief, and asked UNO to intervene and revoke his banishment.
>
> Expulsion of Yugoslavia from the IUS: WISU refuses to support the expulsion of Yugoslavia student organizations and instructed the delegate to vote for their return. Suggestions should be made that a neutral deputation of IUS member

organizations be sent to Yugoslavia to investigate the charges of the IUS against Yugoslavia Youth organizations and government.

The instructions to our delegates to the IUS were approved, and after passing a resolution *condemning the banning of books in the West Indies* as an attack on freedom of thought, the general conference proceeded to the elections.

This matter of communist sympathies and affiliation still remained a matter of some controversy. The communist sympathizers as well as the innocents within the Union found that their actions received an appreciative if incorrect interpretation from the Communist Party itself.

The WISU sent a delegate to the second World Student Congress. He reported:

The most striking characteristics that have come out of the 2nd Congress are the magnitude of the peace movement among students and the solidarity of IUS with colonial students some of whom are even now actively fighting for freedom. The Congress also exposed those student leaders who, under the guise of a politicism, divert students from the vital tasks concerning them, namely peace, national independence and the maintenance of living standards, saying that students object as citizens and not as students.

Colonial student delegation had a dominant and major say in the Congress and contributed a great deal to the formulation of IUS policy.

A French colonial student from North Africa was elected to one of the IUS's vice-presidencies on the joint nomination of WISU, WASU and the Nigerian Union of Students.

The mark of the beast was also here quite clear, but still the Union decided to continue its affiliations. At the same meeting, a line more acceptable than that taken after the Budapest dispute to the communists was adopted. The communist news-sheet came out with the following description of the conference:

WEST INDIAN STUDENTS VOTE FOR INTERNATIONAL SOLIDARITY

The bi-annual conference of the West Indian Students Union meeting in London in January voted by a 3–1 majority to continue affiliation to the International Union of Students. Those who sought to split the solidarity of the International Student movement were themselves exposed for as the hackneyed phrases about communist domination etc. fell from their lips it was already evident that they were not voicing their own ideas.

This vote of the students is more than just rubber stamping continued affiliation to the International Union of Students. It means that the pusillanimous policy of the old executive was finally thrown overboard.

The conference was shocked when it learned that the Union had been offered five scholarships and had not made any move to offer them to West Indians. This is a criminal act when hundreds of West Indians in London and at home cannot get places in the overcrowded universities.

This description angered the executive committee who felt that it was inaccurate and gave a false picture of the decisions of the conference as well as of the attitude of the executive. Protest letters were despatched and the communists in their turn indicated that they had not intended to offend or to misrepresent.

Here again we have an illustration of how 'the innocents' have been led astray. The report of the communists was not a misrepresentation of fact so much as a distortion of interpretation for political purposes. In the world of politics, this could only be expected. The indignation of the leadership of the WISU may have been righteous. It was not realistic.

Chapter 11

Colonial Student Hostels and the Problem of Housing

The colonial student comes up most sharply against the problem of discrimination in the sphere of housing accommodation. In the years immediately following the war, the housing problem was particularly acute. Moreover, it could not be expected that newly arrived students, coming very often from small towns and rural areas, would be able to find their way around the big city without aid and assistance of some sort.

During this period, these services of providing accommodation to the incoming student were undertaken by the Colonial Office. In point of fact, there was a dual administration which was to lead to certain characteristic problems. The Victoria League assumed responsibility for the running of the hostels. The impulse and initiative in establishing and maintaining them came, however, from the Colonial Office. Eventually, the whole field of student accommodation and welfare was turned over to the British Council and this proved a much more satisfactory arrangement.

With the growth of the West Indies and other colonial areas towards self-government, and the drive towards the establishment of autonomous centres and hostels of their own, the problem of student welfare administration is likely to undergo sharp changes. Nonetheless, the characteristic problems of segregated hostel residence are likely to continue although in a somewhat transmuted form.

The Case of Nutford House

There have not really been any of the more dramatic episodes arising from segregated hostel accommodation. This has been largely due to the divorce of the Colonial Office from the administration. Yet, familiarity with contemporary hostels would lead to the belief that the prevailing emotional tone is not unlike that existing in the immediate postwar years.

For this reason, an account is given below of some of the incidents in the life of Nutford House, a hostel which existed for three years, from 1945 to 1948. The types of problems outlined here are, however, general to colonial hostels and for this reason, certain other parallel incidents in existing hostels of that period are given as well.

When Nutford House was opened, it was done with a great fanfare of trumpets. Originally, the home had been designed under the terms of a tryster of housing establishment for working girls. During the war, it had been used as a service hostel and it became a colonial hostel with the large influx of students during the immediate postwar period. It appears that the extent of the demand for accommodation for colonial students was not correctly assessed because many of the original students were told that they would be able to remain in the hostel during the full duration of their course. In each succeeding year until the hostel was finally closed down, the problem created by the influx of new students precipitated a crisis. The Colonial Office was anxious for the already established students to leave and look for digs independently in order that the newcomers would have the comfort and haven of hostel accommodation. In spite of all the protests of colonial solidarity, it was clear that such a sacrifice on behalf of the newcomers was not welcome. Invariably, the 'colonial solidarity' turned out to be an assertion of the hostel acting as a group against the proposals of the Colonial Office.

In spite of this, there was a certain number of people who quit the hostel in the course of the year. This movement out of the hostel was due to several factors:

(a) Students, especially married students, desired a greater amount of privacy in their relations with women.

(b) The odd student found it impossible to study under hostel conditions.

(c) Student who had a friend from home who was unable to find accommodation at the hostel. Friendship might lead him to leave what he considered the assurance and comfort of the hostel for the perils of life with a landlady.

Occasionally, there was the student anxious to integrate with British society who was glad for the orientation which the hostel offered in the initial period but who felt that there was some stigma attached to living in a colonial hostel and who therefore decided to move out as soon as he had found his bearings. There was also from time to time, the individual student not ashamed to identify himself as colonial, but who became depressed by living in the little colonial island in a state of constant conflict with the authorities and who consequently moved out in order to find a change of atmosphere.

The fates of those who moved out varied. Some who had been imprisoned by their own fears of discrimination found the outside world freer than they anticipated and never worried to come back. More found the colonial hostel a convenient place because of the dances that were organized there and as a general comfort in their loneliness, and continued to keep in contact with the hostel. From the outset, however, most students viewed Nutford House as their permanent home. This legitimized many of their grievances and their demands; for they had every right to be concerned in the details of management of an institution which was to be their own.

The hurried nature of the establishment of the hostel led to a great deal of student collaboration with the warden of the hostel. But soon, there arose a series of conflicts. First, the warden had been chosen partly at least because he had colonial experience. This experience had been of West Africa and the West Indian students came from an area where the radical tradition was that administrators from 'backward' Africa came to the West Indies in order to treat them too, as 'natives'. This predisposed the West Indians to see prejudice at the slightest provocation.

Second, the warden had been a school teacher and expressed fatherly interest in the students. The fact was that some of the students were fathers themselves. In any case many were on postgraduate or special courses and the average age of the student was much higher than that of normal university population. The treatment of the students as boys by certain persons in authority (for example, when they were charged with impertinence) also had overtones of the general derogation from adult status so often given to natives in the colonies.

The students felt that the warden considered himself superior. He seemed to set himself up as an interpreter of British culture to the benighted natives. There were reports that he insisted on all references to English people in conversation being made in the correct form and so on.

It was his decision to set up the notice, Colonial Students Hostel in a prominent position at the gateway. He felt that it was necessary to let the residents, in what was a respectable neighbourhood, know that the coloured folk who had suddenly been placed in their midst were not merely working men. The traditionally high place accorded university students would then be given them. In the course of time, the students became more willing to accept the label 'colonial' which the host society gave them, but at this stage there was resentment. Moreover, they argued, if that was the justification for the notice it would have really been just as well to eliminate the term colonial. There was some talk about physically removing the offending sign but eventually the students became reconciled to its existence.

Further, the warden sought to bring to the attention of the students habits which he considered undesirable. Thus it soon became the practice of the students to congregate at the entrance and sit on the steps and chat. Besides this, there were the multifarious rules which had to be made to control the running of the hostel. Two of these which seemed to the majority of students to be unnecessary and particularly irritating were, the rule preventing the introduction and consumption of alcohol on the premises and the rule confining female visitors to certain public rooms only. The first rule was soon eliminated and the interpretation given was that the warden was himself extremely partial to the consumption of liquor and merely wished in self-defence to allay the fears of those in authority over him that he was prepared to take a strong stand on the matter. The latter rule led to one of the first incidents at the hostel when a student entertaining a group of female students in the library, was called upon by the warden to take them away. The problem remained with the hostel until the very end of its days, however.

Student Protest

The most serious clash with the students, however, arose over the eviction of a student from the hostel. Words passed between the student and the warden who threatened him with eviction. However, the student had already paid his rent for a period in advance to the secretary of the organization. In spite of this, the student was still given notice to leave. The student happened to be reading law and consulted his teachers about it. He was assured that he was on sound legal ground in ignoring the notice. However, he returned to the hostel one day to find that his room had been locked, his bags packed, and his key seized, while the warden informed him that he was only prepared to open the door for him to take away his bags and leave immediately.

This incident aroused the greatest possible resentment among the residents. Just as among West Indians as a whole there was a need of a common culture of protest, so among the residents of the hostel any incident which helped to focus attention on the 'hostile' hostel authorities helped to create a common fund of experience and sentiment. Moreover, the issue affected an African student, but was of such a nature that the dominant West Indian group had to give its wholehearted support.

The incident soon assumed major proportions because some of the law students approached Professor Harold Lasky, who advised them on the legal aspect of the matter and promised to speak to the secretary of state for the colonies on the matter.

The reaction of the students on the night when the student was locked out of his room was extremely aggressive. After bitter denunciations of the warden at a specially summoned meeting, it was decided to send a delegation to the warden to discuss the matter. The warden's wife reported that he had already retired to bed as he was feeling unwell. The students saw this as an insult or a sign of weakness – in any case, it increased their anger against him. There were proposals that the students refuse to break up the assembly until he made his appearance, that all the doors in the hostel should be continuously banged until the warden was awakened and agreed to meet with them, and for the boycott of meals and all official functions.

The boycott which most students had in mind was the official opening of the hostel scheduled to take place in a few days. This was an important occasion because the secretary of state for the colonies was himself to declare the hostel open. Many important people connected with the colonies and the administration of the hostel were to be present. The fear of the consequences of such a flaunt of official authority prevailed over the opinions and desires of the more radical elements, however. It was argued that such drastic action was not required since the substance of the students' claim was so well grounded.

In spite of the decision not to take boycott action, when the ceremony took place there were very few students present and the majority of those attending were there more by accident than by design. It was reported that the secretary of state had actually commented on the absence of the students and had sought an explanation, so that the dispute entered high political consideration.

Shortly after this, the warden was replaced. Although no official word was ever given the students involved, they preferred to believe that he had been relieved of his post because of their action. This incident was very similar to others which arose from time to time in the various colonial hostels. One of the earliest to arise after this opening was the famous "Earls Court Incident". The following account is taken from the WISU newsletter:

> Early in May, the WISU received very disturbing reports concerning certain incidents that were the aftermath of the ejection of a West Indian student from the Men's Colonial Centre at Earls Court, where nearly 100 students reside.
>
> The facts as reported to the Union were that following an altercation between the student in question and the warden, the student was served with a notice to quit. On account of illness and intervening examinations (both of which the warden was aware), he did not find it possible to terminate his stay at the hostel by the date appointed nor was he able to find accommodation elsewhere.
>
> Accordingly, he stayed on for a few days after the termination of the notice. Though fully aware of the student's position and the difficulty that anyone encounters in finding digs in London these days, the warden summoned the police to eject the 'trespasser' from the centre at about 11 pm one evening.
>
> The patent unreasonableness of ejecting anyone, much less a student and a colonial at that, at midnight in a strange city, quite naturally evoked protest from some of the other students resident in the hostel. By their combined efforts in peaceful persuasion, they were able to prevail on the police to postpone their unpleasant duty for the time being. There the situation rested for a further period of two days, the student still having failed to find somewhere else to go.
>
> In the meantime, alarmed by the 'constitutional' demonstration of unity amongst the colonial students that had occurred on the earlier evening, the authorities decided that strong measures had to be taken to prevent the recurrence

of what seemed to their lively imagination a native rebellion. And, the student concerned having temporarily left the building on some errand, they quickly seized their opportunity, took his baggage down from his room, placed it on the street in front of the hostel, posted a notice to the effect that non residents were from now on not allowed to enter the hostel, and summoned a policeman to stand guard at the door. On the student's return, he was accordingly denied admission by the policeman, and when some of the other residents in the hostel once again addressed the warden on his behalf (the time was about 7 pm) that gentleman once again summoned the squad car from the neighbouring police station, and after further argument the ejected student departed, destination unknown.

This ban on the entry of 'non-residents' into the hostel was maintained for some time further, and so we understand were the services of the police. The following telegram sent by WISU to the Secretary of State for the Colonies on 17 May tells the story of the restrictions and some of its effects.

From President, WISU to Creech Jones, Secretary of State Colonies. WISU protests scandalous ejectment of (name of student) from Earls Court Colonial Hostel and existing state of police guard. Visitors to residents denied access. Coloured doctor refused admission to tend sick resident. Request immediate investigation, and prompt remedial action.

After the lapse of a few days, we were favoured with a reply from the Welfare Department of the Colonial Office which stated, inter alia, that:

1. There was no police guard at Earls Court *at present* (Note there was no denial of the fact that a police guard had been employed).
2. The refusal of admission to the doctor was due '*to a regrettable misunderstanding*'.
3. It had been decided that no visitors would be allowed to enter the hostel for the time being.

In a letter to the president of the Earls Court Students Committee, the Colonial Office explained that in view of the then unsatisfactory state of affairs, it was feared that outsiders might have gone in to stir up trouble.

Subsequent facts which have come to light make it indeed arguable whether the ejection of the student was justified or not, but this is of course a matter within the discretion of the warden.

The points on which WISU takes issue are:

(a) the method and manner of ejectment which was and is odious – an unhappy combination of cunning, force, and patent unreasonableness.
(b) The ban on entry of all nonresidents, a measure clearly not directed only at the ejected student or his friends, but intended as a type of collective punishment. Are students, many of them old enough to be married with children of

their own, to be 'punished'? And for what? And why punish *all* for the sensible protests of a few against high-handed and arbitrary action?

(c) The refusal of admission to a doctor on his errand of mercy is of course quite indefensible, and indeed 'regrettable'. Suppose his patient had died!

Further, the mere fact that the warden and the authorities concerned thought the measures which they took were justified by the situation which they faced must raise serious doubts as to their suitability for running hostels of this kind.

Wise administrators by the use of a little tact, sympathy and understanding, and firmness where necessary, are never placed in positions where resort to measures smacking of cunning, the use of force and collective punishments are necessary.

The result of this first major incident at Nutford House was to bring about a greater measure of student participation in the running of the hostel. At that time, the colonial hostels were run by the Victoria League on behalf of the Colonial Office. An advisory committee was set up for running the hostel and the students were given representation on it.

Meanwhile the students themselves articulated their demands through the warden and through their representatives to the advisory committee. The students found that the measure of self-government granted was not enough. They found an unreasonable attitude in the advisory committee and suspected something of the same patronage which they had complained of in the warden. The net effect of the arrangement, however, was to give the students an appeal over the head of the warden, but the battle with the latter still went on.

Reason was not always displayed by the student even when he was most righteous in his indignation. For instance, there was a continuous debate over the use of the public rooms. It was frequently found that the toilets were kept in an insanitary condition. When the warden rightly drew the attention of the students' committee to the highly unsatisfactory state of affairs and about which the students themselves were also complaining, the committee denied on behalf of the students all responsibility on the matter. Faulty cleaning by the maids, faulty plumbing and clogged drains were responsible. It was several months before the students' leaders could be brought to believe that faeces on the toilet seat could not be the result of faulty plumbing, or that some colonial students might actually be unaware of how to use certain facilities.

There was the problem posed by the persistent tendency of the student leadership to take the sides of members of the domestic staff against the warden. Whenever a dispute arose between the housekeeper and the warden, the Union almost invariably came out on the side of the housekeeper. In the case of the first housekeeper, resolutions were passed protesting against her dismissal and demanding her reinstatement. The agitation was done with the connivance of the housekeeper who tried to make it an issue of colonials versus Englishmen, herself posing as a true friend of the colonials. She had deviated from the prejudiced code of the warden by being too friendly with and looking too carefully after the coloured students. This was the reason why she was being fired and therefore she expected all the students to rally to her cause. When the warden was adamant the matter was taken to the advisory council. This support of the housekeeper was all the more surprising because of the way in which food was continuously made an issue of conflict, and the constant complaints made on this score.

The problem of tenure which arose in the early days at the hostel was to crop up again. Thus we find in 1947, a further discussion of the problem arising from the expulsion of a student from the hostel by the students' union. The latter's point of view was:

> In effect, Mr Bulleid's letter (Mr Bulleid was regional officer in the Colonial Office) implied that henceforth, the warden could at any time terminate the residence of any student and the Colonial Officer and the Victoria League (advisory committee) would have nothing to say or do about it except merely to endorse the warden's decision. Obviously, this meant that the warden had the absolute power in the matter of deciding who should continue his stay in Nutford House and who should not, merely because he did not like his face or the colour of his tie, as apparently was being done in Pershad's case; nobody could check upon him. This was very hard on us. It might be noted further that the implications of Mr Bulleid's letter contradicted the assurance given to the Union by the advisory committee of the Victoria League in its letter dated 12 November 1945 that besides the conditions of gross misconduct and nonpayment of the financial commitments in connection with a students' residence at the hostel, the warden could terminate residence only on instruction from the advisory committee.

Rule 7: The Issue of Morality

Another source of friction between students and warden related to Rule 7. Of all the rules, the one that caused the greatest controversy was the one regulating women visitors. The hostel itself started with the shadow of the fate that befell another colonial hostel hanging over it. A widespread belief among the students was that one of the reasons for the closing of Aggrey House was that relationships between loose women and coloured folk developed to such an extent that the hostel obtained a bad reputation and had to be closed down.

It was perhaps for this reason that Rule 7 permitted the visits of female students only in one public room. The first assault on the rule was the demand for the right to entertain in all the public rooms. Because of the numbers involved and the impracticability of the idea, this initial breach was made early. But except among the most unconventional, the rule held good for the first three months – until the first Christmas dance was to take place. In view of the large numbers attending, and the need to relieve the dancing hall as far as possible of private entertainment, the rule had to be temporarily, even if informally, suspended. From thenceforth, there was no possibility of enforcing it.

At the regular Saturday evening dance, students continued to entertain their friends in their rooms, protesting innocently that they believed that the rule applied to all dances. Gradually, the tradition grew that female visitors were allowed in the rooms provided it was not flaunted in the face of the authorities. One warden formally gave this interpretation of the rule to the committee. This arrangement worked in a highly satisfactory manner since the arrangement and physical layout of the rooms were such that the transition from a visit to one or other of the public lounges to the students' private rooms was easy. Under these circumstances, only a warden waiting to trap students – and thus bring trouble upon himself – could have been able to enforce Rule 7 with any rigour.

In spite of the existence of this working arrangement, there still continued to be conflict. One reason for this was that the rule came from time to time to be absolutely neglected, so that visitors to the hostel who were aware of the regulation and who were directly or indirectly concerned with the administration of the hostel had to be placated. One warden worked out what was in fact the most effective technique for the agreed observance of Rule 7. Having openly stated that he was in favour of discreet breaches of the rule, he enjoyed the wholehearted support of the student body. Whenever the matter got out of hand, he would inform the students' committee that the neighbours had complained that discarded contraceptives were being thrown into their gardens. The more responsible students were themselves highly conscious of the carelessness of students within the precincts of the hostel itself, and they were able to use these reports from the warden in order to bring a sense of realism into the conduct of these delinquent students. In actual practice, the physical circumstances of the place were such that it was highly unlikely that any such complaint could have been lodged. If there had been such complaints, in fact the warden would hardly have treated the matter in such a cavalier fashion. Because of his 'reasonable' approach to the problem, however, the students' leaders never queried the accuracy of his reports but gladly acted upon them, in order to induce a greater sense of discipline among the students. With such flagrant and foolish abuses to attack, all united against the 'imaginary' culprits, all deplored their lack of discipline and all promised to keep to the spirit of the informal agreement for the violation of Rule 7.

Again, in spite of the working arrangements, there were periodic calls for the revision of the rule. One reason for this was the feeling among some of the senior students that it was below their dignity to sneakingly violate Rule 7. It was thought that a sweet and reasonable approach to those in authority would be successful in obtaining its total elimination. Just at a period therefore, when everything was quiet and working smoothly, a newly elected and dignified student broached the subject anew. The following account of a general meeting of the commission to discuss the position following the breakdown of negotiations gives some idea of student opinion upon Rule 7.

> The meeting commenced at 8:15 pm.
>
> The president gave a summary of what the executive committee of the Union had been able to do in its efforts to get the unpopular Rule 7 modified by the Victoria League. He mentioned the occasions on which representatives from the committee had interviewed the members of the advisory committee of the Victoria League and read copies of letters written to and received from the Victoria League in connection with Rule 7. The Victoria League in its last letter to the union dated 6 July 1947 had categorically refused to accept the modifications to the rule suggested by the Union and rather insisted that the rule be obeyed to the letter.
>
> The president deplored the fact that the Victoria League and the Colonial Office had both failed to see this question of enforcing Rule 7 from a practical point of view; that the Victoria League had displayed a total lack of understanding and sympathy for the committee of the Union by asking it to enforce a rule which was impossible to observe. The president made it clear that the committee had exhausted all possible constitutional means and exploited every possible point in

argument to win for the Union the favourable consideration of the Victoria League in this matter but the League had remained apathetic and altogether indifferent to the point of view of the Union. The president had been free in these circumstances to throw into open discussion the future line of policy the student body would like to follow as regards their attitudes to Rule 7.

Mr Pershad said it was clear from the results of the reference in Rule 7 that the Union was unanimous in its objection to the rule as it stood, and it was that important fact which should guide members in making suggestions in connection with the future attitude of the Union to the rules. He moved a resolution that the student body should pledge itself to stand behind any student who might be victimized for breaking the rule within the limits prescribed by the student body. He made it specific that his "standing behind any student" implied picketing the hostel and refusing to allow the forcible ejection of any student who might break the rule within the limits set by the Union. The president observed that the effectiveness of Mr Pershad's resolution would depend on how willing all the members of the Union would be to stand together when the necessity for picketing etc. arose.

There were two counter-resolutions: the first . . . was that the rule be ignored, that should any student who observes the rule within the limits prescribed by the Union be victimized the members of the Union in protest must invite their lady friends on an appointed day and march with their lady friends into their rooms.

Mr C (British Guiana), observed that it would have been absurd for the Victoria League as a body to grant officially and on paper the modifications to Rule 7 that the Union demanded. He was assured that it would be possible to get the members of the Victoria League round in this matter through discussions rather than by correspondence. He moved the second counter-resolution that the question of Rule 7 be brought on a personal basis, that it be pointed out to the Victoria League that its rigidity in sticking to its opinion in this matter could only be explained by a prejudice against our colour and our race, that had the residents in the hostel been other than coloured students it would have credited them with sufficient self-respect and not associated so much suspicion with their relation with their women guests. The first resolution was carried.

Mr Wijenatre suggested that a sub-committee be appointed to draw up a scheme for giving effective backing to any resident who might break the rule within the prescribed limits. (Mr W pointed out the difficulties of enforcement, Mr Charles the impossibility since the majority were government scholars.) The president appreciated these difficulties . . . which might easily have made the scheme workable but was quite certain that once every student was convinced about the worthiness of the cause for which he would pledge his support he was sure that only an insignificant number would resort to blacklegging at the expense of their integrity and conviction. The rule was taken up by the West Indian Students Union. There was a general belief that the hostels run by London University did not enforce such a rule. Everyone cited the case of a well known institution where visitors of either sex were permitted until ten o'clock. It was thought that an impartial investigation would reveal the existence of colour discrimination. In practice, the investigation revealed that there was a wide range of practices with regard to university hostels and the intention to build a case on the simple grounds of discrimination had to be abandoned.

Another reason why there was resentment against the rule was that there was the widespread belief at one period that many of the people concerned with colonial student welfare were homosexuals, and that their interest in the boys at the hostel was often highly immoral. It seemed to the students strange that there should be this concern with morals with regard to their relations with womenfolk when the obvious immorality of some welfare officers attracted no attention whatever.

These allegations of homosexuality were in fact merely an expression of aggressive feelings. It was this sort of allegation that went down well with the residents, and it was not an allegation that was directed against welfare workers alone. But in the latter case, it seemed to the students to have a much firmer foundation. On that account, they suggested that Rule 7A should be introduced which would restrict male visitors, or male visitors with known immoral intentions, to the rooms of the hostel.

In actual practice, there was some reason for concern about Rule 7 and its maintenance. In this hostel as in others, there was a very real problem, whatever the merits of formal rules in helping to achieve a solution. Many students, particularly African students, had great difficulty in making contacts with English women. Consequently, there was a tendency in their loneliness to engage in conversation with the domestic staff. In most cases, the relationships with members of the domestic staff were impeccable. But inevitably some of the domestics, surrounded by men who constantly made playful passes at them, fell to temptation. At one stage in one hostel, nearly all the domestic staff, on several levels, found themselves noticeably interested in one or other of the students. In one or two cases, maids engaged in cleaning the rooms were openly promiscuous. On a somewhat higher level, there was the development of relationships between students and senior staff who had legitimate grounds for visiting the room. It is clear that under such circumstances, the enforcement of the prohibitory Rule 7 became doubly difficult. The position was rendered more difficult because the maids became more brazen in their approaches as time passed by and no disciplinary action was taken. Not only did they violate the rules during working hours but they returned at night to visit their friends and introduced female acquaintances. It became a popular joke on the hostel that, while the official charge was £2.10/- for bed, breakfast and supper, there were students who paid "£2.10/- for everything".

The problem of these relationships with the hostel maids were present from the very start of the hostel. At the first dance, given a few weeks after the place was officially opened, an African student invited a maid and she attended – much to the surprise of the warden and most of the students. There was talk of taking disciplinary action against the maid and this in itself caused concern. But there was also the fact that some of the students were very class conscious and abhorred the development. This was particularly the case among West Indian men who had West Indian girlfriends. The latter objected most strenuously to attending dances to which maids were invited, and many disparaging remarks were passed on the character of residents of hostels who would allow such things to happen.

In spite of this, the leaders of the Union, including the West Indians, thought that while it was highly undesirable for students to mingle freely with the domestic staff on social occasions, it should not be made the subject of a formal regulation. The radical egalitarian feeling that there was too much stress on the social distinctions in the West Indies conquered over the class distinctions which had been brought over from the homeland. It is doubtful whether with the social cleavages in the West Indies such social mixing could have ever taken place. In spite of the protests of the radicals against class prejudice, there can be little doubt that the fact that there were white women involved and that the student faced a serious sex problem influenced the student attitude on this problem.

Rule 7 and the Neighbouring Community

The indiscretions of the students did not seem to cause much concern among the neighbours except for the reported complaints already mentioned. Occasionally, a story would circulate of a woman living in an adjoining block of flats who would undress without drawing her curtains so that she might be visible to the students. Stories of such indirect invitations to students to make advances circulated but caused no action. More dangerous was the odd student who by design pursued this particular form of self-advertisement; or where students unaccustomed to the use of curtains or being surrounded by flats violated Rule 7 in view of the whole world.

Working girls in a nearby factory showed a strong interest in the students which suddenly ceased. No one knew exactly why, but the students were led to believe that because of the simultaneity and unanimity of the withdrawal of interest, the management had officially frowned upon it. The hostel was actually situated in a transitional zone. On one side of it were some extremely up to date flats, on the other, the houses of working class folk. The latter had on all matters relating to the hostel, an entirely different attitude from the upper class group. In so far as there were relations with them at all, those with the upper class tended to be antagonistic, those with the lower class friendly. The working class families thought it not undesirable for their children to mix with university students. Their laxness in controlling the contacts of their daughters led to what the students called "the problem of the juvenile delinquents".

Suddenly, a group of young girls from the neighbourhood started visiting the place and attracting the friendship of the students. It was clear that in this they had the faint encouragement of their parents. But they soon became a nuisance in the hostel generally. They were welcomed at first because they served a useful purpose by providing dancing partners at the regular Saturday night dances at a time when contacts with the opposite sex were low. But when they started violating Rule 7 in a most conspicuous manner even the students started to be annoyed. They would visit their friends in their rooms and their shrieks and laughter could be heard resounding throughout the hostel. Moreover, some of the girls appeared to be below the age of consent and this aroused the fear of possible police action. Much to the annoyance of those students with whom the girls were most intimate, the executive committee of the Union voted to ask them not to return. In actual practice, the more senior of the delinquents continued to visit the hostel and developed stable and enduring alliances with students.

The "case of the juvenile delinquents" was always cited as proof by the more moderate students of the need for the maintenance of the formal provisions of Rule 7 which they argued, however, should only be enforced in cases of emergency. There can be little doubt that some students acted irresponsibly in this matter. One introduced a prostitute into his room and allowed her to ply her trade therein; others, unable to distinguish between various types of Englishwomen, obligingly gave their names and telephone numbers to pick-up girls who later caused embarrassment. Desperation often threw discretion to the winds; one student who attended a general meeting in which students pledged themselves to violate the rules discreetly and voted in favour of the resolution was seen half an hour later flagrantly violating his undertaking.

The subject was always one of high emotional interest and of potentially explosive significance. When one warden introduced a threatening notice stating the punitive action he proposed to take in order to prevent violation of the rule, there was an uproar. The notice was taken down and in its place anonymous insulting notices placed. Notices appeared also scrawled upon the walls likening the hostel to the concentration camps of Belsen and Buchenwald. Faced with this pressure, the warden eventually saw reason and the hostel returned to its former situation in which the rule was violated with impunity and, in some cases, discretion.

The problem raised by the agreed implementation of Rule 7 by the students was paralleled in other fields as well. Students would agree to carry their dirty crockery back to the kitchen, in return for the privilege of taking meals to their rooms. In practice, they were always prepared to accept the privileges but not quite so eager to accept the responsibility, or rather the responsibility was accepted in resolution and in theory, but not carried out in practice. Nor were these attitudes confined to the rank and file. The welfare officer who was supposed to see that the arrangements to which he had agreed were carried out by the students openly violated such rules and considered himself something of a hero for doing thus.

Food

Food was one of the problems which all colonial hostels had to face. All institution-produced food tends to be of poorer quality and there can be little doubt that from the student point of view, eternal vigilance is the only way to prevent hostel standards from deteriorating. Yet even when this is allowed for, much of the student attitude still remains to be explained. The symbolism of food and its suitability as a subject of protest must be considered. The problem of food was one feature which fitted neatly into the common culture of protest which helped to unify the student group and this undoubtedly was one reason for its popularity as a subject of complaint. The importance of the symbolism of food can also be seen in the fact that when disputes arose proposals for the boycott of the food would inevitably arise although the actual implementation of the threat would have led to a financial loss on the students' part, and might strike at individuals in the administration well disposed to the students.

The following is an account taken from the minutes of the Students Union of one of these disputes over the supply of food:

> Mr Burnham read a memorandum which was sent by the committee to the warden on the question of food. He next went on to read the reply he had received from the warden. Mr Phillips congratulated Mr Burnham for his invaluable services as Food Officer and asked for the others' attitude on the matter. The President then called on other members to air their grievances.
>
> Mr Hall mentioned the fact that the service in the dining hall was deteriorating. He pointed out that good meals at Lyons were sold for 1/9d and moved the resolution: 'Whereas the overbearing and insolent manner of the Central Administration of the Domestic Staff is incompatible with the prestige of the Victoria League and the dignity of the residents, and whereas the domestic administration seems to be creaking on every rivet as is indicated by such factors as the almost daily increase of staff, yet the progressive deterioration of the service and of the food on the other hand, be it resolved that this home respectfully requests the Victoria League to have removed those members of the domestic staff so that the efficiency of Nutford House and the welfare of the students be secured.'

This was passed unanimously.

Student Solidarity

With the subjects of food and the regulation of female visitors always at hand, the effect of continued residence in the hostels was to develop a feeling of group solidarity. This was shown not only by the development of such self-descriptive titles as the "Nuts of Nutford House", but also in the real influence that the leaders of the student movement had upon the conduct of the members.

This solidarity was imperiled at the end of each academic year as a certain number of the residents returned home. The new student vaguely seething with discontent would turn to the radical element among the older residents. It could be prophesied for certain that the new academic year would bring a new crop of discontents and agitation. Usually, the established leadership had settled down to a certain degree of objectivity and responsibility. But there were always others prepared to challenge this leadership when the opportunity arose. People who never complained about the food or the administration of the hostel would suddenly develop into pioneer revolutionaries. The anti-authoritarian value system of the hostel was potent and it was always possible to obtain a certain amount of status by taking a leading role in creating and formulating grievances. The situation in some respects resembled that in trade union movements[27] which have developed in recent times where the union leader has to continuously create issues and present demands if he is to maintain his role as labour leader in the face of competing leadership.

The solidarity of the hostel naturally manifested itself most markedly when open battles were being fought. Some of the issues over which battles were fought are extremely revealing since they show that the hostel came to be a little island, a haven of protection which was much loved. It was not a ghetto that was resented in spite of the eloquent protests about the inadequacy of the accommodation. In a sense, what hostel students wanted was not a cessation of this form of segregation but the creation of bigger and better ghettoes.

English Residents at Nutford House

On one occasion the Colonial Office arranged accommodation in a colonial hostel during vacation time for some Colonial Office cadets who were about to go into the colonial service. The idea behind the arrangement appeared to be that it was important that people going out into the colonies should be able to mix with 'natives' as equals and that residence in some of the hostels and personal acquaintance with people from the areas to which they were assigned would be a good beginning for the new colonial civil servant.

Whatever the motive, there can be no doubt about the violence of the reactions which it provoked. The writer first became aware of the presence of these English residents when on a visit to the hostel in question, he heard an African doctor declaiming on the steps of the hostel, after the fashion of a madman, to everyone in general and no one in particular, that "this thing cannot happen here", that "these people" could only take up residence in the hostel over his dead body. If the students were prepared to put up with this, it would show that they were a spineless lot fit only for the treatment that the English deservedly handed out to those who accepted colonialism.

On enquiry, it turned out that the English residents had arrived a few hours before and that they were met with general hostility by the students on their arrival. The first allegation and the one most widely accepted was that the Colonial Office had planted Englishmen in the midst of the students to spy upon them. They were afraid of the progressivism and the radicalism of the students and therefore they had sent their spies. This allegation about spying, although repeated with particular vehemence on this occasion was one that was frequently made in colonial hostels. It is clear that the Colonial Office, the warden, and others concerned with the administration of a hostel, were always anxious to know about the genesis of a dispute and there was also an inordinate desire to identify the ringleaders and the particular form which protest was likely to take. But on this particular occasion, there were no serious issues brewing within the hostels and the conspicuous planting of Englishmen in the hostel would hardly have recommended itself to people interested in obtaining information. In the circumstances, it is not clear exactly what the functions of the spies were. The accusation seemed to be a means of classifying the ambiguous person as belonging essentially to the enemy camp. The English residents provided a target around which the general anti-British sentiment could coalesce.

Fear of spying was not the only reason for opposition to these English residents. There were also subsidiary arguments. One of these was that the placing of white people in hostels reserved for coloured students was adding insult to injury. While coloured students were waiting eagerly to enter the hostel and were exposed to racial prejudice, the few places open to them were being eliminated.

On the same night that the new English residents arrived, a meeting of all the students was called to discuss the new development. The hall was crowded and the issue created such a furore that many other colonial students in no way connected with the hostel attended. Speaker after speaker roundly condemned the nefarious policy of the Colonial Office. It was demanded that the administration terminate the tenancy of the residents and, if this was not possible for any legal reason, then the Englishmen should be invited to leave. Knowing the sentiments of the students, it was inconceivable that any of them should wish to stay.

Strangely enough, in spite of the belief that the Englishmen were spies, they were permitted to attend the meeting and to state their case. Constitutionally, as residents, they were entitled, it was argued, to take part in the affairs of the Union. Further, if they were spies they would be able to take back to the Colonial Office a true picture of the hostility and resentment which their nefarious proposals provoked.

The English speakers on their part pointed out that they had not been sent by the Colonial Office. On the completion of their courses, they had thought it a good idea to take up residence in one of these hostels in order to get to know the African people better. They had been assured that at that particular moment there were a number of empty beds in the hostel available for temporary residents and that the supply far outran the demand. There was, indeed, a great pressure for permanent places but their stay in the hostel was not depriving any colonial of accommodation. If this could be proven, they would be prepared to give up their rooms.

The highlight of the meeting was an impassioned speech, which was well received, in which the speaker alleged that "it is all right for these Englishmen to go out into the colonies and lord it over the people there, but are we going to allow them to come *here* and take away the roof from over our heads". The ludicrousness of the situation was quite above the heads of the participants. This was home, the haven, their fatherland. Exploitation was all right in the colonies. It could not happen *here!*

It should be noted that the exaggerated respect paid to constitutionalism on this occasion cannot be accepted at its face value. There can be little doubt that the violent attacks upon Englishmen and upon the Colonial Office were all the more gratifying because of the presence of the presumed representatives of the latter.

It should not be thought on account of the incident recorded above that complete segregationalism was always a set policy of the students. Indeed, at one of the leading hostels from which many of our main illustrations have been drawn there was no such policy. Occasionally, English friends stayed at the hostel and there was never any resentment shown towards white colonial residents. Rather, it was the belief of the students that it was highly desirable that the hostel should come under the direct control of the University of London. Thus we find students in one hostel debating the matter:

> Mr J moved the resolution demanding that the hostel be brought under the direct control of the University of London in coordination with the other institutions of which the residents were members. The request for this change of control should be passed through the inter-university council.
>
> Mr R pointed out that not all the residents of the hostel belonged to the University of London, and the position of those who did not belong to the University of London might not be very secure when the London University took over the control of these hostels.
>
> Mr P explained that arrangements could easily be effected by which the position of the nonmembers of the University of London living in the hostel might be safeguarded.
>
> Mr F thought that the resolution was asking for the impossible. He pointed out that the Colonial Office could easily recognize in the resolution a challenge to its efficiency in running the hostel and since yielding to the transfer of its authority might imply its open admission of such inefficiency, he was quite sure that the resolution would fail to gain the objective for which it was intended.
>
> Mr B said that at least the resolution would be an effective means of showing the Colonial Office how dissatisfied the residents in the hostel are with the management and how disgusted they were with the increasingly rigid control it exercises over them. For this reason, he thought the resolution was worth a favourable consideration.

There were also proposals from time to time that the London University hostels should be asked to exchange students with the colonial hostels but nothing ever came from this proposal.

Other instances in which there was always a great deal of solidarity among residents were the occasions when the proposal was made that a particular hostel should be closed. This was most marked in the case of Nutford House but the incidents which attracted the most public attention and received the most press publicity were the incidents surrounding the 'expulsion' of students to make way for newcomers. Since nothing could shake this interpretation of events, the students decided to do battle. At the time, there were in London frequent newspaper reports of squatting by tenants and students decided that they too, would squat. On the expiry of the lease, they would refuse to abandon their rooms. This would possibly, indeed was likely to bring them into conflict with the police. But where their rights were involved this would be a small sacrifice to make – so the argument ran. There were proposals for picketing and demonstration and the general mood was one of extreme hostility.

In actual practice the scheme fizzled out. Towards the end of the academic year when the hostel was scheduled to be closed, there was a great depletion in the ranks of the residents. Moreover, there were many fainthearted souls who were willing to be present at public meetings and to be loud in their approval of battle, but who made sure that they were not be around when any real fighting developed. Furthermore, the attitude of the Colonial Office was scrupulously correct and even indulgent in manner. They declared that if in point of fact there were students who were unable to find lodgings before the closing date, such students would be allowed to stay on for a few days. Addresses of people willing to rent rooms to colonial students would be furnished by the Colonial Office Welfare Department.

The agitation fizzled out, much to the regret of some revolutionary souls. To some of these, the 'surrender' of the students was a major crisis. One leader of the agitation who had taken a leading part in the opposition visibly degenerated. Having been one of the best dressed and most presentable of the students – he was a professional doing a postgraduate course – he became ill kept and unshaven, sullen and morose, on the verge of a nervous collapse. A few other students followed a similar path. To the majority, however, the surrender was accepted with good natured grumbling. It meant little for they never had seriously considered before, the consequences of giving battle.

Relations with Neighbours: The Problem of Noise

While the relationship with women and its effect on the neighbourhood appeared to give the officials the greatest concern, in practice the problem of noise appeared to be of much greater significance. Students were unaccustomed to dwelling in the big city and the loud laugh or call in the street which would pass unnoticed in the tropics, was used in a fashion which caused a certain amount of annoyance to neighbours. The students themselves had to complain about this.

But the general problem of noise was of less importance than the specific problem of dances. The very first proposal for a formal dance led to conflict.

The students wished the first Christmas dance to be an all night affair. They insisted that the warden should give permission for such a dance. He was prepared to sanction a dance only until 2 a.m. out of consideration for the neighbours. Such a proposal was considered impracticable by the residents because there would be no transport available. The only alternative was to permit female guests to sleep in the rooms. Even this threat, however, could not bring the warden to sanction the all night session. Yet the students went ahead making their own arrangements and when the dance was officially pronounced ended, they proclaimed its continuation. The following week there was a New Year's Eve dance in which the same pattern was followed.

At the time, most students did not appreciate that public dances followed quite a different pattern in the UK than that to which they were accustomed in the West Indies. It is unlikely that such knowledge would have made any difference. Feeling so much 'at home' in the hostel, the students felt confident enough to demand that in their own home things should be run according to their specifications. When in later years this factor was appreciated, the all night dance came to be a standing feature of the hostel despite the neighbours' protest.

There was only one occasion when note was taken of the neighbours. On this occasion, in response to the Africans' protest that the West Indians were dominating the hostel, and that the dances were too West Indian and the music too heavily calypso in character, it was decided to employ an English rather than a West Indian band. One student discovered a group of young musicians who offered for a fairly high consideration to play at the hostel dances. They were engaged and turned up complete with manager and tuba. The latter, together with the general cacophony of sound which emerged was too much even for the students. Nobody danced. Each gazed at the others in wonderment – and then the protests from the neighbours by telephone and in person started pouring in. The students could not in all conscience continue the outrage. The orchestra was asked to leave and did so uncomprehendingly. One student bringing his girl to the dance passed them on the way out. "We played nigger music," one of the rejected musicians was heard saying in consternation as he left, "Funny, they don't like nigger music." On this occasion, between neighbours and students there was a united front. More generally, the attitude of the students could be illustrated from the incident when a neighbour called out in irritation to the 'niggers' to make less noise and was told to go to bed and give comfort to her husband.

In summary, the case in favour of colonial hostels is this:

(1) Newly arrived students coming into the metropolitan areas need a point of reference. The existence of the colonial hostel gives them breathing space so that they do not have to face all their problems at the same time. This of course does not constitute an argument for hostels as run at present. The difficulty is that it is possible to run a hostel merely for a few months in order to accommodate newly arrived students. If the time limit of an academic year is placed, students by this period have developed a certain amount of group spirit and are in a position to give troublesome if not successful resistance to the rule.

(2) It permits students to have a wide range of contacts with other colonials. At first glance, it would appear that the development of a solid colonial mentality is a drawback, but this is not the case. In spite of the tendencies to national segregation, residents learnt a great deal about other areas of the world. In all hostels, there were some informal friendships which overrode national affiliations; in all there were individuals who could comment from a different and more informed point of view on current items of colonial interest than if they had relied solely upon the press and the radio. In all there were organized lectures in which important visitors from the colonies and students themselves gave lectures on the places from which they came. Without the existence of colonial students' hostels, it is difficult to see how the stereotype of the African held by the West Indian could have in any material way changed. There were few points of contacts with the African and hence unless they were thrown together by residence, cooperation and understanding would never have been so close.

(3) The colonial hostel being residential remedies a great many of the deficiencies of the University of London. Students are brought together not only from different areas but also from different disciplines. This is of particular importance in the case of colonial students because the vast majority of students are engaged in some form of professional training. Students of medicine and law predominate. The training in both these subjects is notoriously narrow and although the amount picked up from other students may appear to the initial observer to be minimal, there is undoubtedly discipline.

(4) The colonial hostel provides a ready meeting place where colonial students may meet to discuss their problems. It is inevitable that students should meet to discuss these problems. A certain amount of group identity is bound to persist in the British movement no matter whether hostels exist or not. Such discussions are not in themselves harmful. Indeed, conducted in a university atmosphere, they can be highly beneficial.

Attitude of West Indians to West Africans

The relationship between West Indians and Africans in the hostel followed the general pattern of West Indian and West African relationships generally.

On the whole, the West Indians tended to regard the Africans as a backward group. Indeed, the student having become disillusioned about the 'superiority' of the British and having had his stereotype of the inferiority of the Africans reinforced by casual contact, declared that the effect of his visit to England was to convince him that the West Indians were 'the master race'. The stereotype of the African was brought over from the West Indies where the textbooks in use in the schools in so far as African life was dwelt on at all, depicted the African as an illiterate savage, rescued from heathenism and barbarism.

Again, the historical experience of the West Indian people had led to certain conventional interpretations of the African background. The West Indians, in spite of slavery, had been rendered Christians. So, far from hating the European, it was sometimes argued, West Indians should be grateful to them since whatever civilization they possessed was European. The conservative would often tell the radical that if it were not for the British he would still be a cannibal in Africa. The conservative point of view never had wide acceptance, but the argument was sufficiently widely used for it to act as a reinforcement to the idea of the African as a barbarous savage.

Moreover, the social system in the West Indies put the black element at the very foot of the social ladder. 'Black' became almost synonymous with lower class. The rejection by people placed higher on the social scale was never in terms of class alone. The biological fact of colour was of the greatest importance. There was a negative evaluation not only of colour but of other negro 'racial' attributes, for example, the broad nose, the thick lips, the kinky hair and so on. The ideal marital partner and children desired should be as fair, as

European and as non-African as possible. This traditional picture is changing somewhat in the West Indies but it is safe to say that the majority of students from the West Indies were from the middle class and shared this scale of values.

This was particularly true of the women. One girl recently arrived from the West Indies danced and mixed with all West Indian students. On interview, however, she was quite forthright in claiming that she would never have any black man, West Indian, or West African as a real friend. Disparaging remarks were often made by West Indians in private about the Africans. This was one of the reasons why African dances were never patronized strongly by West Indians. The newly arrived student, if he was interested in going to dances was quick to attend one of the public dance halls in the hope of picking up an English girlfriend. The idea of developing a friendship with an African girl was abhorrent and few alliances developed between West Indian men and African women.

The refusal of West Indian girls to dance with West Africans at public functions and particularly at colonial hostel dances was one of the greatest points of friction between West Indians and West Africans. Most West Indian girls remained adamant in this, however, and found some easy rationalization for their position when accused of prejudice.

Even among the most politically conscious of the West Indians and those who believed in the expression of colonial solidarity, there still remained much of a prejudice against the Africans. "Solidarity with Africa" was an ideological slogan without reference to any personal action. There were many reasons for rationalization of this prejudice which included the following:

(1) The Africans were more 'primitive', less at home in English culture. They felt less assured. The epithet 'mission-trained' which came into current usage reflected the belief of the West Indian in his superiority as compared to the priest ridden, English-oriented African. It must be remembered that this was particularly true of the period before the vast advances of the West African towards self-government. But in spite of these advances, the belief in the African as culturally backward, continues. More important than the changing political status of the African colonial as a source of modification of these attitudes was the desire to find cultural features symbolic of the West Indies. The realization that most of West Indian culture was European derived led to a stress on the African element and

through this there developed an interest in those aspects of West African culture of which there were obvious retentions in the West Indies. The music and dancing, the 'glorious' aspects of West African history attracted attention. These were items which in a sense could be made respectable and drawn into line with Western tradition. Their acceptance involved no basic alteration in the value system of the West Indian. There was a much less marked interest in West African religion although there were obvious African cultural elements in some aspects of lower class religious life in the West Indies, and some of the dance creations in the area were dependent upon these religious practices.

(2) The Africans as a whole were not as personally presentable. A large proportion of them never combed their hair in the 'civilized' fashion of the West Indies. Resentment at the 'African' haircut has already been mentioned. This belief of the West Indian in his more presentable appearance and his greater ease in Western culture, led to the view that West Africans would always lose out in competition with West Indians for English girls. Any girl brought to a hostel dance by a West African remained attached to him only through the good grace of the West Indian men. A favourite pastime during the early postwar influx was to try to put this belief into practice. It is clear that whether these sentiments were well or ill grounded they inevitably disposed to conflict rather than cooperation.

(3) The Africans aped the British, as indicated in their more English patterns of speech and dress. Among the West Indian, there was a curious ambivalence which led on the one hand to pride in being at home in Western culture, and on the other a resentment at being too British.

In manner of speech, for instance, West Indians were only too eager to resent the fact that Britishers did not appreciate that English was their mother tongue, and just as quick to criticize those who lost their provincial accents and sought to speak BBC or Standard English.[28] There was a failure to appreciate that the language problem in Africa was essentially different to that in the West Indies. The speech pattern of the African either appeared (in the worse cases) to be broken English or (in the best cases) to be servile imitations of Englishmen. The same hostility which would be directed towards lower class West Indians on the one hand, or upwardly mobile West Indians seeking to change their speech patterns on the other, were directed against the Africans.

Attitude of Africans to West Indians

The attitude of Africans to the West Indians appears to be of a somewhat more defensive kind. One of the things held against the West Indians was that they were the descendants of slaves. Here again, the rationalization developed that the people exported to the West Indies were really of the domestic slave class. Some of the African students could claim noble descent; most, if not all, were able to see in West Indian slavery a clear reflection of their superior social standing. Moreover, many of the students had come from areas on the West Coast to which there had been West Indian migration. The West Indians were considered on the basis of this experience to be a group considering itself superior and desirous of keeping apart from Africans.

With the rise of nationalism in Africa, there tended to be an aggressive display of African culture. In the hostels, this led to some controversy. The wearing of traditional African dress not merely on special occasions but whenever the individual felt so disposed, was an aggressive assertion of nationality, not only to the British but to the West Indians as well. West Indians in moments of anger could be conceived in their turn as pale imitations of the European while the Africans possessed a distinctive culture of their own. The reaction of the West Indians to this wearing of traditional costumes was mixed. On the one hand, there was an identification with the African who was flaunting his nationalism in the face of the British and, to some, a feeling that the West Indians could take legitimate pride in their ancestry, because their ancestors had not been so backward and primitive after all. On the other, there were sentiments of jealousy, a revival of feelings of inferiority because "West Indians themselves had nothing to offer", and a belief that the unnecessary flaunting of African costume only helped to make even more visible, an already 'highly visible' group. The wearing of distinctive dress stressed differences whereas in their personal adjustment to the surrounding conditions, West Indians were more concerned with stressing similarities and points of identity.

Within the hostels themselves, the degree of mixing depended largely on the numbers involved. In Nutford House, where West Indians were the single largest group there was a strong tendency for West Indians to dominate the students union. West Indians had a great deal more confidence in their own leadership and in that of the Ceylonese (that is, Sri Lankans) than in the leadership of West Africans. In general, they found themselves much more at ease with the Ceylonese students, who in the superficialities of everyday life at any rate seemed to share more of a common culture with the West Indians than with the West Africans. Perhaps it was that the Ceylonese students were drawn from a middle class which had been established for a longer period, and was more Westernized. But both formal and informal contacts with Ceylonese and West Indians were better than those with West Africans.

Not only did the West Indian dominate the students union at the initial stages but they tended to attract the stray (Chinese, Arab, Turkish) student to them as well. One Indian student from Mauritius in the course of his residence became so 'creolized', so imbued with West Indian values that he avowed that he could now consider residence in no other place but the West Indies.

Within the African group there were of course internal divisions. Just as on the organizational plane there was an assertion of West African unity which tended to break down into separate national identities, so there was frequently within the hostels alternative assertions of 'African nationalism', of 'regional nationalism' and of 'tribal nationalism'.

African nationalism showed itself in the desire to have an African selected to the presidency. The first presidents of the Union had been West Indians. Then, largely because of informal contacts, the presidency was passed over to a Ceylonese. To many of the Africans, the fact that there had never been an African president was galling. It reflected on the 'inferiority' of the group. Consequently, in the third year of the hostel's existence, there was an organized attempt by all African groups acting jointly to get an African selected as president. They knew that if they turned out *en masse* and voted in a block they would be successful in getting their candidate elected. By that time, however, colonial solidarity had overcome sectional differences to some extent. The Africans came to the election to show battle but they found that all the other residents shared their opinion that it was high time that an African was elected president. Consequently, the African candidate was returned unopposed.

The constitution of the Union did not provide in any way for regional representation. Such representation had been supported when the hostel was first started but had been rejected on the grounds that it would encourage sectional differences at the expense of a hostel group spirit.

The identification of Africans as a self-conscious group only took place on isolated occasions such as these. On the political level, there was a differentiation between the militant and progressive West African students, and the East Africans who were looked down upon as being politically backward. Within the West African group, the Sierra Leonian stood out as quite separate. The 'creolized' Sierra Leonian seemed to consider himself, like the West Indian, more at home in Western culture and much less anxious to identify with African traits.

In actual everyday practice, tribal grouping and nationality appeared to be the most important item. While the Nigerians were an easily identifiable group, the internal differentiations were most marked. The Hausa fold were marked off by their distinctive national dress which they wore on every possible occasion. This was a close-knit group and with them even their Muslim affiliation seemed to be more powerful than their Nigerian ties. Unlike the case of the West Coast Africans, their wearing of national dress did not appear to be an aggressive, radical, flaunting of nationalism, but simply a reflection of the fact that they felt more at ease and at home in their own costumes. An indication, however, of the existence of national Nigerian feeling arose early in the existence of the hostel when West Indian students not appreciating the title of address and respect used the term 'Malam' as a 'Christian' name. No objection to this was taken by the Hausa concerned but another Nigerian of a different tribal affiliation promptly rose at the public meeting where the incident occurred to correct and castigate the West Indians who were at fault. The other tribal distinctions within the Nigeria group were not as marked but readily apparent. The same applied to the students from the Gold Coast.

In all cases, there was a very marked tendency for students to fall back, in the strange foreign surroundings, on the most familiar. People from their own school, their own tribe, their own homeland – whichever of these points of contact brought back the best possible rush of familiar associations was developed as a basis of friendship.

These factors of group background and affiliation were much more powerful than any other tie, such as attendance at the same college, pursuit of the same course and so on. Once there was a handful of people from the social group with whom they would have mixed in their homelands, these earlier ties dominated any other contacts made in the host country.

The degree of group identification reflected most conspicuously in the manner in which groupings spontaneously developed in the students dining hall. Among the West Indians, there was an almost total neglect of insular origin. This was not so in the very first phases of the hostel where the tendency to cling to insular contacts was more marked. As the hostel developed and the West Indian group emerged, personal friendships between people of the same origin were never identified as such, either by the individuals concerned or by others.

The fact that West Indians all dined together in a separate section of the hall led to the belief among many Africans that West Indians were prejudiced and seeking to separate themselves from the Africans. This suspicion of prejudice was held in spite of the fact that the whole of the dining hall was divided according to national groupings. The prejudice of the West Indians was real but it had little or nothing to do with the seating arrangements that were adopted.

The majority of West Indians were not aware that this interpretation was given to their actions. Indeed, it was usual among them to deplore the lack of mixing that took place and then to proceed as usual to dine only with old friends. When this situation was brought to their notice by some Africans, the latter were told that they had as much responsibility in the matter. Africans should themselves take the initiative in freely mixing with West Indians. The Africans in their turn replied that if they took the initiative and sat at a table usually used by West Indians, they found it deserted, or if already occupied, conversation flowed with a complete disregard for their presence.

On the other hand, West Indians found that when they made approaches to the Africans they were frequently rebuffed. The same indifference and antipathy which the colonial so often used against the well disposed Englishman, was used by the African against the well disposed West Indian. The unprejudiced West Indian individual who sought to break down the barrier was conspicuous and some Africans detected overtones of patronage. Many West Indians found that when they joined an African group at dinner, the group which had previously been speaking English relapsed into their native tongue. Frequently, there was suspicion that personal references were being made. Always, speaking in an African tongue was identified by the West Indian as an act of aggression, intended to exclude and to embarrass him.

The question of the colonial hostel has a special significance for West Indian students. The problem of the colonial in Britain tends to be regarded as one of getting to know Britain. Bearing in mind the particular background of the West Indian, we have seen that this question of endeavouring to achieve a successful adjustment may in fact divorce him from the West Indian community. The residence of the West Indian in a colonial hostel frequently brings him face to face with the colour and shade discrimination as practiced in the West Indies, and with the prejudice against things 'black' and 'African'. The depth and strength of these sentiments are such that even prolonged residence in a colonial hostel may not serve to overcome them but generally, there is a tendency to accept the colonial classification and to reduce the prejudice against Africans. In terms of the social structure of the West Indies, one of the main problems is to achieve a bridge over the gulf separating the predominantly brown middle class and the predominantly black lower class. The change in attitude towards Africans helps in building this bridge. It is a point for argument which form of adjustment in terms of the developing social system of the West Indies is the more to be desired: the good adjustment to the British which maintains and fortifies his own particular set of prejudices, or the poor adjustment to the British which through solidarity with other colonials frees him of some of his insular prejudices.

Hostels for Female Students

The problem of the hostels is in large measure a male problem because of the preponderance of men among the student body. The largest single group of women students are the nurses for whom institutional provision in the regular nurses hostels is made. In London, there is a colonial centre for women patronized by the Colonial Office. At this centre, there never occurred any of the incidents which made some of the male colonial hostels famous: there were no strikes, boycott of meals, refusal to pay rents. But the main problem of colonial hostel accommodation remained the same.

Although women students came up against the same prejudice in accommodation as men, they seemed somewhat more acceptable to landladies. In any case, the women with their ability to cook and to do housework were much more inclined to seek places where they were on their own. Moreover, this was frequently an economical measure. As a result of this, there was not that steady pressure on available hostel accommodation as in the case of the male students – a pressure which provoked several of the crises that occurred.

However, the existence of a relatively self-contained unit without the hostel led to certain characteristic situations; to the development of hostility with the management and to an identification of administration of the hostel with the Colonial Office and with white society generally; and hence to a hostile attitude towards the whole of the outer world itself.

The Case Against Colonial Hostels

The cases against the existence of hostels are:

(1) They hinder the development of contact with the host society. There is often talk of the establishment of good relations with the host society as if it were the prime purpose for which the colonial student is seeking education. There is, often, the easy assumption that the existence of the hostels is a main stumbling block in the establishment of such relationships. It is doubtful, however, whether the abolition of the hostels would increase significantly the number of profitable contacts of the students with British people. Indeed, it might result in considerably less intimate contact since hostel dances and socials were often a means of developing contacts. For many students, it would certainly increase the loneliness and hence the possibility of being drawn into really revolutionary channels.

(2) The colonial hostel, by fostering segregation, builds up an attitude of antagonism towards the host society. Here again, there is often an assumption that if colonial hostels were abolished the amount of anti-British hostility would be considerably reduced. Sufficient evidence has been given above to show that there is real ground for the feeling of colonial solidarity. By uniting the students under a central administration directly or indirectly associated with the British Government, the colonials are given a common focus of discontent for their grievances. Yet, colonial students are now present in the UK in such large numbers that the existence of large and viable national organisations of colonial students is inevitable. Again, the development of self-government and protest movements within the Empire is such that colonial students are inevitably drawn into developing political interests and taking some part in 'nationalist' political action.

(3) It should again be stressed that the development of a colonial attitude is not necessarily the development of antiwhite and anti-British sentiments. In some respects, some of those who lived and identified themselves as 'colonials' had a finer grasp of the realities of the world in which they lived, than those who strained all efforts to make sure that they possessed at least one British friend – no matter of what calibre – with whom to keep up correspondence.

One eminent English academic pointed out to the West Indian students that he wished to see an end to the ghettoes and such a free mixing of West Indians with English, that sociological and anthropological studies of the British could be made with the same objectivity and insight of studies made in other lands. He challenged the West Indian to come out of his shell and look at the world as it really existed. In so far as the challenge was directed to West Indians at large, it had its point and significance. It is doubtful, however, whether London students who lived on their own were more knowledgeable about British life than their hostel dwelling colleagues.

The existence of the hostel and the confidence and security it gave did, however, influence the type of contact that was made. To the provincial student, the hostel in London often was a place where he could relax after the tension of term time. To the hostel resident himself, vacation was a period in which he did not feel the urge to face the perils of the larger world. There can be little doubt that at one stage a greater proportionate number of nonhostel residents travelled to the continent than residents. However, with a little encouragement, the pattern soon got a foothold in the hostels, and the nature of the contacts made there will probably mean that in future the position will be reversed. The solidarity that is born in hostel life can be used for many and not necessarily anti-British purposes.

(4) Closely linked with the former point is the belief that the existence of these focal points of agitation permitted communists to rally behind colonial student causes. In actual practice, the communists did in fact attempt to use these issues, but they were never successful. Because of the development of strong ingroup feeling, the hostel students looked upon their fights with the Colonial Office and other branches as purely domestic issues and resented the attempt to use them for larger political purposes.

In a sense, the creation of these hostels was due to the deficiency of accommodation provided by London University. It has been said of America that there is no Negro or Puerto Rican problem but a problem of race relations. In the same sense, there is no problem of colonial students but a problem of providing adequate residential accommodation for the students of London University. In the course of our general survey, we have seen that within the university itself there was little experience of discrimination, and in spite of the nonresidential character of the university, sentimental ties of great strength have the opportunity to develop. Where in practice there is residential accommodation, the students have no difficulty in integrating themselves.

Limited experience would point to the need for much greater residential accommodation for London students. This is a problem of which the university authorities are not unaware and the case of the colonial student was in large measure only a special case, because of the peculiar circumstances of the general case of London's students.

The West Indian Student Centre

From its very first meeting, the WISU found that there were many who were anxious for the development of a special West Indian centre. There was much irritation and resentment of a guest speaker who spoke of a West Indian home as necessary because of the existence of racial prejudice and discrimination. The students did not deny the existence of those factors. Indeed, they were more inclined to stress than to ignore them. But they wished to see some sort of West Indian centre because they felt that they needed a place where they could get together, get to know one another better, and hold discussions where a real and true West Indian nationalism would be forged.

At this time, the League of Coloured Peoples had schemes a foot for such a centre but the students wished to share a separate one of their own. The use of the colonial hostels to some extent satisfied this need but there were two problems which made them unsatisfactory.

(1) The use of the hostel meant that meetings had to be nonpolitical. Although WISU was a 'nonpolitical' body, it was clear that its own interpretation of nonpolitical was likely to conflict with that of the Colonial Office and the hostel administration.

(2) The use of the hostel also precluded privacy and to that extent reduced the element of independence. In most cases, the use of the hostel conflicted with the needs of the hostel residents themselves.

Further, the hostel with its conglomeration of non-West Indians introduced an alien theme into the picture as far as the West Indian was concerned. One of the main reasons why a centre was needed was the fact that students, extremely conscious of their status, wanted to repay hospitality to English friends in a manner in which they could be proud. A West Indian centre, serving West Indian food and so on, was a symbol of national pride. On the other hand, residence in a colonial hostel aroused suspicions of segregation and stressed the fact that in the relationship, the friends came from groups of unequal social status. Consequently, even among hostel residents there was the feeling that a West Indian centre was necessary in order to return hospitality. Except in the case of the very few who lived in self-contained flats, entertainment also introduced the element of the 'English overlord' (the landlord). Students preferred to entertain their friends either in complete privacy or in a central public place.

At first, the scheme of a student centre was as cockeyed as the belief that an adequate university in the West Indies could be achieved by pooling the available resources of the students. It was thought that students out of their own efforts and resources would be able to provide a suitable centre.

It is interesting as an illustration of the interplay between personality and social action to recount the story of the establishment of the centre. The first impulse in favour of the establishment of the centre soon spent itself. It is clear that there would have been no further discussions of a centre had it not been for the obsession of having 'a room of one's own' (for purely idiosyncratic reasons) of one of the leaders of the union. At a time when there was no conceivable possibility of its establishment, he kept playing away at the idea – to the irritation and amusement of his colleagues.

Eventually, the visits of local politicians and administrators to the UK, the problem of organizing colonial hostels and the consultative and welfare work of the union led to a certain amount of recognition being given to the WISU. The situation changed very sharply in favour of the establishment of such a centre when the secretary of state for the colonies issued a circular to West Indian governments recommending the establishment of such a centre. This

move may have been inspired by the decision to delegate as much responsibility as possible for the running of colonial student welfare to 'national' units
of the colonies. The appointment of liaison officers for the individual territories or areas was the first step in that direction. The rise of colonial nationalism
and the progress of self-government in the decade following the end of World
War II encouraged it further. The move was also in line with developments
in other areas. The Malayan students possessed a centre; the West Africans
had one (organized on a purely regional basis).

The official blessing of the Colonial Office led to the individual governments agreeing to the establishment of such a centre. Money was voted in
1953 but there was great difficulty in obtaining suitable premises. Eventually,
suitable accommodation was provided and the centre was opened in 1955 by
Princess Margaret.

It is an illustration of the peculiar situation in which the colonial finds
himself in England that although one of the highest dignitaries of the state was
associated with the occasion, the establishment of the centre, although it did
not of course give any sanction to segregation, marked out the West Indies as
a separate and distinct unit having a special problem of adjustment.

Moreover, Princess Margaret in her speech assured those present that they
would meet with the same hospitality which she had enjoyed on her recent
West Indian tour. The West Indian centre would provide them with a home
away from home. The fact of the matter was that the loneliness of the
metropolitan area, coupled with the existence of the colour problem, meant
that the home away from home could not be found within the English
households. A special island of colonial solidarity – different in shape from the
colonial hostel but essentially similar in conception – had to be created.

Chapter 12

The Colonial
Student in
Broader Perspective

In the course of this study, an attempt has been made, albeit in impressionistic form, to identify some of the important factors influencing the adjustment of students from the colonies and in particular from the West Indies. In the course of our discussion, we have seen that the existence of racial discrimination is only one and possibly not the most important factor influencing relations.

The racial factor enters primarily not only in the question of discrimination, but through the individual's culturally derived conception of his own role and status as a member of a racially subordinate group; and again in the fact that, the racial factor renders the West Indians as a group very highly visible and thus lays a basis for solid relationships.

The migration of students to the UK is a temporary migration and therefore cannot be placed on the same basis as other migratory movements where people move in order to take up permanent residence. Even in the latter cases, there is frequently a conception of domicile as temporary and an emotional involvement in the affairs of the fatherland. In the case of the temporary migrants from the West Indies, this factor is accentuated. The conception that the West Indian student has of himself and of his social role is intimately bound up with the understanding of West Indian social structure. This gives the problem a peculiar flavour of its own.

This peculiar flavour does not prevent the assimilation of the temporary migrant from being compared with the assimilation of other migrant groups but makes the problems susceptible to a different analytic form of reference as well. In this connection it is interesting to reflect upon the comments of Professor W.J. Sprott in discussing the problems of assimilation in Israel. Based on the writings of Eisenstadt and others, he points out:

> It is clear that assimilation is a complex process depending on, (a) the attitude and aspirations of the immigrant, (b) the attitude of the receiving community, (c) the opportunities offered to the immigrant to satisfy his aspiration and to mix with the society into which he has come, and (d) the degree to which the immigrant has a sense of security derived either from his own people or from the receiving society. It is clear also that the immigrants respond to the situation in different ways and that one way is to cling together if there are significant numbers of them. Lastly, it is clear that the situation in Israel is in many ways peculiar. There are certain common elements – their common religion and common plight among the Gentiles – which give the situation there a peculiar flavour though one which by no means ensures an absence of bitterness as we have seen. This very peculiarity of the Jewish problem was one of the reasons for choosing it; it calls attention to the fact that the problem of assimilation is bound to vary from one context to another. (Sprott 1954)

This common feature of immigrant problems makes it feasible to make some brief comparison with features of other immigrations of a similar nature. We have seen that much of West Indian nationalism is borne only in the foreign environment as the individual takes over the definition of the host society as 'coloured', and 'colonial' and asserts his West Indianism as a form of protest against such definitions. In this respect, the migration to the UK has been of importance because of the temporary nature of the migration, because of the special political relationships; and because of the fact that the temporary migrants to the UK were in some sense an elite. This West Indian nationalism may have been only temporary but as the number of students increased and the social structure of the West Indies changed in a more democratic direction, this source of nationalism became of increased importance. It used to be the gibe that more African nationalists were to be found in London than in Africa proper and something of the same sort applied in the case of the West Indies. The interplay of metropolitan experience and the colonial social structure makes this particularly meaningless now. In the case of West Indian students attending American and Canadian universities, we get glimpses of the emergence of exactly the same problems and the counterassertion of West Indian nationalism in spite of relative differences of the host society with regard to racial discrimination. Moreover, it has long been noted that West Indian immigrants in the USA on a permanent basis have shown precisely the same tendency to form a West Indian community separate and apart not only from American white society but from Negro society as well.

This separation of West Indians from American Negroes shows how little the racial question is involved. In so far as they meet racial discrimination, there is nevertheless a tendency – although American citizens – to retain their British connections as a point from which to proclaim their superiority – in some respects at any rate – to their pure American counterparts. In the case of Marcus Garvey, we have a figure who was significant both on the metropolitan and on the colonial level. In the case of Jamaican politics, the interaction is most marked as it is clear that West Indian emigrants in the USA significantly influenced the pace and development of the radical 'nationalist' movement in Jamaica. It is clear that there is a cultural difference and consequently a basis of group identification among West Indians. In the case of the London experience, we have seen that the cultural differences between the coloured immigrant countries were largely ignored. It was the different segments of this coloured community itself which led to the differentiations of the national groups. In the case of the USA, although there was the definition of the host society of West Indians as Negroes, the latter group made distinctions among themselves. The American Negro aspect of the host society was quick to seize upon differences and to stress and accentuate them. The West Indians were labelled 'monkey-chasers'. The West Indian group, partly in reaction to this labelling, partly because of differences in culture as an immigrant group, tended to separate themselves from the host society.

It would be interesting to carry further a comparison of the adjustment of the West Indian – permanent and temporary – in the USA and Canada, and the UK. Unfortunately, interest in the problem of adjustment of immigrants from the West Indies ceased with the virtual cessation of migration from the islands when the quota system was abolished, and sufficient data are not at hand to make any definite comparison of even the temporary student migration and the permanent working class migration.

It is of interest to note, however, certain gross distinctions that immediately became apparent in the working class migration; that is the distinctions between old and new migrants, and secondly, the greater militancy of the latter groups. It is clear that the scale of numbers is an important factor in welding the group together. Certainly, among the working class migrants, before the recent impetus there was a tendency to compare life in the UK favourably with life in the West Indies provided the initial physical adjustments to the climate were made and the cultural differences interpreted.

There is, however, another comparison which would perhaps render the data on West Indian students with that of students from different areas. Some indication of the nature of these problems has already been given incidentally in our discussion on relations with Africans and the problem of colonial students hostels. The subject has been the focus of some research. Dr Kenneth Little in *Negroes in Britain* (1947), devoted a chapter to the problem of colonial students. Later research includes that done under his leadership at the University of Edinburgh, and the more ambitiously conceived scheme of the PEP (1967). The results in so far as they are known do not in any way contradict the factual basis or the interpretation that has been presented.

From the writer's own experience, the African and Ceylonese (that is, Sri Lankan) problems can be conceived within an identical theoretical framework. This of course does not mean that the actual content of the experience and attitudes of all groups are alike. But even where there are differences, there may be a tendency for them to even one another out.

The West African may be perhaps a little more sensitive to the term 'native' and to the stereotypical picture of 'primitive' peoples held by the host society. There is a correspondingly greater strength of reaction. Among the Africans, there was to be observed a range of reaction which was not to be found within the West Indian group. There was the student from one African colony who persistently refused to think about politics or to take part in any student discussion because this was something for the 'bigger-ups', the higher-ups, to study and take action upon. He was a nobody who by the grace of God had become privileged enough to obtain a professional education. Insults, prejudices, student agitations, passed him by. The limitation of his conception of self to being a 'nobody' who had no right to interfere with the governance of the world at large made him meet the buffets and the storms as if they did not exist.

At the same end of the scale was another African student who was accustomed to a sharp separation of racial groups in his native land. He felt that the African at home had been badly treated, and there was much resentment at his experience of discrimination. He felt, too, that he had been grossly mistreated by the missionaries. Yet he was grateful to them for the education he had received and considered their work irreplaceable. Injustices were inevitable in the very nature of things, they had to be put up with. One should strive for the best terms possible without giving offence to those in power upon whose cooperation future progress rested. This acceptance of a situation may not have been unrelated to the fewness of numbers of the scholars from that part of the world from which he came. The development of self-confidence that undoubtedly arose from participation in the larger world was largely a personal one and did not lead to that exaggerated form of group identification which, in the case of so many West Indians, was the way in which the problem of anxiety about their own worth was solved.

In spite of this almost philosophical and maturely reflective attitude to the situation, this student was actively courted by the communists precisely because he was one of the few students from his area. Eventually, this student returned home to take an active part in defence of African interests. It was not that these students were not subject to the stresses and strains of living, but that their aggressive feelings were to a much greater extent internalized, and directed against the self.

On the other hand, we can contrast with these cases two examples of extreme radicalism. The first case is that of a student from East Africa who was on a special colonial office course. It was intended that he should return to the colonial administration service but he intended to leave the government service and enter into the field of business and political activity. He conceived of himself as a future leader of his people. The exact origins of his bitterness against the British were not discernible but of the reality of it there could be no doubt. It was clear that his conception of himself was intimately bound up with his native land.

In the other case, the student came with the erroneous belief that he had made an important scientific discovery. The professors to whom he was referred all assured him that he was mistaken, but he conceived that they were all trying secretly to obtain possession of his solution to the problem. Eventually, he antagonized his potential friends in the academic world.

His radicalism, although accentuated by his visit to the UK, did not have its origin there. One suspects that his radicalism really had its origin in a psychological predisposition to revolt against established authority, and that emerging nationalism in his home country had satisfied his need. Before proceeding to the UK, he had taken external degrees at an age which showed – and this was known by subsequent experience – that he was a person of exceptionally high ability. This had further convinced him that his radical position was convenient. One of his English masters at school had stated that because of the language barrier and the nature of the educational system it would be impossible for an African to obtain certain degrees within specified times considerably larger than the usual period for English students. The expression of this point of view was taken as another indication of the inevitable prejudice of the Britisher. This student's success was proof of the fact that Africans were much better than they were conceived to be; and that these conceptions based on the limitations of circumstance were in reality only part of the dastardly attempt to retard the progress of the African.

His early experiences in Britain accentuated this attitude; the 'hostility' to the acceptance of his scientific contribution clearly sprang from prejudice and the fact that he was an African. Clearly nothing better could be expected from the Britisher. Eventually, this student settled down to the establishment of good personal relationships in the university to which he finally became attached. This did not influence his radicalism in any way. In spite of the good personal relationships, England was a really benighted country, the people were hypocritical and prejudiced; there was only one good thing left for them to do – and that was to get out of the colonies. Following the experience of sharp disassociation in another European country, he became even more bitter and returned home to become, among other things, the leader of an extreme nationalist party.

Such expressions of emotion as we find in the case of many West Africans was only paralleled by those West Indians who actually became communist. West Indian nationalism never took on a very violent form.

The wide variety of reactions reflected in part the very different stages of development within the different 'national' territories as well as the wide variation within each colony itself. It appeared that the West Indian group, although naturally not coming from a completely homogeneous society, were more nearly identical in culture and outlook to the host society.

These differences in background made a great difference to the conceptions of themselves which Africans and West Indians had, to the level of expectation of what the host society had to offer, as well as to the conception which the students possessed of their specific abilities to adjust to and cope with their abnormal situation.

The sensitivity to the African background sometimes existed despite the aggressive assertion of African characteristics. Thus students from the Gold Coast who frequently wore national dress, became extremely silent and embarrassed at the time of the 'ritual murder' trials in the Gold Coast. Just as in the case of the West Indians there seemed to be a reluctance to have any publicity of the local environment which fitted into the stereotype of 'the backward native'.

Again, the conceptions of themselves and their social roles changed rapidly with social changes within the African territories themselves. Just as the developments toward self-government in the West Indies brought a change in attitude in West Indian students, so it was obvious that the development of constitutional changes and the spread of radical anticolonial political movement in Nigeria and the Gold Coast affected these students tremendously. The rapid Africanization of the services made them perhaps more deeply involved emotionally than they would otherwise have been.

The studies so far published have been more concerned with the experiences of the colonial students in Britain. Because of the temporary nature of the migration, it is just as necessary here to take into account the students' conception of their ultimate social role in the colonial social structure if we are to make sense out of some of the most important effects of the education of colonials in metropolitan countries.

We have seen that to some limited extent, the host society differentiated between Africans and others, but that the overall tendency was to treat all markedly coloured people alike. It does not follow that similar treatment produces similar results. We have seen that in the case of West Indian students the question of personality and individual aspiration and background were of great importance in influencing the type of reaction to the characteristic problems which colonial students face. It is likely that differences in culture and political background are of major importance. For this reason, the large-scale survey of students by the PEP was executed with some curiosity. However, the treatment of this subject in their report is disappointingly slight.

On the basis of impressionistic observation, one would expect to find both a difference in evaluating the experience of discrimination say, and in the violence of reaction to such discrimination.

The stereotype of the 'native' for instance was particularly galling to middle class West Indians who accepted the dichotomy of native and civilized peoples but placed themselves in the latter category. In the case of the African, the greater self-assimilation to the 'native' background produced more ambivalent attitudes. On the one hand, the use of the term 'native' as in native authority was quite common among African students without much of an emotional overtone. The distinction corresponded to something real and was accepted. On the other hand, whenever the term native was used by a European in such a way that it provoked the slightest suspicion of an assumption of superiority or the speaker was thinking in terms of backward natives, the reaction of the African was usually much more aggressive than that of the West Indian in a similar situation.

One of the most important differences was the difference of language background. The West Indians had been Europeanized for such a lengthy period that they came to think of themselves naturally as part of the stream of western civilization. English was their language. Even among the working class where there was much less justification, this identification of the individual as English speaking was most marked. One working man for instance was heard protesting in Jamaican dialect about the conduct of an English club official: "Him think him civilized but him can't even speak English properly." Consequently, the Englishman who attempted to correct the West Indian in his use of the English tongue, not on the basis of superior education and knowledge but on the basis of being English usually met with short shrift from the West Indian student.

On the other hand, the African student through hearing the conversation of other African groups became deeply impressed by their dependency upon English. The status given African languages in the school of Oriental and African studies, and the fact that some Africans were engaged in the teaching and study of their own languages gave many African students pride in their language and in their cultural background. At the same time, they became aware that in their discussions of institutional and administrative changes their own languages were highly deficient and relied heavily on the use of English.

English being one of the more visible aspects of culture and a highly important instrument in effecting adjustment to the host society, the attitude of the West Indians to the English language seemed to be a factor which would have to be considered in comparing the differential adjustment of West Indians and Africans.

The inadequacy of the published material on the role of foreign students in the UK is to some extent compensated by the studies made in the USA. There, the problem has not been conceived as one of 'colonial students', although there are students from the 'underdeveloped' territories of the USA, for example, Hawaii and Puerto Rico. Rather, the studies have been made of the foreign students in the USA. Perhaps the best procedure would be to give some account of the reported results of these studies before comparing the data with the materials and framework of the present study. This should be all the more rewarding since the material on the foreign students in America was only examined after the material in Britain had been written up.

One of these studies is of special interest because it included students who had been educated both in the UK and India. Ruth Hill Useem and John Useem made a study of people within a small area of Bombay province who had been educated in Britain and the USA. The results of this immigration have been published in *The Western Educated Man in India 1955*, and "Images of the United States and Britain Held by Foreign-Educated Indians".[29]

The Useems state that a majority look with favour on certain attributes of the British character. The Indian designation for these are 'personal integrity', 'self discipline', reserved but helpful and thorough in whatever they do.

The question of racial discrimination is discussed and they made the following observation:

> The one outstanding social weakness of the West, both the UK and the USA, that most of the foreign returned mentioned is that of racial discrimination. Racial relations serves the foreign student educated as an acid test of Western attitude and values. Racial prejudice is a hypersensitive spot whether the Indian is the object of discrimination or merely a spectator of discrimination imposed on other colonial people. Around this issue high interest can be aroused, lurking suspicions activated, and a whole train of antipathies concerning colonialization set under way. (Useem and Useem 1955: 75)

They noted further that

The colour bar in the UK before independence aroused resentment as being proof of the ranking of Indians as a subject race, since independence is viewed as being an unfortunate flaw in British character that is offensive to a few people. The colour line in the United States for the earlier generation of students was not a serious one so far as they personally were concerned, but in connection with the Negro was deemed analogous to the British-Indian relation in India.

The later students point to racial discrimination as an anachronism in a nation that is holding itself up to the world as the prospect of democracy. (Useem and Useem 1955: 74)

What was the overall effect of the education in Britain on the relations between peoples? As compared with those educated in the USA, education in Britain did appear to lead to positive feeling towards the British and to better international understanding.

The experiences of the colour bar as experienced by West Indians is very similar indeed to those described by the Indians with British experience, for the Useems had observed that

The United Kingdom cases who experienced racial discrimination said that the colour bar was no worse in England than what they were used to in India before Independence – and in some respects not so bad, or that the behaviour of the Englishman was pretty much what they expected from a people with the reputation of being prejudiced and thinking of themselves as the 'master race'. Many add that it was not easy to distinguish between British reserve with strangers and racial prejudice, but that in most instances since they got to know an Englishman well they were accepted as equals. Nearly all report no discrimination in their intellectual relations with professors and fellow students; a number remember that their teachers took a special interest in them because they were Indian. Although away from the college, they might encounter children who yell, "Look Mom, there is a black man", or "Look at the nigger", adults did not talk that way. The chief area of discrimination seemed in trying to get housing accommodations in which the obvious reasons for rejection was race. (Useem and Useem 1955: 76)

In addition they revealed that

Those trained in the United Kingdom feel fairly sure that they know what the British are like but those trained in the United States are not equally sure that they know what makes Americans tick. One plausible though interesting hypothesis is that the British culture may be more homogeneous than its American counterpart. And as a result, perhaps the Indian has a more standardized set of expectations in the United Kingdom than in the United States. It may also be that the British in their personal conduct in varying types of situations are more consistent and Americans more flexible. (Useem and Useem 1955: 77)

Both countries, however, trade what the writers describe as "a favourable image". Thus they wrote that

Eight out of ten of the foreign returned have a favourable image of the British and Americans as people, as distinguished for their social and political patterns. Those back from the United Kingdom respect the British people (whether they like them or not) and those returned from the United States like the Americans, (whether they respect them or not). Before going overseas, the students tended to be antagonistic toward the British and idealistic about the Americans. After being in the West, approximately 80% reorganize their images losing much of their antagonism to the British and being more realistic about the Americans.

Three out of four now distinguish between the characters of the foreigners in their homeland, who are seen most often in a favourable light. The Britisher at home appears to be a more decent person than the Britisher abroad. (Useem and Useem 1955: 77–78)

It is clear from the foregoing that the authors have placed their fingers on and stressed the importance of, certain factors which have been brought out in this study. For instance, it is clear that the level of expectation of the students was of great importance. The research, however, it must be remembered, was conducted in India and was based upon interview material. This may be responsible for the apparently strange contradiction that the former students apparently feel more strongly about racial prejudice experienced and reported to them and still report favourable attitudes to the British. The point raised in connection with the West Indians is that the disruption of primary group and the suitability of racial discrimination as a point of focus cause a great deal of group unity to develop around an anti-British basis. This culture of protest is temporary and the symbolism of racial discrimination and its function not appreciated by the individual student. The pinning of all their discontents on racial ideology persists in spite of the fact that back in their home country the attitudes to England assume possibly a different character to what they did in England. The question of evaluating the opinions and beliefs of the Indian are rendered difficult because of the inability to check their beliefs and statements of attitude, against their experience in the UK.

The Useems' report bring out quite explicitly the identifications of the student with the home country and the interplay of changes in the social structure of the latter with experiences abroad.

In connection with studies of Indians in the USA, two other authors, Lambert and Bressler (1954), bring out some theoretical considerations which appear as equally valid. These pertain particularly to "the sensitive area complex" which they explain as follows:

> It is difficult to determine the extent to which perceptions of major but segmental aspects of American life contribute to the development of an overall 'favourable' or 'unfavourable' attitude towards the USA. Elsewhere we have advanced the theory that visitors from low status countries develop their attitudes towards the USA not so much on the basis of their reactions to American life, but rather as the end-product of the 'looking glass' process of temporary international migration characteristically impels the visitor to re-appraise his own culture appreciatively and is usually marked by a heightened identification with his own country and an increased sensitivity to its status. Very early in his visit, the student perceived an American image of India which contains elements appearing to him to imply low status for his home country and by extension for him. Americans, in talking with him about India, allude to certain specific subjects (such as caste, untouchables, population expansion) which are associated with colonial status and reactive nationalism and thus have become 'sensitive'. The mere mention of these subjects even in a natural or favourable context will cause the visitor to feel that Americans are hostile to India, a condition which will in turn predispose him to a general negative view of the USA.
>
> If confirmed by subsequent research, the implication of this theory is that so long as Indian students and writers from other 'low status' countries correctly or incorrectly perceive that Americans hold an unfavourable image of their home countries, even extravagantly favourable assessments of American life will be largely irrelevant to the formation of 'friendly' attitudes towards the USA. Therefore, our foreign policy and public pronouncements with respect to countries recently emerged from colonial status, must carefully avoid these emotion laden areas of cultural conflict.
>
> For amity, contact is not enough, especially if prolonged contact serves only to accumulate as a series of assaults on the self-esteem of natives of low status countries. Among other things, friendliness is a function of both personal and cultural security and only after the viewer has a minimal feeling of security can the hostile elements of an image surrender to a more objective assessment. (Lambert and Bressler 1954: 71–72)[30]

The same authors also stress the importance of the family experience of the Indians in view of the large cultural difference between the Indian joint family and the nuclear family of America. In the case of the Indian students from the West Indies, the remarks are significant but of lesser force since the joint family pattern has been considerably modified. But even in the case of the ordinary 'creole' West Indian, there is some appropriateness in their comments that

> The Indian student is not likely to become sufficiently intimate with any one American family to observe the subtle interplay of 'real' family relationships. Few American families can resist the temptation to display the 'typical American family at home', a dramatization which frequently results in an exaggerated caricature of the official norms. (Lambert and Bressler 1954: 69)

In the case of West Indian students in Britain, this phenomenon of artificiality in family relationships is reported in cases where entry into families is through the organized efforts of voluntary agencies and do not develop spontaneously. Getting into 'a good English home' in this way is often more harmful than productive of good results.

The study, *The Mexican Image of Americans* by Norman Humphrey (1954), relies on interview material of students. He stresses the difference in culture between the immigrant Mexican and their host American society. Among the most important factors affecting adjustment were length of stay, closeness of contacts and background of interest. The most important point, however, that emerges from this paper is the relative reaction to discrimination. Humphrey writes

> In view of the discrimination they experience in the United States, surprisingly few of the vast population of working class and rural ex-migrants have come back with unfavourable reports. In fact, as a group they bear amazingly good will to the country. One reason for this is that they are used to class discrimination at home. Moreover, Texas and Texans are regarded separately and known only vaguely as belonging to the United States. The semiliterate ex-migrants are regarded with favour by their working class peers for their American knowledge and they institute a great reservoir of goodwill for the United States. (Humphrey 1954: 116)

Two other studies bring out points of relevance to our own material. The first are the studies of Japanese students in America and of foreign educated Japanese in their homeland, and the others, the study of Scandinavian students. Hubert Pursier and John W. Bennet, in their article "The America-Educated Japanese: The Student in America", make the important point that there is no single attitude to America but a complex of sentiments.[31] They write that to describe images:

> We have distinguished between image *content* and image *judgment* or type of critical perspective and image *attitude*. When describing image content we will often use the terms 'stereotypic' and 'realistic'; for image judgment the terms 'negative' and 'positive' and for attitude 'friendly' and 'unfriendly'. Although these three aspects of the image often follow the same direction,[32] there are important cases in which they don't. (*Annals of AAPSS* 1954: 84)[33]

The rest of the studies, particularly in relation to the position of women bring out clearly the importance of understanding the social origins of the students and their social role in their home country in order to get the reaction as well as the effects of education abroad in perspective.

In the Scandinavian student,[34] there is a point of contrast. All the other bodies of students studied came from 'coloured' countries outside of the main stream of Western civilization. In the case of the Scandinavians, this is not so. The reports on the Scandinavian students bring out the point clearly that there can be quite a critical assessment of a country's way of life without being in any way bitter, resentful and antagonistic to it. The individual student although aware of the reality of America as a great power, does not bring with him a low status evaluation of his own country, nor does he meet it. The fact that both of these factors are present makes it difficult to separate out the relative influence of each. The author of the paper on the Scandinavian would appear to point at the former function as being the most important. In terms of the study of West Indians, we can see that high status evaluation of the self and of the student group combines to produce and not to eliminate hostile feelings when the host society gives a lowly evaluation.

In the case of the Scandinavian, it is indeed likely that their own high status evaluation would turn to resentment if they entered into a society in which there were low status evaluations given them. As pointed out in the article too, Scandinavians are not highly visible as a group. This factor would appear to be of importance because the existence of such visibility leads to the establishment of group unity on a 'nationalist' basis, by separating out the immigrant group and pitting it against the host society. Second, high visibility leads to status evaluation of the individual not as an individual but in the first place as the member of a group. Where such visibility is absent the status evaluation of the group by the host society naturally assumes less importance.

The thesis of the effect of the disruption of primary group relationships advanced in this study would appear to be supported by the study of Watson et al. (1942) These writers point out that among the German visitors to the University of Michigan,

> There was strong need to find a friendly warm host figure who would be a good guide in meeting the many strange situations and finding physical and social satisfaction. The hosts always seemed too busy with their own affairs to give them the attention and audience they really needed and the hosts lacked the warmth to make them really at home – friendliness never seemed to develop into the intimate support they sought.

In the case of these German visitors, the hosts found that instead of the appreciation and gratitude that they expected, they found hostility and misunderstanding. This led to further efforts on their part to provide adequate services. But the degree of hostility or appreciation apparently bore no relation to the value of the services rendered. The prime needs of these visitors were for sources of affection. These abnormal needs of the person displaced from his own society cannot easily be satisfied.

Chapter **13**

Conclusions
and
Recommendations

The education of West Indians abroad is a process that is likely to continue for a considerable time to come in spite of the establishment of the University College of the West Indies. It has been part of the argument here presented, that granted the level of political development in the West Indies and the attendant political consciousness of the West Indian, the education of such students abroad will inevitably lead to the growth of nationalism. There should therefore be continuing concern with the problem of the effects of education abroad and its effects on the social structure.

Psychologically, one effect of education abroad is to lead to a tremendous access of self-confidence. This self-confidence arises from several sources. There is in the metropolitan-colonial relationship, much of the big-country small-town rural relationship. Participation in the larger world removes much of the parochial interest in the small community background. Those who welcome the relief from the ideology of rural life in the small town find that they can make their way and hold their own in the big city. Those who philosophically, if unsystematically reflect, on life in the small community evolve positive and real appraisal of its values. In nearly all cases, the students are forced by participating in two different, albeit similar cultures to have a more consciously developed and reflective attitude to life. Further, students have been forced to compete with other students possessing somewhat different standards. Although the students have competed in the West Indies in English examinations and some may have taken external degrees, this distant impersonal competition is nothing like the personal competition in a well defined and familiar situation in which the individual feels at home. This is of all the more importance because of the tremendous stress in the West Indies on objective examination results.

Another source of increased confidence comes from the feeling of participation in the world that has been read about and thought about but in which one has never lived. It must be remembered that for their literature, and to a large extent all their entertainment, the middle class of the West Indies from which the bulk of students are drawn are entirely dependent upon the metropolitan centres. Paris and Piccadilly, the London West End are not mere words but highly charged emotional symbols. This high evaluation of the metropolitan community may result in some cases in a counteracting tendency to denigration. In these instances, the self-confidence arises from the realization that the British are merely human and that the world of the colonial's imagination has created a superman and superculture which do not correspond to reality. By bringing this world of imagination down to the level of personal experience, the sojourn in England makes the world at large appear a safer, more manageable one in which the student feels more at home. There are of course some students who still maintain, even after personal experience, their imaginary world of a superculture peopled by supermen. This is particularly the case with those predisposed to their English experience as a means of increasing their social status on their return to the West Indies. Even in these cases, however, there is an access of self-confidence because prestige and status arise from their familiarity with the British superculture.

This gain in self-confidence is intimately related with the larger perspective inevitably arising from foreign travel. It is not merely that the person in the small island evaluates his own experience lowly and that of the metropolitan world highly. The position is somewhat similar to that of the boy who moved from New Orleans to Boston, expecting to find a bigger and better carnival in the larger city. The nature of the metropolitan-colonial relationship is not seen in overall perspective. As long as the individual remains within his own island he is really imprisoned by the social structure thereof. He comes from a colonial society and the metropolitan power is evaluated purely in terms of the colonial society as viewed by that society.

There are other sources of this self-confidence. One relates to the general ability of the student to mix freely with whites. The psychological consequences of the colour-class system in the West Indies are profound:[35] the generalized feelings of inferiority that result from this can hardly be worked off by formal education, but only by a significant emotional experience which participation as a free and equal person in a white society affords.

In addition, there is the factor of emancipation from the home. The problems of education in a foreign country presents some special problems and dangers but one of its results is that it releases the student from the control of the home. It was almost the universal experience of the West Indian student that the English student of a similar age was more 'mature' than he was. In the small community in which there is an organized middle class family, the pressures to conformity on the part of the adolescent are very great. Moreover, in all relations with adults there is the tendency to carry over the titles and respects accorded to adult kinsfolk. This renders the gap between childhood and youth on the one hand and adulthood particularly difficult to bridge. Education away from home releases the student from these pressures and forces him to stand on his own feet. The effect of this emancipation is often only partial. Young girls in their loneliness keep up frantic correspondence with their family. In the case of private students, the dependence on the family allowance tends to keep correspondence more regular and the orientation toward the homeland greater than would otherwise be the case. But taking all factors into consideration, there is a disruption of emotional dependence upon the family.

We have seen that preoccupation with the colonial problem is one of the most important forms which student discontent takes, but this very fact is of importance. The newly arrived student inevitably identifies his own community as the most important in the metropolitan-colonial relationship. Eventually, in spite of all the contradictions and confusion we have described, the colonial problem comes to be seen in much larger and hence more realistic perspective.

Moreover, the broadening of horizons is not merely in a colonial direction. There is a much more realistic appraisal of British social structure. Even when contact has been minimal with the British society, there is a much more realistic appreciation of it. Those who share in the subculture of protest that develops among the students are nonetheless thrown into some sort of intimate contact with Britishers. It may be purely with maids, or with fellow students, but as the ideal development for the West Indian is to have an English girl if not an English wife, strenuous efforts are made to get into intimate personal contact with at least one member of the host society. Quite apart from this, however, the relatively impersonal contacts with British society are of great importance. The student who declared critically that he had never known before his visit to Britain that the terms 'thank you' and 'please' could be used so often and mean so little was himself profoundly influenced by the high standards of public manners and civility to be found in British life. The newspaper, the press, the radio, the types of films he saw, the conversations he overheard – all these were significantly different to his experiences at home and helped him to understand some of the forces which go to shape the English character.

There is conveniently a much greater appreciation of social differences within the British society. Although many students continue to carry around with them the stereotype of the Britisher, this stereotype is much more realistic than the original one which saw in the Englishman *merely* an exploiter on the look out for a good job in the West Indies. The possession of an unfavourable stereotype of the British is in fact compatible with a realistic assessment of concrete situations. An appreciation of this fact is important because of political consequences. The West Indian who developed an 'anti-British' attitude must not be prejudged as likely to develop consistent hostile political attitudes. An appreciation of this point would appear to be very relevant in evaluating the methods of 'fighting' against communism in the West Indies. It would appear that the expression of sentiment sympathetic to communism is often taken to imply a politically anti-British loyalty. In our discussion of the relationship of the communists with the colonials, we did in fact see that there are very real possibilities of the 'anti-imperialist' sentiment of the colonial being brought in line with the communist cause. But in general, the anti-British sentiment does not imply a forthright and consistent policy on all matters. The majority of those who took 'the communist line' in the Budapest festival could not by any stretch of the imagination be conceived of as communists and their stress on this fact was quite genuine. Subsequently, most of these students have returned to their homelands. While still showing (in some cases more than others) marks of their radical ideology sufficiently strong to influence their practice, they have not in fact become communists or taken part in any form of communist activity. If communist hunters were to visit the West Indies they would have a happy hunting ground digging up the 'communist' past and former communist affiliations of prominent politicians. One minister who dabbled in radicalism in England openly described himself as a communist in a public speech in the West Indies. Another, as an aftermath of radical student days took part in 'communist' activities before entering politics and achieving responsibility.

This tendency again is not 'West Indian' and has been repeatedly commented upon (or rather used to be repeatedly commented upon) before the threat of communism developed into a fear of anyone who had had any communist connections whatsoever. The need to distinguish between these idealists who have been drawn into the support of communist and other 'progressive' causes but who have learnt in practice the difference between the ideals to which they gave allegiance and the actual working of the party machine and the real communist is of paramount importance. In the case of the West Indian student, the 'idealism' which he professes tends to be very much a psychological form of adjustment to a temporary situation and hence it is unlikely to have any consequences for practical political action in the West Indies.

For this reason, in so far as the communist movement needs to be fought in the West Indies – and its strength is negligible – a strategy of indirect approach is indicated. In so far as acceptance of the ideology of communism is an 'ideal' and a form of psychological adjustment, the direct frontal attack is likely to lead to a reinforcement of communist belief rather than to its elimination. The frontal assault by striking at the psychological adjustment of the individual and offering nothing in its place puts him on the defensive. Such an attack is interpreted as coming from an 'enemy' and the individual idealistic 'communist' has an ideological label ready for use.

We have seen how the position of the colonial student leads to a mild and temporary form of paranoia, to the vision of a world peopled with colonial office spies and the suspicion of prejudice everywhere. So far as the ready-made ideologies integrate into this picture, they are successful in increasing the individual's allegiance. The converse is also true. If by any means the psychological background can be changed acceptance of such ideologies becomes highly unlikely.

Threats and punitive action of any kind are likely to lead to a reinforcement of the vision of a hostile world. What is also conceivable is that such frontal assaults may drive such 'idealistic' communism underground and transform it into something dangerous. Among the few hardier souls already engaged in straight communist activity, it is unlikely to cause much of a change of attitude. In the case of the others, the 'innocents', it will lead not so much to a publicly correct attitude but to a private adherence to the ideology of a more sustained character than what would otherwise have been.

This statement is made in spite of the developments in British Guiana, the only place in the West Indies where 'communism' ever became a really live issue. Some of the characters who figured prominently in that country's crisis were indeed among the sample of students selected for study. One suspects that the peculiar structure of British Guiana was in part responsible for the prolongation of the communist sympathies of returned students.

In sum therefore, we can state that the overall effect of education in Britain is to strengthen the political ties between the two countries, and that those who have to play the most important social roles in the communities learn to evaluate the metropolitan-colonial relationship more realistically.

The Emergence of West Indian Nationalism

The West Indian student learns to identify himself as a West Indian. Education abroad is therefore one of the most fruitful sources of West Indian nationalism. The way in which this nationalism is evaluated will naturally depend on our political and philosophical position. West Indian nationalism has never taken that sharp turn or developed such bitterness of tone as the emergent nationalism in some other colonial areas. For instance, there has never been, except in the case of British Guiana, any move for a complete severance of the ties with the UK. Even in the latter case, the 'Guianese' nationalism was not what inspired the extremists but their adherence to communist ideology. The appeals to nationalism of the leaders there read more like carbon copies of patriotic speakers in the socialist fatherland or the people's democracies rather than the expression of a deeply felt sentiment.

Within the West Indian group, in so far as it has become articulate, West Indian nationalism has sought to create a federation in order to achieve dominion status for the federal unit. In view of the large dependence of the economy of the West Indies on the imperial relationship and the intimate cultural ties between the two countries, the case could hardly be otherwise. In so far as there is any further development of this West Indian nationalism, it is unlikely to lead to withdrawal from the British Commonwealth, or to display any ferocious antiwhite sentiments. The position of the white minority in the West Indies although changed is not one in which they are threatened with immediate or total destruction.

All we can say is that the development of a limited form of West Indian nationalism is desired by the majority of thoughtful and reflective people in the West Indies, and is also desired by the Colonial Office. There is no formal disagreement (except in the cases of British Guiana and British Honduras) on the need for a federal unit and for ultimate dominion status. Indeed, it is becoming increasingly clear to all concerned that one of the main obstacles to the creation of a viable federal structure is the persistent insularity of the separate units. The creation of a common West Indian sentiment therefore hastens a development desired by all. It must be remembered that it was the secretary of state for the colonies in a Conservative government who stated that the object of colonial policy was to create "good West Indians, good West Africans and not imitation Englishmen". It is true that the conservative Englishman's conception of a good West Indian is not likely to be identical with that of a radical West Indian, but there is a large (even if for the radical, unacknowledged) measure of agreement.

The Content of West Indian Nationalism

The fact that students learn to identify themselves as West Indians in a foreign environment is a fact of profound consequence for themselves and for the West Indian social structure. The nationalism that develops while professing a great love of the people is in reality quite ignorant of West Indian conditions. This nationalism may have some of the violence of appeal as 'communism' since it is a defensive psychological reaction to a given situation. Much of it, therefore, as in the case of 'communism' is a temporary phenomenon soon shed if it threatens to interfere with the privileged social life which the middle classes enjoy in the West Indies. However, the pace of political development, in the area where there is no increasingly greater access to job opportunities previously denied to the West Indian, acts as a spur to the perpetuation of the nationalism which has its origins in education abroad. Someone interested in the problem of colonial students once remarked regretfully that West Indian students (like other groups with which he was familiar) measured the progress of their country by their personal achievement in seducing females of the metropolitan group and obtaining lucrative posts in the colonial service.

Such a remark may be born of disillusionment but there is some connection between the phenomenon. It points to the identification of the personal interest with the national cause and the function of competition for jobs (and to a very limited extent, women) in keeping alive the 'nationalist' cause.

The fact that West Indian nationalism is largely born in a foreign environment would be of much less significance were it not for the fact that the students are so heavily from the middle class. In the highly stratified West Indian society, the middle class is more than usually unconscious of "how the other nine-tenths live". This is particularly true of the young student who lives a secluded life and is expected to concentrate on getting through his examinations. The type of educational system with its heavy reliance on foreign text books and its general neglect of social studies particularly on the secondary level does nothing to overcome the lack of personal familiarity with the West Indian environment. As a result of the ignorance of his own country, this transition from the 'nationalism' of psychological adjustment to a genuine nationalism with a live and largely disinterested concern in the welfare of the 'nation' is particularly difficult.

It also means that the nationalism is so largely a formal matter that it is forced to take over a great deal of its content from the host society. The exact manner in which the 'radical' and 'progressive' movements have developed in the West Indies still remains to be written but there can be little doubt that the higher education of West Indians abroad has been one of the main factors in introducing into the community principles of social organization more appropriate to a highly industrialized economy. This of course has not been the only source of radical ideas but it is important in understanding why the most radical leaders seeking to serve the cause of the masses and to assert the cause of the local man as against the foreigner, have remained so firmly united to the traditions of British radicalism. To this extent, the radical concept of the 'good West Indian' implies not a rejection of personal and intimate contacts with members of the upper class, but a reception on the basis of equality.

Here again, we meet with a point of some importance. The issues of 'personal radicalism' or radicalism in social life on the one hand, and political, ideological radicalism on the other, are often confused by the radical himself. The British administration, too, although skilled in accommodating itself to radicalism, has not been free of sin in this regard. One source of West Indian nationalism is, we have seen, the sense of personal rejection which develops through education in a country where direct or indirect experience of discrimination is high and where stress on racial discrimination and prejudice becomes an effective means of adjustment for the majority of students. West Indian social structure is based largely on the principle of colour as a determinant of social status. For this reason, the psychological predisposition to participate in white society is very high. The radical turn away from such participation does not undo a lifetime of education and social pressure. Everyone knows, although it is less galling to some than others, that economic, political and professional success cannot be validated by social acceptance, without conforming to the required standards of colour or at least to the code of colour values.

Because of this, West Indians are aware that in spite of all their boasts of rapid constitutional advance towards self-government, of the standards of their professional work and so on, that the vast majority of West Indians stand rejected in social life because of colour. There is little bitterness about colour because the rejection is so largely self-rejection with a real if not complete acceptance of the colour values of the society. Because of this self-rejection, the *seduction* of social life has a particular attraction to the radical. There is always the suspicion that political nationalism and, indeed, any form of public service are being used by individual leaders as a means of social mobility, that is not merely as a means of advancement professionally and politically but as a ground for social acceptance. The fight against this tendency within the self means that the symbolic or open rejection of intimate association with the white society tends to be proof to the radical of the genuineness of his radicalism. Generally speaking, it is not conceived that one can mix freely in social life with whites of the upper classes or obtain a public decoration without having been 'bought' by the other, the imperialist side. Radical rejection of such contacts must be viewed in this light and should not be adduced as further evidence of the viciousness and extent of the radical affiliation.

In this respect, the increase in numbers of educated West Indian students has important consequences. The majority of West Indians do in fact enter into sufficiently intimate relations with British people and British culture to make it possible to conceive of mixing in social life without surrender of radical values. In the past this was not the case. The adjustment in the days when students went as individuals was fundamentally different to what occurred when there was a mass of students involved. In the case of the earlier students, the degree of mixture and integration with the British society appears to have been high except in the case of the isolated radical. But this integration and familiarity with British culture was used primarily as a means to individual social mobility.

Precisely because of this development in the past, the fears of the radicals that social mixing would lead to the development of conservative attitudes appeared fully justified. The two things seemed to hang together. Social mixing and conservativism had occurred together in the past and therefore they were likely to occur together in the future. Such was the logic with which the radical assessed the position.

The new situation in which the most intimate contacts are with fellow West Indians or other colonials, while contacts with Britishers tend to be secondary and subsidiary, carried with it some danger. There is the possibility that the growth of nationalism may lead to a voluntary segregation which will lead to the minimum possible contacts with Europeans. Such a development would be highly unfortunate from several points of view. In the case of those training for, or likely to enter into higher administrative posts, it is highly important, during the process of transition to full self-government while the process of West Indianization of the civil service is taking place, that such people should be able to enter into free and easy relations with Europeans without being beset by needless anxieties. Even with the West Indianization of the civil service completed, the need for responsible mature persons will continue. This is particularly the case because the area is likely to be dependent like other underdeveloped areas on the need for the technical services of experts from metropolitan countries. Experience in the West Indies shows that by and large the attitude of the West Indian to the Englishman is highly ambivalent. On the one hand, he is evaluated as a competitor who must be denigrated in order to reduce the threat to the local man. 'Nationalism' calls for group unity against the stranger. At the same time, the halo of the superior race follows the

Englishman around. The feelings of inferiority of the West Indian cause all sorts of desirable – and sometimes nonexistent – qualities to be projected upon the incoming individual. There is consequently a characteristic overevaluation of the role of the expert. Nearly anyone coming from abroad with the slightest semblance of competence becomes an expert better fitted to advise and to solve the problem of the area than the local people whose primary concern it is. The psychological problem centring around the evaluation of the expert is only one of the many problems surrounding the wise use of the expert in the West Indies, but it is an important one in the present stage of development when inexperienced ministers and newly appointed civil servants are beset with anxieties produced by their rapid rise to power.

The rise of West Indian nationalism is only one of the significant emotional experiences which the students obtain when abroad. To most, the irresponsible student days are a period of much if superficial intellectual endeavour. Their horizons become broadened. It is true that participation in the host society could be greatly increased, but nearly every student becomes acquainted for the first time with the European union, with the drama, opera, ballet, and the like. Political philosophies which at home are contacted, if at all, only in slogan form are encountered in reasoned statements. Much of this contact is superficial and much of it is used for the seizing of symbols which will allow the assumption of superior status, but much of it is permanently illuminating and significant emotionally. The student who during the carefree student days has some of the most significant experiences of his life in a foreign country continues after his return to the West Indies to have his life bound up partially at any rate with a foreign country. This is one of the factors which helps to promote the retention of the symbols of visits abroad. It is one of the reasons why people in the area who have been to universities follow with some eagerness the futures of their 'alma mater' without showing a similar concern for higher education within the West Indian area; or even with the provision of adequate facilities for higher education abroad. The significant thing about this is that each student identified his own university experience with the whole range of possible experience. Those who have attended American universities consider that American university education is the best and its systems are compared favourably, albeit somewhat defensively, with that obtained in other lands. Those who have been to Oxford and Cambridge extol the virtues of the British university, with their own universities at the summit of it all. Those at provincial universities more or less accept this evaluation too, but make sure that the reputations of their own universities should not fall by default. We have seen that in the case of Canadian students coming to Britain they were faced with the problem of adjusting their scale of values and had difficulty in conceiving their 'highly prized' Canadian education as in some sense 'inferior' to British university education.

The mere fact that so much of the emotional life of the student is bound up with a foreign country may not in itself be a bad thing. Indeed, it may be an important contribution to the promotion of international understanding and to the prevention of any harsh form of West Indian nationalism. In the particular context of the West Indies, however, the result has been to further the traditional neglect of the local environment and a further heightening of interest in and orientation towards the foreign country. As a consequence, there is a dearth of informed opinion about the social role of higher education in the area, and little enthusiasm about its development.

This attitude towards higher education is in its turn merely a reflection of more deep-rooted attitudes towards the foreign country as a whole. At a time in which there is a great demand for self-government and a parallel development of nationalism, the increased opportunities for study in England continues to encourage the old tendency to use the sojourn in that country as a means of ensuring social status for the individual and differentiating himself from the masses of the people. The growth of nationalism is the more obvious, the more exciting development; the capture of the soul of the West Indian elite in the superficialities of metropolitan life is more liable to pass unnoticed.

The symbolism of class consequent upon the visit to the UK varies. To a small proportion of students, the English wife remains important; the number of such alliances is still sufficiently high to keep the issue of interracial marriages a matter of extremely high emotional interest for West Indians. But there are other less visible badges. There is for instance the tendency to retain some of the outward symbols as for example the drinking of tea, the failure to use sugar in the quantities considered normal in the West Indies, the type of dress used, and so on. In spite of the rapid changes in attitude to dress and the move towards wear more appropriate for the tropics, some students, at least for the first few days of their arrival, insist on wearing the three-piece tweed suit. In other cases, the uncut hair (a remnant of the barber problem) becomes a style cultivated because it proclaims the individual as 'different' with a background of study abroad.

This is not, of course, a universal phenomenon. There are older students rising in social status somewhat late in life and therefore more appreciative of the criteria for social differentiation in the island. These often come to hold the belief that in some sense a hoax has been perpetrated on them. They discover the essentially commonplace nature of so many of the highly charged emotional symbols of the West Indies.

They discover that their social superiors who have enjoyed status because of their contact with a superculture had often lived deprived of those gadgets which the West Indian identifies as the mark of civilized progress. But on return to the West Indies, they are not vociferous in proclaiming their discovery because they find that they too can profit from the 'myth' of a superculture. The spread of opportunity indeed has awakened curiosity about life in England in much larger circles than heretofore, and the social influence of these groups is correspondingly greater. The more outlandish claims have had, however, to be forsaken.

Even in cases where there has been a sharp reversal of attitude, the emotional involvement with the host society continues to be paramount. In the case of the two most articulate radicals in the West Indies (Dr T.G. Achong and Dr E. Williams), we have illustrations of the reaction to the foreign environment.

Thus one leading radical invariably makes reference to the situation as it existed in Boston, Massachusetts, when evaluating in his inimitable fashion the problems of the island or the area. For instance, after a speech in which the newly established university college was described and presented as a revolutionary new conception likely to have a profound influence on the area, he duly observed that the people did not have the matter in proper perspective since in Boston, Massachusetts there were several universities in close proximity.

Unlike most other educated West Indians, Dr Eric Williams[36] has addressed himself quite specifically to the problems of higher education in the area. His concept of a university is that it should be completely autonomous without any ties to London. He was expensively educated at public expense at Oxford and, as a public duty, he points out that in terms of the West Indies, a residential university is a misconception. Of course this topic does not exhaust

Dr Williams' contribution to the discussion but is in reality the central core of the criticism of the administrative form in which higher education has developed in the area.

Recommendations

The purpose of this study was not to give guidance in policy formation. Its main practical purpose was conceived as the giving of illumination and insight to the colonial students themselves, of the nature of the problems with which they were faced. However, it may be worthwhile to mention some aspects of the research which appear to have some relevance to administrative practice.

(1) It should be one of the concerns of West Indian governments and people as to whether the services provided for the West Indian students are adequate enough. In terms of the student educated abroad, there is heavy public expenditure and a considerable amount of wastage. A large part of this wastage is caused through the failure of students to complete their courses, and the refusal of students who have graduated to return to the West Indies. There is the additional factor that the community (not without some justification), expects that the most highly educated members of the country should make some contribution other than personal professional success to the development of their country. This idea is very often conceived as a direct political contribution but the appreciation of the lack of contribution on a voluntary basis generally is recognized. The need for appreciation of their role in the West Indies in a realistic fashion can be helped by the provision of other welfare services than those presently utilized.

At the moment, the liaison officers for West Indian students perform the function primarily of catering for the material rather than the social and psychological needs of the student. This factor is not neglected but with the volume of work involved, the officer is ill-equipped to pay adequate attention to psychological needs. From the side of the students, there has developed a demand for a careers officer who would help to place people in employment but what is needed is something more. The development of psychological counselling and of student counselling has never been a feature of British university life. In many American universities, it performs a useful function and some adaptation, not to British university life, but to the needs of West Indian and other colonial students should be considered. Indeed, in the writer's opinion, it is a highly necessary and desirable development.

The difficulty involved in the development of such a service is great. For an adequate service, somebody of both high intellectual attainment, psychological insight and maturity is needed. Moreover, a knowledge of the West Indian or the general colonial background is highly desirable. Such a development, in so far as it encouraged the development of personal maturity, would help to lead the student from a nationalism serving the psychological needs of the student to a balanced non-xeno-phobic nationalist feeling which will not merely pay lip service, but will render true service to the development of the West Indian community.

(2) There is need for the development of such services as exist and the introduction into the welfare services more of that psychological feeling which will render these services of more meaningful. Thus at the present moment, courses are being run in the West Indies by the British Council for intending students. There appears to be a heavy reliance on the 'successfully adjusted' in the development of these courses. There should also be a development of the line of approach dealt with in the very brief booklet by Carberry and Thompson on the West Indian in Britain.

(3) There is still a stress in some quarters on the 'Best of Britain' approach. In view of the nature of the relationship, this approach is hardly likely to have useful results. The most usual reactions are either to encourage 'successful adjustment' at the price of personal self-esteem or to provoke the radicals into an anti-British reaction.

In the approach by the British side to the colonial, there should be as personal and individual an approach as possible. Although the individual Englishman who comes in contact with the student may in fact be an ambassador of his country, he should not proclaim himself as such. The way in which he may best serve his country's cause is by forgetting he is a Britisher and trying not to get under the skin of the colonial.

In this respect, the saying that the expectation of gratitude is an absolute bar to friendship must be remembered. In so far as the colonial student problem is approached in Britain with the idea of winning political friends and gaining commonwealth allies, to that extent West Indians and other colonials will feel that they are being 'used'. Like other similarly placed people, they will accept hospitality and probably abuse it without in any way considering this as something wrong. The suspicion that an approach is not genuine favours the development of such attitudes since the rationalization of conduct proceeds from the premise, "If the individual is seeking to manipulate me, then it is perfectly legitimate for me to 'use' him." Indeed, any other course of action appears submissive.

(4) The rise of West Indian and other colonial nationalisms must be accepted. We have seen how students wished to have their own West Indian centre set up so that they could repay adequately, on the basis of equal status, hospitality received from their British friends. This is only one of the ways in which national feeling actually advances the cause of international understanding. In the light of the persistent emotional preoccupations of the West Indian and other colonial students, it would be wise to arrange courses, lectures and discussions dealing with the West Indies and linking this with an analysis of British social structure. The direct approach in lecturing at any rate to introduce the student to the British way of life will almost inevitably be considered by the student as patronage, or another version of 'The Best in Britain' approach. Whatever of excellence is self-consciously labelled awakens in the colonial mind his early training that 'whatever is British is best'. It immediately leads him to believe that this view is shared.

In the same manner, the protests about colonial student hostels, the WISU and other manifestations of 'colonialism' should not be fought against but accepted as the starting point for leading the student to wider perspectives.

In the last resort, the only satisfactory answer to the problem is the provision of adequate facilities for higher education within the West Indies itself. Even under the most ideal circumstances, it would still be necessary for students to go abroad for certain special subjects and for postgraduate work. Under these circumstances, greater care would be taken in the selection of the individuals and in the case of the postgraduate students at any rate, the students would approach their problem with a greater degree of maturity. This point has been possibly made by Sir Raymond Priestley in *The Making of a University* in which he discusses the progress made towards the establishment of a university college in Jamaica. The problem, however, is one of such large dimensions and so important in its own right that it will be treated in a separate paper.

Notes

1. See Duncan Hall, *Mandates, Trustee-ship and Dependencies* (London: Longman, 1948).

2. Logically, there is no necessary con-nection between the belief in inevita-bility and action to bring about the inevitable situation. Indeed, the opposite position could be more strongly held. The fact is that belief in 'inevitability' like belief in the omnipotent government can be used to strengthen either position.

3. In a penetrating article, "Africans Want to be Clerks", in *Round Table*, no. 157 (1949), this position is rightly attacked. The African, it is agreed, merely takes over the scale of values of the dominant group.

4. Carnegie Corporation of New York, "The Foreign Student in America", *Quarterly Report* (April 1955).

5. See his autobiography, *The Story of My Experiments with Truth* (Ahmed-abad: Navajiman Publishing House, 1940); also Sebastian de Grazia, "Ma-hatma Gandhi: Son of his Mother", in *Political Quarterly*, n.p., n.d.

6. Eric Williams, *My Relation with the Caribbean Commission* (Trinidad: TECA, 1955).

7. The following are given as:
   Reasons for Starting this Enquiry:
   The responsibilities of leadership in the swiftly developing countries from which they come must fall to a large extent (and fall early) upon the shoulders of the relatively small number of colonial stu-dents who are gaining the advantage of higher education and specialized training in Britain. This is in fact happening already. Young men who two or three years previously were students in Lon-don, have found themselves occupying ministerial posts in West African govern-ments and many others begin to play an influential part in public and professional life very shortly after returning home. This fact has greatly influenced our enquiry . . .
   However, in view of the limitations imposed on the study they undertook, the original emphasis was altered. The group believed that the scope should be widened so as to comprehend factors other than the effect upon the students of a sojourn in Britain and that it should be restricted because . . . research would have to be confined to work in the United Kingdom . . . Consequently, the group decided to undertake a systematic and factual study of the arrangements made for colonial students (or made by themselves) to find out what students think of these arrangements and of the courses which they are following and more generally, of the society in which they are living.

8. For the best accounts of these social distinctions during slavery see:
   Lowell. J. Ragatz, *Fall of the Planter Class in the British Caribbean 1763–1883: A Study in Social and Economic*

History (New York: Octagon Books, 1977); Mrs Carmichael, *Domestic Manners and Social Conditions of the White, Coloured and Negro Population of the West Indies* (London: Whittaker Treacher, 1833); R. Pares, *A West Indian Fortune* (London, New York: Longman, 1950); Elsa Goveia, *Slave Society in the British Leeward Islands at the End of the Eighteenth Century* (London: Yale University Press, 1965).

9. Section 7, 1932 Report, p. 20.

10. As for instance:
   1st Student: A glass of water please.
   Waiter to 2nd Student: For you too, sir?
   2nd Student: No, I never touch the stuff.
   Waiter: I do, I bathe in it.
   2nd Student: Well you see, I bathe in milk.
   Waiter: Oh, I wondered where you got that lovely complexion.

11. On this point see the important study of Morroe Borger, *Equality by Statute: Legal Controls over Group Discrimination,* (New York: Columbia University Press, n.d.)

12. See S. Collins, "The British-born coloured", *Sociological Review* 3, no. 1 (July 1955).

13. Dr Clarence Senior and Douglas Manley, *A Report on Jamaican Migration to Great Britain* (Kingston: The Government Printery, 1955).

14. Michael Banton, *The Coloured Quarter* (London: Jonathan Cape, 1955).

15. Note how the allegation of only *one* experience of discrimination is immediately contradicted by the listing of other experiences.

16. Thomas S. Simey, *Welfare and Planning in the West Indies* (Oxford: Clarendon Press, 1946).

17. Within recent years there have been a series of murders which have demanded international attention.

18. This idea was based on a realistic assessment of professional people they know and on books like *English Justice* by Solicitor. As far as the writer was able to discover, there was never any official statement on the tightening of examination standards. The belief was based on a regularity of percentage passes and the numbers of students who had difficulty in passing.

19. The main outlines of the scheme of stratification in the West Indies have been examined in: L. Braithwaite, "Social stratification in Trinidad", *Social and Economic Studies* 2, nos. 2 & 3 (1953); F. Henriques, *Family and Colour in Jamaica* (London: Eyre and Spottiswoode, 1953).

20. For a recent discussion on this point, see *The Working Party Report on Education* (Port of Spain, Trinidad: Government Printery, 1954).

21. The attitude of the intellectual towards the UCWI was ambivalent in the extreme. Where an academic career was strongly desired there was a measure of self-interest and nationalism which seemed to make the establishment of a West Indian university highly desirable. In so far, however, as integration into the university system of the UK appeared feasible, the enthusiasm for a separate university college did not seem of such immediate and pressing concern. In one case, a former proponent of the idea denounced fellow West Indians as traitors for accepting facts which a few years before he had considered highly desirable.

22. It must be remembered that this is largely used as a generic term for all white Britishers.

23. Phillip Garique, "The West African Students Union", *Africa* 23, no. 1 (1953): 55–69.

24. This embarrassment over the slave past was shown in the preoccupation of many students of history and social science with the slave past. Historical research was frequently conceived as research into the regime of slavery.

25. In point of fact, one student appears to have had strong communist leanings. This student wrote to the *Spectator* 30 September 1949: 420 as follows: Mr ? states that "a number of British colonial students refused to take part in a demonstration in favour of national independence because they did not want independence under the Hammer and Sickle." I was myself one of the British colonial students in Budapest but I know of no such refusals. Furthermore, I think it would be true to say that all the British colonial students who were at the festival fervently desire the national independence of their countries; and that most, though not all of them, seeing no difference between labour and conservative colonial policy, looked to the British Communist Party for support in their struggle for independence.

26. Incidentally, one of the members of the majority group was a white West Indian.

27. For a good discussion of this problem, see A.M. Ross, *Trade Union Wage Policy* (Berkley: University of California Press, 1948).

28. On these points see above.

29. "Our information is based on life histories of a sample of Western educated Indians who reside in the small towns and cities of Bombay State located in the central-western section of India. The cases include persons who were trained in the West both before and after India attained independence (1947). The majority are currently employed in colleges and universities, the government, business and industry; a few are unemployed and the rest are engaged full time in political affairs, as editors of newspapers and in the social services. They stem from a variety of social classes and subcastes; most rank now as members of the middle-class in their communities" (*Annals of the AAPSS* 295 [September 1954]: 73).

30. See also by the same authors: "The Sensitive Area Complex: A Contribution to the Theory of Guided Culture Contact", *American Journal of Sociology* 60 (May 1955).

31. *Annals of the AAPSS* 295 (September 1954).

32. "When people are positive and friendly they speak of them as favourable. When negative and hostile, as unfavourable" (*Annals of the AAPSS* 295 [September 1954]: 84).

33. "The conservative position in Japan today is often 'negative' towards American civilization but 'friendly' to America for political reasons; the liberal is often positively disposed towards the democracy of American life but 'hostile' to America because of her foreign policy in Asia" (*Annals of the AAPSS* 295 [September 1954]: 84).

34. See William H. Sewell, et al., "Scandinavian Students' Images of the United States: A Study in Cross-cultural Education"; and Franklin D. Scott, "The Swedish Students' Image

of the United States", *Annals of the AAPSS* 295 (September 1954).

35. For some account of this see: A.A. Campbell, "St Thomas Negroes: A Study in Personality and Culture" , *Psychological Monographs* 55, no. 5 (1943); Madeleine Kerr, *Personality and Conflict in Jamaica* (Liverpool: Liverpool University Press, 1952);

L. Braithwaite, "Social Stratification in Trinidad".

36. Dr Eric Williams' *Capitalism and Slavery* (Chapel Hill: University of North Carolina Press, 1944) is an attempted refutation of the narrowly moralistic interpretation of the abolition of slavery and the slave trade, shows in his radicalism something of a violent reaction away from the British tradition.

Bibliography

"Africans Want to Be Clerks". *Round Table* 157 (1949).

Annals of the American Academy of Political and Social Science 295 (September 1954).

Attiyah, E. *An Arab Tells His Story*. London: John Murray, 1946.

Banton, Michael. *The Coloured Quarter*. London: Jonathan Cape, 1955.

Borger, Morroe. *Equality by Statute: Legal Controls Over Group Discrimination*. New York: Columbia University Press, n.d.

Braithwaite, L. "Social Stratification in Trinidad". *Social and Economic Studies* 2, nos. 3 & 4 (1953).

Cameron, N. E. *The Evolution of the Negro*. 2 vols. British Guiana: Argosy Press, 1929.

Campbell, A. A. "St. Thomas Negroes: A Study of Personality and Culture". *Psychological Monographs* 55, no. 5 (1943).

Carmichael, Mrs. *Domestic Manners and Social Conditions of the White, Coloured and Negro Population of the West Indies*. London: Whittaker, Treacher, 1833.

Collins, S. "The British-Born Coloured". *Sociological Review* 3, no. 1 (July 1955).

Crocker, Walter R. *On Governing Colonies: Being an Outline of the Real Issues and a Comparison of the British, French and Belgian Approach to Them*. London: Allen and Unwin, 1947.

Crocker, Walter R. *Self-Government for the Colonies*. London: Allen and Unwin, 1949.

de Grazia, Sebastian. "Mahatma Gandhi: Son of His Mother". *Political Quarterly* n.d.

Desai, A. R. *Social Background of Indian Nationalism*. Oxford: Oxford University Press, 1948.

Eisenstadt, S. N. *The Absorption of Immigrants: A Comparative Study Based Mainly on the Jewish Community in Palestine and the State of Israel*. London: Routledge and Kegan Paul, 1954.

Evans, Geoffrey Sir. *Great Britain Colonial Office Report of the British Guiana and British Honduras Settlement Commission.* London: H.M. Stationery Office, 1948.

Gandhi, K.M. *The Story of My Experiments with Truth.* Ahmedabad: Navajiman Publishing House, 1940.

Garique, Phillip. "The West African Students Union". *Africa* 23, no. 1 (January 1953).

Goveia, Elsa. *Slave Society in the British Leeward Islands at the End of the Eighteenth Century.* London: Yale University Press, 1965.

Hall, Duncan. *Mandates, Trusteeship and Dependencies.* London: Longman, 1948.

Henriques, F. *Family and Colour in Jamaica.* London: Eyre and Spottiswoode, 1953.

Humphrey, Norman O. "The Mexican Image of Americans". *Annals of the American Academy of Political and Social Science* 295 (September 1954).

Kerr, Madeleine. *Personality and Conflict in Jamaica.* Liverpool: Liverpool University Press, 1952.

Lambert, R., and M. Bressler. "Indian Students and the United States: Cross Cultural Images". *Annals of the American Academy of Political and Social Science* 295 (September 1954).

Lambert, R., and M. Bressler. "The Sensitive Area Complex: A Contribution to the Theory of Guided Culture Contact". *American Journal of Sociology* 60 (May 1955).

Lewin, Kurt. *Dynamic Theory of Personality.* New York: McGraw-Hill, 1935.

Little, Kenneth. *Negroes in Britain: A Study of Racial Relations in English Society.* London: Kegan Paul, 1947.

Nehru, J. *An Autobiography.* London: The Bodley Head, 1936.

Pares, Richard. *A West Indian Fortune.* London, New York: Longman, 1950.

Park, Robert. "Magic Mentality and City Life". *Publications of the American Sociological Society* 18 (1923).

Priestly, Raymond Sir. "The Making of a University." Paper read to the Cambridge Branch of the Royal Empire Society, 1951.

Pursier, Hubert and John W. Bennett. "The America-Educated Japanese, I. The Student in America: Theory, Background, Images." *Annals of the American Academy of Political and Social Science* 295 (September 1954).

Ragatz, Lowell J. *The Fall of the Planter Class in the British Caribbean 1763–1883: A Study in Social and Economic History.* New York: Octagon Books, 1977.

Richmond, A.V. *Colour Prejudice in Britain: A Study of West Indian Workers in Liverpool, 1941–1945.* London: Routledge and Kegan Paul, 1954.

Ross, A.M. *Trade Union Wage Policy.* Berkeley: University of California Press, 1948.

Scott, Franklyn D. "The Swedish Students' Image of the United States". *Annals of the American Academy of Political and Social Science* 295 (September 1954).

Senior, Clarence, and Douglas Manley. *A Report on Jamaican Migration to Great Britain.* Kingston: Government Printery, 1955.

Sewell, William H., et al. "Scandinavian Students' Images of the United States: A Study in Trans-cultural Education". *Annals of the American Academy of Political and Social Science* 295 (September 1954).

Shand, F. *The Foundations of Character: Being a Study of the Tendencies of the Emotions and Sentiments*. London: Macmillan, 1926.

Simey, Thomas S. *Welfare and Planning in the West Indies*. Oxford: Clarendon Press, 1946.

Sprott, W.J. Science and Social Action. Watts, 1954.

Stonequist, E.V. *The Marginal Man*. New York: Scribner, 1937.

Taylor, Edmond. *Richer by Asia*, 2nd ed. Boston: Houghton Mifflin, 1964.

Useem, R., and J. Useem. *The Western Educated Man in India*. Dryden Press, 1955.

Useem, R., and J. Useem. "Images of the United States and Britain Held by Foreign-Educated Indians". *Annals of the American Academy of Political and Social Science*, 295 (September 1959).

Watson, A.R., et al. *West Indian Workers in Great Britain*. London, 1942.

Williams, Eric *Capitalism and Slavery*. Chapel Hill: University of North Carolina Press, 1944.

Williams, Eric. *My Relation with the Caribbean Commission*. Trinidad: TECA, 1955.

The Working Party Report on Education. Trinidad: Government Printery, 1954.

Collected Works of
Lloyd Braithwaite

"Social Stratification in Trinidad: A Preliminary Analysis". *Social and Economic Studies* 2, nos. 2 & 3 (October 1953): 5–175.

"The Problem of Cultural Integration in Trinidad". *Social and Economic Studies* 3, no. 1 (June 1954): 82–96.

Review of L. Constantine's *Colour Bar, 1954. Social and Economic Studies* 4, no. 2 (June 1955): 191–92.

Review of A.V. Richmond's *The Colour Prejudice in Britain, 1954. Social and Economic Studies* 4, no. 2 (June 1955): 191–92.

"Progress Towards Federation, 1938–1956". *Social and Economic Studies* 6, no. 2 (June 1957): 133–84.

" 'Federal' Associations and Institutions in the West Indies". *Social and Economic Studies* 6, no. 2 (June 1957): 286–328.

"Sociology and Demographic Research in the British Caribbean". *Social and Economic Studies* 6, no. 4(December 1957): 523–71.

"The Development of Higher Education in the West Indies". *Social and Economic Studies* 7, no. 1 (March 1958): 1–64.

Roberts, G.W., and L. Braithwaite. "Fertility Differentials in Trinidad". Report of International Population Conference, Vienna, 1959.

"Social Stratification and Social Pluralism". *Annals of New York Academy of Science* 83 (1960): 816–36.

Roberts, G.W., and Lloyd Braithwaite. "Fertility Differentials by Family Type in Trinidad". *Annals of the New York Academy of Sciences* 84 (1960).

Roberts, G.W., and Lloyd Braithwaite. "A Gross Mating Table for a West Indian Population". *Population Studies* 14, no. 3 (March 1961).

Braithwaite, Lloyd, and G.W. Roberts. "Mating Patterns and Prospects in Trinidad". Paper presented to the 1961 Conference of the International Union for the Scientific Study of Population.

Braithwaite, Lloyd, and A. Singham, eds. *Conference on Political Sociology in the British Caribbean, 1961.* Mona, Jamaica: Institute of Social and Economic Research, 1962.

Braithwaite, Lloyd, and G. W. Roberts. "Mating among East Indians and Non-Indian Women in Trinidad". *Social and Economic Studies* 14, no. 1 (September 1962): 203–40.

Review of H.F. Cline's *Mexico: Revolution to Evolution, 1940–60. Social and Economic Studies* 12, no. 2 (June 1963): 221–23.

"The Role of the University in the Developing Society of the West Indies". *Social and Economic Studies* 14, no. 1 (March 1965): 76–87.

"Race Relations and Industrialization in the Caribbean". In *Industrialization and Race Relations: A Symposium,* edited by Guy Hunter. Held under the auspices of the Institute of Race Relations. London: Oxford University Press, 1965.

"Social and Political Aspects of Rural Development". *Social and Economic Studies* 17, no. 3 (September 1968): 264–75.

"The Background of Slavery and Its Implications". In *Caribbean Background I* (Lecture Series). Cave Hill, Barbados: Centre for Multi-Racial Studies, 1969.

"Ethnic Structure of the West Indies in relation particularly to Race and Income". In *Caribbean Background II.* Cave Hill, Barbados: Centre for Multi-Racial Studies, 1969.

Braithwaite, Lloyd, and J.D. Elder. Folklore Research and Archives Project (Present Position and Future Development). St Augustine, UWI, 1969.

"Problems of Race and Colour in the Caribbean". In *Caribbean Background II.* Cave Hill, Barbados: Centre for Multi-Racial Studies, 1970.

"Problems of Race and Colour in the Caribbean". In *Caribbean Background III.* Cave Hill, Barbados: Centre for Multi-Racial Studies, 1971.

Commission of Enquiry into Racial and Colour Discrimination in the Private Sector. Interim Report, October 1970. Port of Spain, Trinidad: Government Printery, 1971. [Braithwaite served as chairman of this commission.]

"Social Stratification and Cultural Pluralism". In *Peoples and Cultures of the Caribbean,* edited by M. Horowitz. New York: Natural History Press, 1971.

Social Stratification in Trinidad – A Preliminary Analysis. Mona, Jamaica: Institute of Social and Economic Research, 1975.

"Introduction to the Trinidad Labour Riots of 1937". In *The Trinidad Labour Riots of 1937: Perspectives 50 Years Later,* edited by Roy Thomas, 1–22. St Augustine, Trinidad: Institute of Social and Economic Research, 1987.

Unpublished Works

1. A Study of Village Life in Blanchisseuse
This is an anthropological work, done using participant observation in 1950. It covers all aspects of village life and the fieldwork lasted one year.

2. A Social History of Education in Trinidad and Tobago, 1833–1930
This is a review of educational expansion from the period of the Negro Education Act to modern times. The study examines the influence of class, race and political factors on the educational system.

3. The Indians of Trinidad: Integration of an Ethnic Group
This is an assessment of the process of cultural change based on participation in Curepe and Caroni Village in 1952.

4. The Federation of the West Indies
This is a long study on the history and experience of Federation in the British West Indies, parts of which were published as "Progress Towards Federation, 1938–1956", *Social and Economic Studies* 6, no. 2 (June 1957) and "Federal Associations and Institutions in the BWI", *Social and Economic Studies* 6, no. 2 (June 1957).

Index